MK
7.65

D1180142

UNIVE~~~~~~~~~~~~~~~~~~~~~~~
PORT~~~~~~~~ALMORAL
WINNIPEG 2. MAN.   CANADA

DISCARDED

INTERNATIONAL REGIONS

AND

THE INTERNATIONAL SYSTEM

JX
1979
.R8
1967

INTERNATIONAL REGIONS AND THE INTERNATIONAL SYSTEM

A Study in Political Ecology

BRUCE M. RUSSETT

Yale University

RAND McNALLY & COMPANY   CHICAGO

RAND McNALLY *Series in Comparative Government and International Politics*

Harry Eckstein, Advisory Editor

THE FUNCTIONS OF INTERNATIONAL LAW: AN INTRODUCTION TO THE ROLE OF INTERNATIONAL LAW IN THE CONTEMPORARY WORLD
William D. Coplin, Wayne State University

INTERNATIONAL REGIONS AND THE INTERNATIONAL SYSTEM: A STUDY IN POLITICAL ECOLOGY
Bruce M. Russett, Yale University

HUMAN BEHAVIOR AND INTERNATIONAL POLITICS: CONTRIBUTIONS FROM THE SOCIAL-PSYCHOLOGICAL SCIENCES
Edited by J. David Singer, University of Michigan

Rand McNally Studies in Political Change
Myron Weiner, Series Editor

PUBLIC LIBERTIES IN THE NEW STATES
David J. Bayley, University of Denver

CULTURAL PLURALISM AND NATIONALIST POLITICS IN BRITISH GUIANA
Leo A. Despres

SONS OF THE ESTABLISHMENT: ELITE YOUTH IN PANAMA AND COSTA RICA
Daniel Goldrich, University of Oregon

CREATING POLITICAL ORDER: THE PARTY-STATES OF WEST AFRICA
Aristide R. Zolberg, University of Chicago

COPYRIGHT © 1967 BY RAND McNALLY & COMPANY
ALL RIGHTS RESERVED
PRINTED IN U. S. A. BY RAND McNALLY & COMPANY
LIBRARY OF CONGRESS CATALOGUE NUMBER: 67–14695

For the other members of our subsystem:

C.

M.

M.

L.

PREFACE

I HAVE TERMED THIS VOLUME "A STUDY IN POLITICAL Ecology." As ecology is defined as *the relation of organisms or groups of organisms to their environment,* I have attempted to explore some of the relations between political systems and their social and physical environment. The book stems from a longstanding interest in the economic and social determinants of politics, and in turn in the influence of political variables on social and economic ones.

More specifically, the volume brings together aspects of research and thought that have occupied me for ten years or more. One is the theory of political integration as it involves the relations between two or more nation-states. Another is a concern with the operation of the international system, with the formation and decomposition of coalitions among nations, and with ascertaining the conditions of peaceful change in the system. Still another is with the use of ecological data on national characteristics, both as a means of hypothesis-testing and as a source of developing better taxonomies for describing national attributes and behavior. Each of these is an extremely broad topic, and I could not hope to treat even one of them exhaustively in a single volume. None of them, however, is wholly independent of the others, so I have tried to find the area of congruence among them and to produce a certain synthesis.

Although the book does indeed represent an area of exploration that has concerned me for a long time, it surely is not the culmination or perfection of that concern. Progress toward a science of international politics has been enormous over the past decade, but it is to a perhaps distressing degree the kind of progress that is dramatic just because it starts from a low initial level. Our present achievements, including those of this book, remain rather tentative. An essential element in the spurt that has occurred has been the development of electronic computers for processing large masses of quantitative data. Without such facilities the inductive taxonomy that forms the heart of this analysis would have been quite impossible. At the same time, the newness of our electronic technology means that its mathematical applications are not always thoroughly understood nor the alternatives fully explored. Furthermore, the potentialities of the computer are so great that refinements and new breakthroughs inevitably follow in rapid order. I have chosen to produce this book at a time when some of its methodological underpinnings are still in the developmental stage. It could not have been done at all five years ago; in another few years it might be done somewhat differently with greater refinement. But that is always the case with a cumulative science, and the rapid rate of development in this field is to be welcomed and not evaded. If publication of this book stimulates work which will make it obsolete, no one will be happier than its author. Card decks with data are on deposit with the Inter-University Consortium for Political Research, P. O. Box 1248, Ann Arbor, Michigan, 48106.

To declare that a science of international politics has in recent years burgeoned from very slight beginnings is not to deprecate the work either of those in the same area in earlier years or of those in other disciplines more recently. For example, on every re-reading of Quincy Wright's work I become more impressed with the degree to which other scholars' products are ultimately derived from it. And my methodological and conceptual debts to those in other disciplines will be apparent in the text and especially in the references, where the political scientists are heavily outnumbered. International relations is truly an interdisciplinary study, and any attempt to explain its political aspects must depend heavily on social and economic variables.

There are three major elements to this book, each of which may weigh heavily on certain types of readers. It contains substantial theoretical sections, extensive methodological discourses, and long pages of descriptive quantitative material. The orthodox method of handling such a variety of material probably would have been to discuss each sequentially in individual sub-sections. To do that here, however, would have been to run too great a risk that the general reader would never make it through the volume, especially that he would find the sustained methodological discussion too turgid and abandon the enterprise. Instead I have chosen to break up these sections as much as possible, following the opening discussion with only as much theory and methodology as seemed necessary for comprehending each descriptive portion. Thus the reader will find methodological and theoretical sections in the majority of chapters, with some of the loose ends gathered together in the concluding chapters. Even so this has required an initial heavy dose of methodology in chapters two and three, but I hope the nontechnical reader, who *is* part of the audience I want to reach, will nevertheless persevere in the knowledge that later sections will be easier. I have indicated that the Appendix to chapter three may be omitted, at least on a first reading. The methodological discussions are there in some detail in order to serve a teaching function; it seems essential that while we are developing new methods and theoretical models we make clear exactly what we have done so that others may understand and be able, if they choose to disagree with any step, to do so in an informed manner.

As an interdisciplinary center *par excellence,* the Mental Health Research Institute of the University of Michigan made an essential contribution to this study. In the mundane sense, it provided me with secretarial and computational facilities for a year; in a less tangible but irreplaceable way it offered me the opportunity to consult, in print and in person, with men working on problems which, though manifested in different kinds of social systems, exhibited many of the same characteristics. If taking a general systems approach to science means being aware of how scientists in other disciplines handle related research problems, then I have been given a unique opportunity to become a good general systems man. I heartily recommend the experience.

Certainly as crucial a contribution, and a prior one, was made by Yale University. It too provided an environment suited to unorthodox research, where I could conceive the project. Most of the data-gathering and much of the computational analysis was performed there, and by awarding me a Junior Faculty Fellowship it allowed me to get away—to Michigan—to think and write about the results. By the facilities provided in its presence, and the subsequent chance of absence from its distractions, Yale made the book possible. And in turn the basic research support, in the form of abundant clerical and research assistance and the critical mass of a professional community, is due largely to the National Science Foundation and its generous grant to the Yale Political Data Program.

If this is in some sense an interdisciplinary effort, it is equally an inter-institutional product. In addition to the contributions of Yale and Michigan, I must mention my debt to the University of Chicago Computation Center, which processed data for me at a point when the programs I needed were operating nowhere else. In this connection I am particularly grateful to Professor Duncan MacRae, who made available his routines for the direct factor analysis of asymmetric sociometric matrices and spent a considerable amount of time in helping me to interpret the results. Another essential computational input came from the System Development Corporation in Santa Monica, California, which processed several matrices that were too large for the equipment available at Yale or Michigan. By asking me to write a consultant's paper on a *furturible* aspect of this study the System Development Corporation also helped me, at a crucial stage, to keep my attentions focused on the general topic. And on the matter of computation, I must express deep appreciation to James Lingoes of the University of Michigan Computation Center for our long and illuminating discussions.

Many of my colleagues also made essential contributions. Rudolph J. Rummel, then of Yale, strengthened my understanding of factor analysis and introduced me to the intricacies of direct factor analysis and of the factor comparison technique employed here. The computer program for the latter was written as part of his Dimensionality of Nations Project. At a critical point several other individuals, including Raymond Cattell, Clyde Coombs, Robert Hefner, and Charles Wrigley, helped me make some methodological choices. While all these people would surely not agree totally with everything I have done—in fact they did not agree among themselves—their multiple consultation enabled me to make better-informed decisions than I could otherwise have done. J. David Singer read the complete manuscript and, during my entire year at Michigan, shared with me his insights and helped me to sharpen my own.

Amos Hawley and Julian Wolpert also read it, to my benefit, and I gained much from the imagination and wisdom of Karl Deutsch and Raymond Tanter, both of whom commented extensively on the early drafts of several chapters. Nor can I omit my research assistants, especially Jean Palmer and Lutz Erbring who carried out most of the data processing with skill and responsibility. Parts of chapters one, two, and four appeared, in earlier versions, as articles (Russett, 1966, 1967).

B.M.R.

Hamden, Connecticut
November 1966

CONTENTS

TABLES AND FIGURES

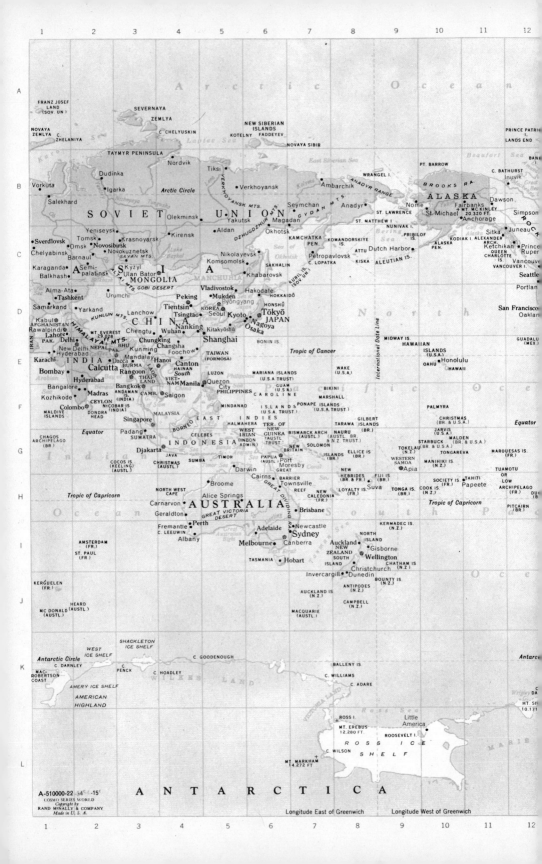

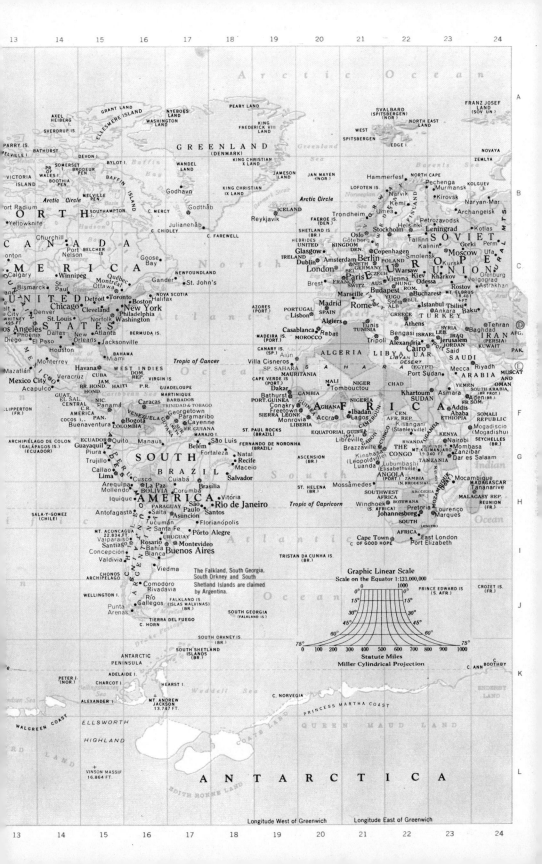

1

REGIONS AND POLITICAL THEORY

WHAT IS A REGION?

THE NOTION OF A REGION, EITHER WITHIN A SINGLE country or a region of the world embracing a number of nations, has provided a venerable tool in the workshed of political and social research. Like most ancient implements, originally designed for specific purposes by their inventors, it fairly soon was discovered to be an instrument useful for a wide variety of tasks—chopping, splitting, shaving, and smoothing diverse bodies of sociological data. In time different workers refined the tool for particular tasks. While they usually kept the basic name "region" for what they were working with, the implements became so specialized that, like the innumerable breeds of *Canis familiarus*, one would hardly know that they all belonged to the same species. The tool for splitting a political body into various groupings became so different from that for smoothing the edges of economic aggregates that to refer generally to the "region" tool was to invite confusion and to risk producing a botched job. Use of an inappropriate version of the implement in otherwise skilled hands has furthermore often unjustly discredited the tool itself.

Some of the results can be seen in a proverb which many Frenchmen enjoy citing to the fury of their southern neighbors: *L'Afrique commence aux Pyrenées*. Actually, though most Spaniards surely take umbrage, the search for a cultural (rather than a geographic) definition of Europe is not a simple one. In "Western Europe" and "Africa" we have two regions which seem, in matters of political and social consequence, to be relatively homogeneous within themselves but different from each other. But how would we draw the boundaries so as to maximize the similarity within each group and minimize that between them? In the words of a recent article, "Where is the Middle East?" (Davison, 1964) Does it extend from Morocco to Pakistan, or should the line be drawn somewhere between? What do we do about Israel which, though right in the middle of any geographic delimitation of the region, still does not fit by any cultural criterion? Or Turkey, which in part is physically on the European continent? Or within a country like the United States: Where is the South? Does it include Texas? Kentucky? And what difference does it make to the politics of a state if it is more, or less, "Southern"?

There is, of course, no simple answer to these questions. Different definitions and different criteria will often produce different regions, and no two analysts may fully agree as to what the appropriate criteria are. This is a problem which has vexed social scientists, both students of international relations and observers of national social and political systems, for decades. In the late 1930's, very substantial research was done on the matter within the United States, under the sponsorship of the Social Science Research Council and the National Resources Committee, with sociologist Howard Odum probably the principal contributor to the body of theory and data which grew up. Yet the various questions involved were never fully answered for the United States even by the distinguished and sophisticated laborers of the time, and nothing comparable to their effort has been devoted to delineating regions of the world. Since the problem is a major one, both in its theoretical and its policy implications, it demands further conceptual clarification and extensive empirical research.

SOME CRITERIA

First we must face certain problems. What definitions of a "region" have been offered in the past, and how can we choose among them? Clearly we want something more satisfactory than the traditional and often non-operationally defined geopolitical or geostrategic regions long familiar to students of international politics (e.g., MacKinder, 1919). One possibility is simply to identify an area divided from another by barriers, perhaps geographic ones, producing thus a definition by *isolation* or separateness. One might find a natural region, such as a river valley or plain. But virtually all social scientists, including geographers, would reject this definition. A region, they might say, must be composed of units with common characteristics. Regions should be areas of relative *homogeneity*. This might still be defined in physiographic terms: "any portion of the earth's surface whose physical characteristics are similar," for example (Vance, 1951, p. 123). More common, however, is the demand for a homogeneity of economic and social structure. Or, the composite social region might combine "a relatively large degree of homogeneity measured by a relatively large number of purposes or classifications. This means it must comprehend both the natural factors and the social factors" (Odum and Moore, 1938, p. 30).

A perceptive critic of the regionalism concept replies, however, in terms akin to those of our opening paragraph: "Regionalism is not one thing, but many things. The failure to discriminate the many distinct factors that underlie the emergence and persistence of regions is a serious fault of present-day research. Areas of homogeneity have been mistakenly represented as areas of integration" (Wirth, 1951, p. 392). Rupert Vance quotes a geographer's reference to "an *ensemble de rapports* between man and the natural milieu." Therefore regions are sometimes explicitly defined by *interdependence,* as areas within which a higher degree of mutual dependence exists than in relationships outside that area, nodes where people are bound together by mutual dependence arising from common interests.[1] This easily leads to a definition of a region according to *loyalties* or patriotism, "an area of which the inhabitants instinctively feel themselves a part," for example (Vance, 1951, p. 123).

Nor is this the end of the possibilities. A region may also be an areal unit defined by an *ad hoc problem.* One suspects that "Southeast Asia's" principal claim to regional status with many Americans is simply the threat posed to the whole area by Communist China. This leads to yet another definition, "a device for effecting *control.*" The term "Middle East" seems to have been originated by the British in the late Nineteenth Century to refer to an area with common implications for Her Majesty's strategy (Davison, 1964). According to the analysts of the S.S.R.C. project referred to above, "regionalism provides an economy for the decentralization of political power" (Odum and Moore, 1938, p. 27). A region can therefore be an area of administrative convenience. Perhaps the baldest usage of the latter pragmatic sort is contained in the following statement about regions:

> There is no particular mystique about identifying them and working with them as units of analysis. They are ordinary, common, practical, geographic areas for which social and economic improvement programs have been conceived, planned, and undertaken. Sometimes these regions are defined by natural features such as river basins, agricultural zones, forest districts and the like. Sometimes they find their identity in terms of trading areas within which economic transactions and flows are numerous and dense as compared to their economic relations with outside areas. In some instances, a metropolitan region is the focus of primary concern. . . . In still other instances, a region will be characterized by relative cultural similarity; for example, a tribal region, an ethnic or traditional area with a high degree of self-consciousness, a remote and backward district, or a distinct political jurisdiction such as a province or republic. . . . In other words, the regional concept . . . [has] been found useful and reasonable under a variety of circumstances (Resources for the Future, 1966, pp. 3–4).

We thus find a combination of description and prescription in the approach of some regionalists. This certainly was true of Odum and Moore, who advocated the delegation to regional authorities—especially one for the

---

[1] Hawley (1950, p. 260) distinguishes between a homogeneous "region" and a functionally interdependent "community area."

Southeast—of political functions which they thought could properly be carried out neither by the federal nor state governments. The same prescriptive orientation is evident in many international relations writings. Much talk, both by scholars and premiers, about regional (e.g., Latin American, Arab) political integration is based upon a presumed homogeneity, or interdependence, or loyalties, which may exist only in the mind of the beholder.[2] The United Nations Charter explicitly allows for security arrangements under regional agreements; NATO is often described as coming under a rather loose interpretation of "regional" in this context.[3]

Even once we finally settle upon a definition or group of definitions—perhaps homogeneity, or homogeneity plus interdependence plus geographical separateness[4]—the problem of finding suitable methods for *delineating regions* remains. The task, in effect, is one of making the definition operational; at best the concept of region is but an analytical device for separating certain areal features thought relevant (Bunge, 1962). If separateness is a primary criterion, physiographic indices might be included. Crop and manufacturing areas might be relevant. The ethnic composition of the populace could be taken into account, as could the level of economic development, the history of the area, and its religious divisions. Frederick Jackson Turner, in discussing possible ways of dividing the West into sections, suggested looking at the way business houses divided up the "territory" (cited from a letter by Turner in Mood, 1951, p. 95). Emphasizing the political aspects of regionalism, he once defined a section as a group of states contending with other groups of states. As measures he suggested homogeneity of votes by Congressmen in their role as national legislators, or areas defined by relative homogeneity of vote in presidential and state elections (Turner, 1932, p. 288). Perhaps if interdependence is to be a major criterion, the patterns of newspaper circulation (To the papers of which central city do outlying regions subscribe?) or mail, trade, or rail traffic patterns would be good indicators. Or if patriotism or loyalty is considered the key, one might, perhaps through survey research, simply ask a large number of residents,

[2] See the criticism by George Lundberg (1942) of Nicolas Spykman (1942) and others.

[3] The term *regional* is not defined in Article 51 of the Charter. When the Charter was drafted an Egyptian attempt to define it was defeated. Egypt's proposed amendment was, "There shall be considered as regional arrangements of a permanent nature grouping in a given geographical area several countries which, by reason of their proximity, community of interests or cultural, linguistic, historical or spiritual affinities make themselves jointly responsible for the peaceful settlement of any disputes which may arise between them. . . ." (United Nations Conference on International Organization, 1945, p. 857).

[4] As for example in the suggestion of Ackerman (1953) that one should be concerned with the "compage," the community of features that depict the human occupancy of space.

especially of the presumed border areas, of what region they considered themselves to be members.

Most of the large-scale empirical efforts to delineate regions have in fact made use of a wide variety of indices, though they have chiefly emphasized that class of indices which might be expected to measure homogeneity rather than one of the other aspects mentioned above. In using a number of variables one can take advantage of the fact that "cultural traits" are correlated among themselves. If no cultural characteristic were related to any other, a region would have to be determined by a single trait and would have no meaning except in terms of that trait (Vance, 1951, p. 129). On the other hand, "while the natural and cultural landscape often coincide they also often clash" (Wirth, 1951, p. 385). And, in addition, different *measures* of the cultural landscape will, though they may frequently correlate, also often clash. "The continental United States cannot be divided into a single set of sizeable regions which meet perfectly all the standards of hypothetical regionality. Compromise is indicated. . . . A region may be delineated upon the basis of many factors, and its extent varies with the factor or factors selected for generalization" (National Resources Committee, 1935, pp. 123, 145). In the Appendix to its report the National Resources Committee gives over 100 maps for what it describes as "proto-regions"; i.e., single-factor regions. The factors in this case are the definitions applied by Federal administrative agencies—virtually all are differently delineated. Again according to Louis Wirth (1951, p. 389),

> Various purposes require different areal scope, and it is difficult to find any single criterion that will satisfy the multiple demands of adequacy. . . . Short of considering the whole world as a single region . . . there is no other regional arrangement of lesser scope that will fully satisfy the many interests that clamor for recognition. The best we can do is to make the most reasonable compromises we can invent, which means weighting some functions more heavily than others, and to keep our lines of demarcation flexible enough so that they can be adjusted to changing needs and possibilities.[5]

Odum and Moore conclude, "The mere grouping together of facts and indices does not give us an organic regional entity, but simply gives us a description, an inventory of what has happened and what *is* under the given forces, which must of course be duly analyzed." They add, furthermore, "Many of the cultural factors, such as personality, folkways, motivation, handicaps, are not measurable in terms of our present objective methods"

[5] A partially dissenting view is expressed by Walter Isard (1956) who, though he recognizes that at present different indices will identify different regions, hopes their proximity, community of interests or cultural, linguistic, historical or spiritual regions on which all the important indices will agree.

(Odum and Moore, 1938, pp. 447–448). In the end, the criteria "must be chosen not by chance, but in close relation to the definition of the region as a functional unit" (Riemer, 1943, p. 279). Perhaps we return to some idea of interdependence.

If there is no agreement about indices for delineation, even more clearly there is no consensus on the *proper magnitude* of a "region." Again according to the National Resources Committee (1935, p. 145),

> The term "region" is not commonly applied to small areas, but there seems to be some disagreement as to whether it should be applied to very large sections such as the Middle West, the South, etc., or to smaller subdivisions of these, as for instance, the Corn Belt, the Industrial Piedmont, the Chicago metropolitan area, etc.

If states (or nations) are taken as the basic sub-unit from which regions are to be built up there is clearly a lower limit to the size of a region. Most often some such political unit is used as the building block, not necessarily because such a course is theoretically most desirable, but because satisfactory data are not readily accessible for smaller units. Even so no consensus on size exists. The size criterion might in large part determine whether "Latin America" emerged as a single region or was divided into several groups like Central America, tropic South America, and temperate South America. Ackerman (1953) and Berry and Hankins (1963) emphasize an alternative to any attempt to specify a "correct" size for a region: the construction of a *hierarchy* of regions, with several levels of regions and, with progressively tighter criteria, sub-regions.[6] Simon (1962) takes a similar position with regard to what he describes as "nearly decomposable systems," defined by a very high ratio of transactions within sub-systems to those between sub-systems.

Finally, there is the sticky problem of *identifying the boundaries* of various regions. If one uses separateness or isolation as a major element in the definition of a region this problem may not be difficult, but otherwise it is. "It seems to be agreed that regional boundaries are usually indefinite, being zones rather than lines. In the majority of instances, therefore, any boundaries which may be drawn will be necessarily arbitrary" (National Resources Committee, 1935, p. 145). "The world does not in fact break easily along neatly perforated lines" (Claude, 1959, p. 113). "It is quite absurd and illogical to seek to establish regional boundaries in detail. They

---

[6] Berry and Hankins provide an extremely useful bibliography of the literature on regions of the United States. Donald Bogue (1955) takes up this suggestion for a hierarchy of regions and urges such an ordering for homogeneous areas of the world, *ignoring both national and provincial boundaries.* For analytical purposes this would have great utility (Brazil is not well described as an average of the industrialized south and the impoverished north) but would, as Bogue recognizes and advocates, require an enormous data-collecting effort.

must remain vague, for they are boundaries of a generalization. If, for practical purposes, one finds that he must draw boundaries, then he should do so in a frankly arbitrary manner" (National Resources Committee, 1935, p. 147, quoting the reply of Preston E. James to a questionnaire). Actually, many researchers would contend that the final decision need not be quite so arbitrary, though neither is it likely to be clear-cut. "The characteristics of a region should be most pronounced in its interior. . . . Regions end in transition, seldom in definite boundaries. The areal complex is substantial, it is only its boundary that is inclined to be capricious" (Finch, 1939, p. 14). Hence we are sure that France is in Western Europe, however defined, but it is hard to know where to put Finland.

All this will sound more than vaguely familiar to students of general systems theory, who have wrestled with the boundary delineation problem for many years and in a variety of empirical domains. These problems are also highly relevant to the efforts of international relations scholars to define and analyze subsystems of the international system. There is no consensus on what constitute the characteristics of an international subsystem, though geographical contiguity, interaction, and perception of belonging to a distinctive *community* are frequently offered. Perhaps a boundary criterion of "differences in the quality or frequency of communications and interactions" (Berrien, 1964, p. 207) is most common. The subsystems hypothesized by various authors are, however, almost invariably geographic regions: Western European or North Atlantic (Hoffmann, 1963); Middle Eastern (Binder, 1958); Western African (Hodgkin, 1961); and South or Southeast Asian (Brecher, 1963; Modelski, 1961a). The usage of system and subsystem in many of these cases is much less rigorous than would be demanded by general systems theory—which would require, for instance, that a variety of operations be carried out, preferably by several disciplines, to establish the existence of a specific system (Young, 1964, p. 239). Our approach in this book is not solely a general systems one, yet the definition of regions by multiple criteria that we shall undertake will be important to all who do wish to apply such an approach.

INTERNATIONAL REGIONS AND COMPARATIVE POLITICS

In this book we shall explore and suggest some answers to the following questions, applying the entire set of questions to five quite different types of data:

1. How many groups (regions) are necessary for an adequate summary description of the similarities and differences among types of national political systems?

2. What countries are to be found in each group?

3. How do these groups compare with those, including the areal group-ings we call regions, now in use by social scientists?

4. What are the discriminating variables for distinguishing groups in general, and in distinguishing between specific groups?

5. What is the relevance of our groupings to theories of comparative and international politics?

At least two kinds of major theoretical issues should be illuminated by the results of this study. Regional cultural, political, and geographic patterns have profound effects both on the nature of a particular national political system and on the behavior of states in world politics. First, there are the questions arising from what might be called the *many roads* problem. Most social scientists become convinced, the more so the longer they are in the profession, that there are "many roads" not just to socialism but to virtually every goal of significance to the analyst of politics or society. Or even more to the point, there are many roads *from* almost every position of significance.

To be more precise, the *meaning* of a variable will be *different in differ-ent social or political contexts.* One of the most striking examples of such a conclusion is found in Brzezinski and Huntington's recent (1964) compari-son of the political systems of the United States and Soviet Union, in which they critically examine the argument that the two countries' systems are con-verging in important respects. The basic argument is that recent *social and economic* trends within the two, but especially the urbanization and indus-trialization of Russia and the increasing wealth and even affluence of the Soviet citizen (beginning to approach the American level), will create similar *political* systems. Most important, they will create the conditions for a relatively pluralistic political system in Russia, leading furthermore to a regime more pacific in international relations.

Brzezinski and Huntington's response to this argument is to emphasize the differences in the political context within which these trends (urbaniza-tion, industrialization, and enrichment) are occurring. The United States is a society where, to an important degree, economics had and still retains a certain primacy and conditioning relation to politics. Thus the American (and also the British) pluralistic political system was made possible by the relatively high level and diffusion of wealth that existed in the Eighteenth and Nineteenth Centuries. By providing many competing centers of economic power it introduced similar widespread competition for political power. But in the Soviet Union, it is politics that has shaped the economy and social system. By enormous sacrifice and a deliberate act of will in the *political* system Russia was industrialized and transformed into a modern urban society. In so doing the economic system was heavily conditioned by the political one (*pace* Marx). Most importantly, the competing pluralistic centers of economic power so typical of the first states to industrialize have not existed and do not now exist within the Soviet Union. Thus the meaning and consequences of the variable *industrialization* or the variable *urbanization* are not the same in the two nations. They may readily promote political pluralism in one but not in the other.

As Brzezinski and Huntington phrase it in their important book this is indeed an *argument* of their own, and their readers may or may not find it a convincing one. But when phrased rather more cautiously, perhaps as a *hypothesis,* if not compelling, it remains an idea deserving of serious investigation. One should indeed not *assume* that the effects of a particular economic or social trend will be the same everywhere, but first should establish whether the social context is essentially the same in all the countries under study and, if not, whether the difference expresses itself by substantially affecting the relationship between the variables we are investigating. The effect conceivably could even be great enough to reverse the sign of the relationship—for example a positive relationship between political violence and per capita income among poor countries undergoing social change might become a negative relationship among richer ones, as the political systems gain the resources either to satisfy demands or suppress them.[7]

No two social or political systems will be exactly alike of course, so there can be no absolutely clear-cut answer to the question whether the social context in two countries is sufficiently similar for one to be able safely to expect the functional relationship between the variables studied to be more or less the same. For most purposes it might be acceptable to ignore this problem when comparing only countries in Western Europe, for instance. But one of the marks of a capable researcher is surely his sensitivity to it and readiness to investigate it where appropriate. The rigorous delineation of regions or groups of countries which have, compared with the rest of the world, a high degree of social and cultural homogeneity should help the analyst of comparative politics to decide in which comparisons he must be especially sensitive to the "many roads" problem and where he can be fairly secure in ignoring it. Similarly, anyone who wanted to commission or undertake an analysis of Haitian politics should find it important to know whether the overall cultural pattern of Haiti was more like that of Latin America or like that of an African country, and thus whether to seek insights especially from a Latin American specialist or an Africanist. Several of the

---

[7] For some preliminary and inconclusive evidence that such a relationship does indeed hold see Russett et al. (1964), pp. 306–07, and for a discussion of the general methodological point being raised see the chapter by Hayward Alker in the same volume (pp. 322–40).

analyses in this book will provide helpful information for making this sort of decision.

INTERNATIONAL REGIONS AND POLITICAL INTEGRATION

The other type of theoretical issue toward which this study is directed involves political integration between national states. This topic has been the subject of extensive research in recent years, and though we still know little enough about the necessary prerequisites for successful integration, or in what sequence they need occur, various authors have identified several conditions as important and perhaps crucial. Probably among others they include: A degree of cultural similarity or at least *compatibility* for the major politically relevant values, economic interdependence, and the existence of formal institutions with substantial "spill-over" or consensus-building effects. Geographical contiguity is also highly relevant.[8]

No one of these is a *sufficient* condition for successful integration, and research has not yet established with certainty whether any are *necessary* conditions. Yet it seems likely that they are essential for any successful formal union (amalgamation) of previously separate political units by peaceful means, and they probably also are extremely important, though in lesser degree, for the long-term maintenance of peaceful and co-operative relations among still-independent states (pluralism). Both conditions fall within the definition of political integration employed in this book, a definition we shall develop in later chapters. Deutsch *et al.* (1957) would maintain that similarity of relevant values and interdependence, if not institutions with spill-over, are necessary for amalgamation or pluralism. Etzioni (1965, pp. 23–36) suggests that similarity of values in general is merely an *enhancing* condition which may grow as a result of political unification, and notes the risk of tautology involved when only the "politically relevant" values are specified. He seems to regard contiguity as virtually essential, though Jacob and Teune (1964, p. 18) emphasize that economic distance or travel time may be more significant than mere physical distance.

Each of these conditions in fact coincides closely with one of our previously suggested definitions of a region. Except for purely physical indices

---

[8] On the importance of these conditions, and their interrelations, see, among others, Deutsch *et al.* (1957), Etzioni (1962, 1963, 1965), Haas (1957, 1958), Jacob and Teune (1964), and Russett (1963). In addition to the empirical studies, two useful reviews of the theory are Bhoutros-Ghali (1949) and Yalem (1965). Eric Stein (1964) suggests that the degree of similarity in countries' legal systems could serve as an index of political integration, and so has studied the efforts of the EEC countries to assimilate their laws more closely. John Wigmore (1928) presented a world map of states identified by broad classes of legal system (English, Roman, Moslem, etc.).

and for some measure of the loyalties and mutual identification of the populace, we in fact have measures for virtually all the criteria offered.[9] In this book we shall make these definitions operational, delineate international regions by each criterion, compare their congruence, and in many cases also compare shifts over time in regions as defined by the same criterion. Attention will be focused upon:

1. Regions of *social and cultural homogeneity;* that is, regions composed of states which are similar with respect to several kinds of internal attributes (chapters two and three).

2. Regions of states which share similar *political attitudes or external behavior,* as identified by the voting positions of national governments in the United Nations (chapters four and five).

3. Regions of political interdependence, where the countries are joined together by a network of supranational or intergovernmental *political institutions* (chapters six and seven).

4. Regions of *economic interdependence,* as identified by intraregional trade as a proportion of the nations' national income (chapters eight and nine).

5. Regions of geographical *proximity* (chapter ten).

In so doing we should be able to identify certain areas of the world where the potential for further integration is high, and perhaps point out other areas where, despite present or projected institutions, some apparent conditions seem weak or absent. Each of these five elements is relevant to the prediction of behavior such as conflict and integration, by serving as a means of facilitating communication and for developing common interests. The policy significance of the observations will be obvious. We cannot, of course, say whether the degree of similarity or interdependence that we find is sufficient to support a given level of integration, but we can point out areas of more and less, and note important discontinuities. Furthermore, we can systematically identify the degree of congruence existing according to each of these criteria, helping to settle the question whether, internationally, these criteria do indeed coincide to form an "all-purpose" region, or whether the National Resources Committee's notion of a proto-region is more appropriate (chapter eleven). By a method to be introduced in chapter three, this degree of congruence can be specified with some precision. And using the same method, we shall compare the results of a single criterion applied at several different points in time—to ask, for instance, whether regions of economic interdependence are stable over a decade. By applying several criteria at various

[9] The physical indices (such as river valleys, etc.) seem too restricted to be of major interest. For the orientation of this book, data on people's loyalties would obviously be of high relevance, but such data are not now available on a comparable basis for enough countries. Before too long, however, a sufficient body of cross-national survey research material may exist to permit work to begin.

points in time we can begin to make some inferences about chronological lead and causation—whether, for example, trade groupings in the early 1950's provides a good "predictor" of political groupings in the early 1960's, or vice versa (chapter thirteen). As one aspect of integration we shall see how closely our regions coincide with areas marked by little international violent conflict, and suggest some theoretical reformulations (chapter twelve).

The method will be entirely inductive; that is, at no point will we interject any *a priori* judgments as to the number of regions which should be found, or what those regions should be. Nor (except of course under point 5 above) will we insist that the countries forming the "regions" so derived be geographically contiguous. In this sense we shall be using the term region very loosely. For historical and other reasons regions of contiguity and socio-cultural groupings often do coincide, and many of the groupings which emerge from our analysis will correspond to generally recognizable geographic regions. But nothing in the inductive procedure for forming the groupings in this book will make any requirement for proximity. Strictly speaking, our groupings will be equivalent to geographers' *regional types*.

Our conclusions will be relevant to several different approaches to the study and organization of world politics. There is a rather widespread view that international integration on the regional level is more likely to succeed than is the worldwide creation of a powerful political institution. Certainly tnere is a long and honorable tradition in the profession which regards regionalism as the proper basis for world order, an alternative both to fragmentation· and to universalistic solutions.[10] Sometimes regional federations are urged not as an alternative, but as stepping stones or building blocks that might later be dissolved or perhaps might even be maintained within a world union. The latter version can be seen in a policy statement of the British Movement of Federal Union, calling for regional units as "constituent and permanent elements of a World Government structure" (cited in de Rusett, 1950, p. 159). This leads easily to the view that regional organizations must be a basic element in a multi-level wider union, sharing the load and handling issues about which there is sufficient regional, but not world-wide, consensus.[11]

In chapter fourteen we shall deal with these contentions without

[10] An early advocate would be Spykman (1942) ; most of the current advocates of European or Atlantic union would probably also belong here.

[11] E. H. Carr (1945) held this view in his influential work. Other representatives of this school are discussed by Claude (1959) and Bloomfield (1960), and Etzioni (1964) and Gladwyn (1966) also expound it. Yalem (1965, p. 141), however, describes contemporary regionalism as "a manifestation of a world in disorder rather than as an intermediate transition to a new universal order."

attempting finally to settle the disputes. But whatever the purpose behind any advocacy of regional unity, the book will help to indicate how one might delineate a region so that, in the light of our current theories, the chances of success may be maximized. In so doing we shall also develop a methodology that will be of use to students of politics *within nations* as well as to those concerned with *international* relations.

The methods and data employed will be derived from a variety of academic fields—sociology, psychology, economics, geography, and, of course, political science. Men from each of these fields have made major contributions and each contributes an essential part. But in our attempted explanation of political events we must engage in truly multi-disciplinary research.

2

SOCIALLY AND CULTURALLY
HOMOGENEOUS GROUPINGS

SOCIAL AND CULTURAL ATTRIBUTES

IF RELATIVE CULTURAL HOMOGENEITY IS TO BE ONE OF
the major criteria by which regions of the world may be delineated, just
what is in fact meant? Though common usage in this context remains
ambiguous, at least two elements can be specified: 1) similarity of nations in
the grouping, rather than identity, is usually sufficient; and 2) the concept is
multidimensional rather than unidimensional (the similarity should apply
over more than a single set of cultural characteristics). Thus close agreement
between two nations on several attributes might permit one to group them
into a fairly homogeneous region despite moderate differences with respect
to another attribute. Close has to be a sufficient criterion because, in the
real world of social complexity, no two units are ever *identical* in anything
of importance. On the other hand, by the most usual applications of the
term even near identity with respect to a single attribute would not be
sufficient grounds for grouping countries together in the face of substantial
disparity on several others.

The emphasis on multidimensionality could of course be challenged,
but it is normally adhered to by those who write either descriptively or
theoretically about regions. More important, it coincides with the demands
regularly made by students of national or international integration. Hardly
ever do they single out a specific socio-cultural attribute—type of political
system, stage of economic development, language, religion, etc.—as being of
such over-riding importance that the others can be ignored. A much more
difficult type of decision arises, however, in the choice of which set of
attributes to concentrate attention upon. It should be clear at the outset that
no inclusive or exclusive set of universally politically relevant attributes of the
socio-cultural sort ever has been or is likely to be identified. Religious differences carried a divisive force in the Central Europe of the Thirty Years
War that they do not carry in the Europe of the Common Market. Linguistic

differences have a greater impact within India than in Belgium, and greater in Belgium than in Switzerland.

If the search for a universal set of politically relevant attributes is bound to end in frustration, a more fruitful approach is to compromise, via a certain element of induction. We can first seek out the major socio-cultural characteristics on which nations vary in the contemporary world, and then decide whether all are relevant to our concern with regional differences and the requirements of political integration. The analyses of this and the following chapter are based upon the data presented in the *World Handbook of Political and Social Indicators*[1] (Russett et al., 1964). In the *Handbook* 70 variables, for up to 133 countries each, were collected, refined, and correlated with each other. They were selected to provide information on a wide variety of social, cultural, political, and economic conditions in the late 1950's, and each was chosen for its relevance to several major hypotheses about comparative and international politics. While it is easy to think of other variables that might have been included, many would correlate quite highly with some already in the *Handbook,* and I believe we were reasonably catholic in our tastes. In the following chapter we shall confirm this point by comparing our results with those from other studies which did use some different variables.

In order to produce for this analysis a set of data with fairly complete information, I limited the study to 54 variables on 82 countries. The countries included most of the world's sovereign states and major colonies except for Sub-Saharan Africa, about which too few reliable data were present to make their inclusion worthwhile. I added several data to the *Handbook* collection from more recently available sources, and, where necessary, I estimated the values for missing data, so that there were no missing observations in the analysis.[2] I intended, however, not simply to use 54 indicators which happened to be available, but to analyze national variation on those variables that 1) were not purely idiosyncratic; 2) bore some relation to basic patterns of social and cultural variation across nations; and 3) seemed relevant to theories of political integration. Hence some method of finding the underlying patterns of association among the variables was required.

Factor analysis is a mathematical technique that has long been used in

---

[1] Fuller definitions of the variables, as well as extensive discussion of the problems of validity, reliability, and comparability, are to be found in Russett et al. (1964). As there, some variables were subjected to a logarithmic transformation before analysis.

[2] One method of estimation is multiple regression. Where this procedure was inapplicable it was often necessary to use the mean observations for countries which had data. If a logarithmic transformation had been applied it was the mean logarithm that was employed. Less than 15% of all observations had to be estimated, however. The effect of erroneous estimates, if random, would be to reduce the correlations among variables.

regional analysis for condensing a large body of data into summary dimensions. Its acceptance for research in international politics is more recent, but it has rapidly gained acknowledgment as a method of great value. It is especially appropriate to the needs of this endeavor, and will comprise the basic methodological tool of the book. In the most common type of analysis every variable is correlated with every other variable, using the product-moment coefficient. Those variables which show high correlations among themselves and very low correlation with other variables point to a single underlying dimension, or *factor*. The initial factors themselves are uncorrelated with (perpendicular to, orthogonal to) each other.

In this study I was able to reduce the 54 separate variables to five orthogonally rotated dimensions which together accounted for 54 variables. Table 2.1 presents the list of variables with their loadings (the correlations of the *particular* variable with the broader *factor* or dimension) on each of the five factors. At the top of each column is a descriptive label for the substantive dimension the factor seems to be measuring, and the percentage of the total variance (variation) accounted for by the factor.[3] For emphasis, factor loadings of 0.50 or higher are underlined, and loadings between 0.30 and 0.50 are italicized. The squared correlation coefficient (r^2) equals the proportion of the variance of each variable that is explained by the factor. Thus by ignoring loadings under 0.30 we are omitting from explicit consideration variables which bear only a very little relation (less than 10 per cent) to the factor and emphasizing only those where at least a quarter of the variance is accounted for.

MAJOR DIMENSIONS

The first factor is labeled *economic development,* from the variables which load heavily on (are highly correlated with) it. They include Gross National Product per capita (variable No. 1); newspapers (2) and radios (6) per capita; life expectancy (4); percentage of labor force in industry (10); pupils in primary and secondary school (11); literacy (12); urbanization (15); infant mortality rate (26); and, with high negative correlations, percentage of G.N.P. from agriculture (7) and labor force in agriculture (8); hospital beds (9) and physicians (19) per capita; and birth

[3] Each factor has an *eigen value* from which one can tell how much of the total variance in the 54 variables is explained by the factor. It is computed by summing the squared coefficients of correlation of each variable with the factor. Since each variable has a variance equal to unity, dividing the eigen value by the number of variables indicates the percentage of total variance that is explained by each factor. By a procedure known as *rotation* to *simple structure* one obtains factors which tend to have either very high or very low correlations with the variables, thus making it easy to identify those variables which contribute most to a substantive interpretation of the factor.

rate (13). It is remarkable, in fact, how high these correlations are for so many variables. Virtually any one of them would, by itself, form a reasonable measure of economic development. Together in this factor they account for 31 per cent of the total variance in the table.

The second factor is clearly a measure of *communist* influence with very extensive government ownership of the means of production and tight control over the electoral process. Variables which load highly on it include votes for communist parties (31) and a negative correlation with non-communist secular votes (34), government expenditure (32) and revenue (33) (including those of publicly-owned enterprises), the rate of increase of G.N.P. per capita (35), and total voting turnout (36).

Factor three could be called *intensive agriculture* (to contrast with *ex*tensive agriculture). Variables loading highly on it include overall population density (38) and density as related to agricultural land (39) and, negatively, area (47). One might call the dimension simply *density* except for the fact that inequality of land distribution (41) is rather negatively correlated with it, emphasizing that in sparsely settled countries there are not only small family farms but a number of great estates as well. Though it is hard to find a perfect label, it is clear that a pattern of agriculture is the dimension at issue here, a pattern that may have important roots and consequences in the general structure of a society. The latter interpretation is supported by the correlations between 0.30 and 0.50 of a number of other variables (40, 50–52) with it.

The fourth factor may best be called simply *size*. Correlated with it are total population (45), total G.N.P. (46), and area (47); foreign trade as a percentage of G.N.P. (48) is negatively correlated with size. (Big countries are more self-sufficient.)[4] Finally, factor five might for convenience be labeled *Catholic culture* because of the variable loading which is highest on it (50). Other high loadings include those for all Christians as a percentage of population (51) and votes for socialist parties (52). The latter, plus the moderately high loadings of television ownership (16), speakers of dominant language (28), Moslems as a percentage of population (negative, 29) and land inequality (41), indicates that a fairly broad cultural phenomenon, rather than a purely religious one, is being measured.

These are the five most important factors; no other accounted for as much as 5 per cent of the variance. Furthermore, no other factor had more than a single variable with a loading as high as 0.60 on it, and in most cases they defied clear substantive interpretation. We shall, therefore, work only with these five dimensions in attempting to delineate homogeneous groupings.

[4] For a fuller discussion of the implications of these correlations see Russett *et al.* (1964).

TABLE 2.1

Basic Sociocultural Dimensions

Variable	Factor 1 Economic Development 31%	Factor 2 Communism 11%	Factor 3 Intensive Agriculture 6%	Factor 4 Size 7%	Factor 5 Catholic Culture 5%
1 G.N.P. per Capita	0.94	−0.00	−0.04	0.06	0.09
2 Newspapers per 1000 Population	0.93	0.13	−0.01	−0.03	0.06
3 Non-Agricultural Workers as % Wage and Salary Earners	0.93	0.00	0.03	0.05	−0.05
4 Life Expectancy	0.92	0.09	0.10	−0.01	−0.02
5 % Labor Force in Agriculture	−0.89	0.12	−0.12	−0.02	−0.04
6 Radios per 1000 Population	0.88	0.09	−0.14	−0.04	0.26
7 Domestic Mail per Capita	0.87	0.11	0.07	0.10	−0.09
8 % of G.N.P. from Agriculture	−0.85	0.04	−0.08	0.03	−0.07
9 Inhabitants per Hospital Bed	−0.85	−0.18	0.10	0.16	−0.11
10 % Labor Force in Industry	0.85	0.19	0.04	0.09	−0.06
11 Primary and Secondary School Pupils as % of Population	0.83	0.12	0.11	−0.08	−0.08
12 % Adults Literate	0.82	0.21	0.07	0.07	0.07
13 Births per 1000 Population	−0.82	−0.26	−0.17	−0.16	0.05
14 Wage and Salary Earners as % of Working Age Population	0.80	0.07	−0.07	−0.05	−0.04
15 % of Population in Cities	0.77	−0.09	−0.11	0.05	−0.14
16 Television Sets per 1000 Population	0.70	−0.01	−0.03	0.26	0.35
17 Foreign Mail per Capita	0.68	−0.09	0.22	−0.30	−0.05
18 Cinema Attendance per Capita	0.67	0.26	−0.03	−0.09	0.03

TABLE 2.1—(Cont.)
Basic Sociocultural Dimensions

Variable	Factor 1 Economic Development 31%	Factor 2 Communism 11%	Factor 3 Intensive Agriculture 6%	Factor 4 Size 7%	Factor 5 Catholic Culture 5%
19 Inhabitants per Physician	−0.62	−0.05	−0.08	−0.09	−0.23
20 Investment as % of G.N.P.	0.60	0.44	−0.21	−0.20	−0.12
21 % of Population of Working Age	0.58	0.30	0.16	0.29	−0.03
22 Deaths from Political Violence	−0.55	−0.02	−0.22	−0.12	0.23
23 Students in Higher Education as % Population	0.53	−0.03	−0.04	0.42	0.18
24 Radios per 1000 Population—% Annual Increase	0.52	0.12	0.05	0.27	0.24
25 Annual Rate of Population Increase	−0.52	−0.31	−0.23	−0.11	−0.02
26 Infant Mortality Rate	−0.52	0.03	−0.14	0.13	−0.07
27 Private Consumption as % of G.N.P.	−0.47	−0.30	0.20	−0.06	0.28
28 Speakers of Dominant Language as % of Population	0.44	−0.06	−0.00	−0.17	0.30
29 Moslems as % of Population	−0.42	−0.05	0.05	−0.13	−0.35
30 Female Workers As % of Labor Force	0.37	0.30	−0.05	0.06	−0.00
31 Communist Votes as % of All Votes	−0.01	0.96	0.00	0.14	0.03
32 Central Government Expenditure as % of G.N.P.	0.11	0.95	0.04	0.08	−0.03
33 Central Government Revenue as % of G.N.P.	0.12	0.94	0.06	0.11	−0.01
34 Non-Communist Secular Votes as % of All Votes	−0.05	−0.92	−0.15	−0.14	−0.05

TABLE 2.1—(Cont.)

Basic Sociocultural Dimensions

Variable	Factor 1 Economic Development 31%	Factor 2 Communism 11%	Factor 3 Intensive Agriculture 6%	Factor 4 Size 7%	Factor 5 Catholic Culture 5%
35 G.N.P. per Capita—% of Annual Increase	_0.31_	_0.61_	0.28	0.10	−0.06
36 Votes as % of Voting Age Population	_0.41_	_0.59_	0.01	−0.02	−0.17
37 Inhabitants per Hospital Bed—% of Annual Change	0.23	_−0.30_	−0.07	−0.09	0.15
38 Population Density	0.02	0.16	_0.90_	−0.03	−0.02
39 Population per Hectare Agricultural Land	−0.07	0.06	_0.89_	−0.03	−0.05
40 Foreign Mail Sent/Foreign Mail Received	0.18	0.19	_0.45_	−0.05	0.08
41 Inequality of Farm Land Distribution	−0.23	−0.12	_−0.42_	−0.24	_0.35_
42 Religious Party Vote as % of All Votes	0.09	−0.13	_0.37_	−0.00	0.10
43 % of Labor Force in Agriculture—% of Annual Change	0.18	0.07	_0.31_	0.22	0.08
44 Military Personnel as % of Working Age Population	0.13	0.20	_0.30_	0.04	−0.27
45 Total Population	−0.14	0.15	0.06	_0.93_	−0.12
46 Gross National Product	_0.35_	0.14	0.04	_0.89_	−0.07
47 Area	−0.11	0.01	_−0.59_	_0.74_	−0.06
48 Foreign Trade as % of G.N.P.	0.15	_−0.38_	0.08	_−0.66_	−0.03

TABLE 2.1—(Cont.)

Basic Sociocultural Dimensions

Variable	Factor 1 Economic Development 31%	Factor 2 Communism 11%	Factor 3 Intensive Agriculture 6%	Factor 4 Size 7%	Factor 5 Catholic Culture 5%
49 Defense Expenditures as % of G.N.P.	−0.02	0.22	0.21	_0.41_	−0.09
50 Roman Catholics as % of Population	0.04	−0.13	0.02	−0.11	_0.87_
51 All Christians as % of Population	_0.47_	0.01	−0.09	−0.17	_0.68_
52 Socialist Vote as % of All Votes	_0.31_	−0.29	0.18	−0.14	−_0.53_
53 Executive Stability	0.04	−0.04	−0.01	−0.21	−0.05
54 % of Farms Rented	−0.03	−0.09	0.15	0.08	−0.01

For Table 2.1, as elsewhere in this book, the "principal components" method of factor analysis was used. The dimensions shown are the orthogonally rotated factors, and ones (unities) were inserted in the principal diagonal. All ten factors with eigen values greater than one were rotated. For a technical discussion of the method see Harman (1960), and for an illuminating handbook written especially for political scientists see Rummel (1967a). See also Denton (1965) and Anderson, Watts, and Wilcox (1966), Ch. 7. For applications in regional analysis see Kendall (1939), Hagood, Danilevsky, and Beum (1941), Hagood (1943), Cattell (1949), Cattell, Breul, and Hartman (1951), Berry (1960, 1961b), Moser and Scott (1961), Thompson, Sufrin, Gould, and Buck (1964), Olsen and Garb (1965), Gregg and Banks (1965), and Megee (1966). For examples and further references in international politics see Alker (1964), Alker and Russett (1965), Rummel (1963, 1964, 1967b), Rummel, Sawyer, Guetzkow, and Tanter (1967, forthcoming), and Tanter (1966).

Yet even this requires a further modification. Although size is obviously a *characteristic* of a country, it is not a *cultural attribute*. Except perhaps in the interplay of international power politics, Luxembourg would be thought of as similar to Belgium or Germany; it is not less European for being small and weak. Nor is there any very convincing theory or evidence about international integration that indicates that the prospective members of a new unit should be the same size. (On the contrary, the idea of a powerful core area to provide centripetal force is rather more persuasive. See Deutsch *et al.* (1957, pp. 137–319), and Etzioni (1965, pp. 294–300).) Thus in the interest of agreement with most intuitive notions of what cultural and social variables are relevant to the delineation of regions, and with existing evidence on what is relevant to integration, we shall hitherto ignore the size factor (number four). This also serves the interests of parsimony, for intellectually we shall be best off with the smallest number of dimensions which can provide an adequate identification of regions. It leaves us with two general cultural dimensions—one political and the other theological, and two which more nearly measure broad aspects of the structure of social systems—development and land use.

Factor analysis was originally devised by psychologists, and at that by psychologists who were interested more in general dimensions of mental ability ("vectors of the mind") than in individual persons. Thus it was, and still is, most commonly used as a method for finding correlations among tests, in a matrix where each item (test-taker, or, in our application, a country) is a row and each variable (test or sociocultural index) is a column. But by turning the table 90 degrees (transposing it) the countries become columns and the indices become rows. When this transposed matrix is factored, the correlations identify countries with similar patterns on the variables and the factors point to clusters of similar countries. The term Q-analysis is usually used to distinguish this procedure from the more common technique (R-analysis) employed earlier, but the mathematical procedures are just the same. Q-analysis has by now been used rather frequently in other disciplines, though to my knowledge the only published applications to comparative or international politics are those of Banks and Gregg (1965) and my own on voting in the United Nations (Russett, 1966).

I transposed the matrix for a Q-analysis,[5] but in keeping with the preceding discussion I employed only those sociocultural indices which were fairly highly correlated (0.60 or greater) with one of the four dimensions identified as relevant to our concern with regional delineation and integration. Use of only these 29 variables seemed a reasonable compromise between brute empiricism (throwing in every available cross-national index) and a priori specification of a few individual indicators—not just broad dimensions—as crucial to integration (a procedure that would not be supportable in the still amorphous state of contemporary theory). The indices associated with economic development are far more numerous than the others, but do not contribute disproportionately to the Q-analysis results. Because countries essentially are similar or dissimilar on all indices associated with a dimension, in the Q-analysis the influence is more nearly equal for each dimension than for each index. That is of course appropriate, since we

[5] When transposing a matrix for a Q-analysis the original variables must be transformed so that all are measured on the same scale. (For example, one cannot use the original figures for both dollar and percentage units in the Q-analysis.) Sometimes this is done by giving each variable the same mean and standard deviation. While this may be appropriate for the applications of psychology, especially where assumptions can plausibly be made about a random sample and a normal distribution of the variable in the universe, it is a theoretically inappropriate procedure for ecological data where some distributions are roughly normal and others (like percentage Christian, or per cent votes for Communist Party) are very bimodal. Forcing both to take the same standard deviation would greatly reduce the range and influence in the analysis of the bimodal distribution relative to the normal one, thus implying that the extreme bimodal cases there were "closer" than the extremes of the normal distribution. It seems to me much more appropriate with these data to assume that the ranges are equal, so I transformed all variables to a uniform zero to one scale.

would not want economic development to be grossly over-weighted, and certainly not weighted merely according to the availability of data for the original indicators.

This second analysis tells us what countries are like each other in terms of a variety of indicators. It provides the number of factors necessary for grouping the countries, and the relative importance of each. We can discover which countries load most heavily on each factor and give them a descriptive regional name or names. The factors and clusters of countries need not be identical. A factor might be bipolar, with one cluster of countries having very high positive loadings on it and another group of countries with high negative loadings. Or, as is in fact the case below, a cluster may be identified by its members' moderately high loadings on two separate factors. But the Q-analysis does give us a parsimonious way of looking in detail at the configuration. Table 2.2 shows four rotated factors, and five clusters, so derived, as well as a few countries at the end which are not closely identified with any single grouping. The map in Figure 2.1 presents the same results graphically.

THE REGIONS AND THEIR CHARACTERISTICS

Except possibly for the fourth one, each of these groupings is readily identifiable as very similar to a region in common parlance. Group one, for instance, corresponds quite closely to Asia and the Arab states, with few exceptions. Of the countries physically located on the Asian continent, its periphery, or Saharan Africa, only Japan, the Philippines, Israel, and China are missing.

Table 2.3 will help explain why some countries were included and others excluded from the groups which emerged inductively from the Q-analysis. It gives the factor scores for each country on the four socio-cultural dimensions originally derived from the *Handbook* (the dimensions, omitting size, given in Table 2.1 and used in the selection of indicators for the Q-analysis). A factor score is a composite index built up from a country's values on the original indicators, with each indicator weighted by a coefficient which corresponds roughly to that indicator's contribution to the underlying factor. Thus it gives us a measure of economic development, for instance, that is related to the original data but as a composite index is less subject to error or idiosyncratic variation on particular indicators. But because they are composites they must be interpreted as rough and general indicators rather than as precise measures. It is not hard to point out where particular rankings might seem more plausible if reversed. This is part of the price one pays for using a composite index (though the same problem often arises, from measurement error, even in simple indicators). Except that it would com-

TABLE 2.2
Regions of Sociocultural Homogeneity

	Factor 1 23%	Factor 2 27%	Factor 3 22%	Factor 4 9%
Afro-Asia				
Tunisia	0.92	−0.06	0.28	−0.03
Iraq	0.91	−0.13	0.21	−0.09
Iran	0.90	−0.09	0.22	−0.11
India	0.87	−0.27	0.24	−0.12
Malaya	0.88	0.16	0.13	−0.09
Turkey	0.88	0.06	0.20	0.06
Morocco	0.87	−0.07	0.28	−0.12
Thailand	0.86	−0.06	0.27	0.02
South Korea	0.85	−0.02	0.21	−0.00
Burma	0.84	−0.27	0.23	0.00
Syria	0.84	−0.05	0.26	−0.19
Jordan	0.84	−0.04	0.19	−0.05
Taiwan	0.84	0.12	0.04	−0.05
Ceylon	0.84	0.18	0.21	0.01
Indonesia	0.82	−0.25	0.18	−0.01
Pakistan	0.79	−0.35	0.24	−0.25
Egypt	0.76	−0.05	0.14	−0.08
Algeria	0.75	0.01	0.33	0.05
Mauritius	0.60	0.25	0.25	−0.11
Lebanon	0.50	0.25	0.29	−0.11
Western Community				
Denmark	0.04	0.98	0.01	−0.05
Sweden	−0.05	0.97	−0.03	0.05
Norway	0.06	0.94	0.05	0.14
United Kingdom	−0.10	0.93	−0.12	−0.14
United States	−0.01	0.93	−0.02	−0.18
Switzerland	−0.12	0.93	0.09	0.00
West Germany	−0.21	0.91	0.00	0.06
Finland	0.11	0.91	0.09	0.26
Canada	−0.10	0.89	0.20	−0.10
Netherlands	−0.06	0.89	0.04	0.16
France	−0.22	0.87	0.30	0.10
Iceland	0.02	0.82	0.12	0.08
New Zealand	−0.04	0.85	−0.06	−0.12
Australia	−0.16	0.81	−0.03	−0.19
Belgium	−0.27	0.81	0.24	0.02
Austria	−0.29	0.78	0.25	0.14
Luxembourg	−0.31	0.77	0.26	0.05
Cyprus	0.44	0.75	0.26	0.13
Ireland	−0.11	0.74	0.50	−0.01
Argentina	−0.19	0.74	0.51	−0.24
Japan	0.36	0.73	−0.25	0.12
Greece	0.42	0.67	0.32	0.15
Italy	−0.27	0.66	0.38	0.20
Israel	0.26	0.62	−0.34	−0.03

TABLE 2.2—(Cont.)

Regions of Sociocultural Homogeneity

	Factor 1 23%	Factor 2 27%	Factor 3 22%	Factor 4 9%
Malta	−0.04	0.61	0.42	−0.03
Trinidad	0.25	0.54	0.10	−0.12
Latin America				
Colombia	0.16	0.15	0.95	−0.04
Honduras	0.34	−0.06	0.92	−0.09
Nicaragua	0.31	−0.04	0.92	−0.05
Ecuador	0.25	0.05	0.90	−0.12
Guatemala	0.34	−0.06	0.90	−0.09
El Salvador	0.34	0.06	0.90	−0.09
Dominican Republic	0.31	0.02	0.89	−0.06
Peru	0.22	0.17	0.88	−0.11
Costa Rica	0.23	0.28	0.87	−0.01
Mexico	0.20	0.10	0.87	−0.19
Brazil	0.21	0.28	0.87	−0.17
Bolivia	0.30	−0.12	0.86	−0.14
Paraguay	0.26	0.01	0.85	−0.08
Panama	0.20	0.39	0.82	−0.10
Philippines	0.43	0.10	0.81	−0.08
Venezuela	−0.08	0.35	0.67	−0.14
Semi-Developed Latins				
Uruguay	−0.17	0.64	0.51	−0.08
Puerto Rico	0.05	0.59	0.60	−0.02
Cuba	0.01	0.56	0.74	−0.14
Spain	0.01	0.54	0.65	−0.01
Portugal	0.13	0.53	0.73	0.08
Chile	−0.11	0.49	0.64	−0.11
Eastern Europe				
Romania	−0.03	−0.00	−0.15	0.97
Yugoslavia	0.02	−0.08	−0.04	0.95
Bulgaria	−0.04	0.00	−0.29	0.92
Poland	−0.41	0.03	0.17	0.83
Albania	0.30	−0.41	−0.19	0.78
Hungary	−0.53	0.24	−0.20	0.73
Czechoslovakia	−0.50	0.30	−0.26	0.71
East Germany	−0.36	0.42	−0.39	0.66
U.S.S.R.	0.22	0.18	−0.55	0.66
Unclassifiable				
Haiti	0.58	−0.34	0.66	−0.06
Jamaica	0.42	0.47	0.50	0.11
Guyana	0.43	0.44	0.29	0.04
South Africa	0.49	0.52	0.14	−0.07
China	0.44	−0.63	−0.17	0.53

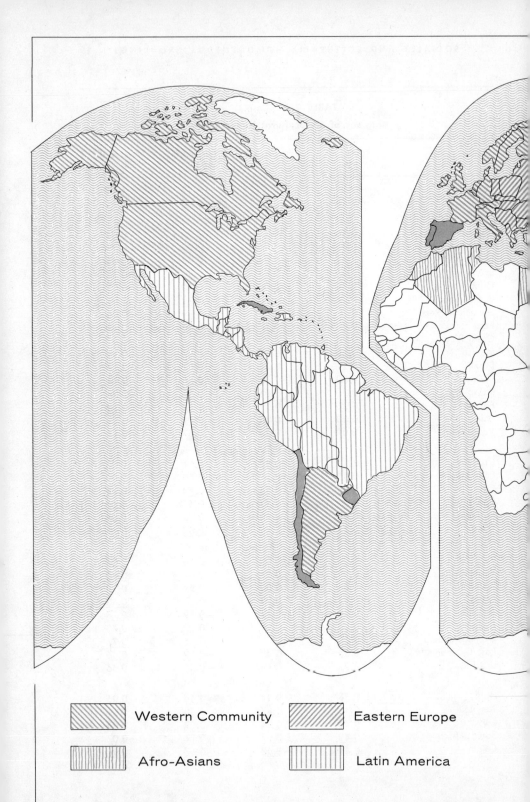

Western Community   Eastern Europe

Afro-Asians   Latin America

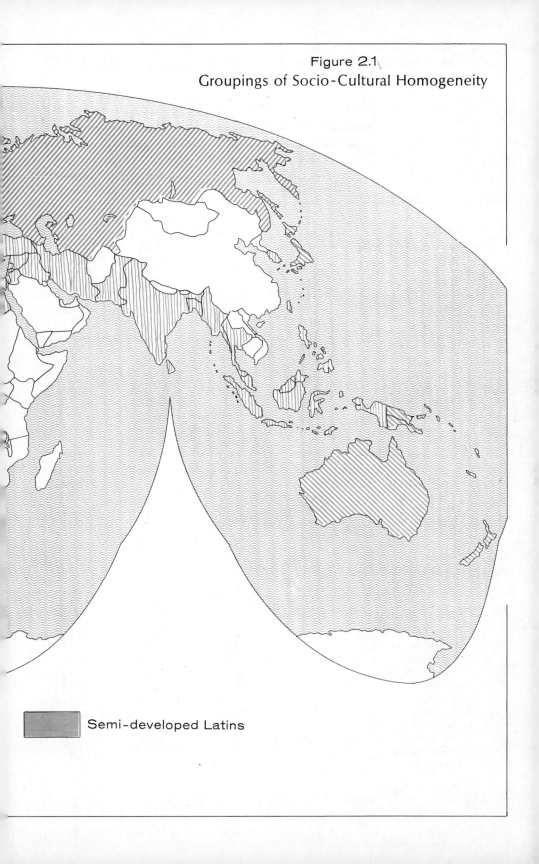

Figure 2.1
Groupings of Socio-Cultural Homogeneity

Semi-developed Latins

TABLE 2.3

Countries' Factor Scores on Sociocultural Dimensions

	Factor 1 Economic Development	Factor 2 Communism	Factor 3 Intensive Agriculture	Factor 5 Catholic Culture
		Afro-Asia		
Mean	−0.93	−0.36	0.27	−0.85
Standard Deviation	0.56	0.37	0.89	0.56
Tunisia	−0.89	−0.27	−0.24	−0.47
Iraq	−0.81	−0.27	−0.57	−0.76
Iran	−0.90	−0.18	−0.90	−1.09
Malaya	−0.50	−0.50	0.23	−1.12
Turkey	−0.84	−0.36	0.22	−0.77
Morocco	−1.03	−0.56	−0.21	−0.77
India	−1.77	−0.61	0.73	−1.20
Thailand	−1.43	−0.50	0.25	−1.13
South Korea	−1.07	−0.64	1.72	−0.15
Burma	−1.56	0.04	−0.30	−1.92
Syria	−0.67	−0.53	−0.80	−0.75
Jordan	−0.71	0.24	0.23	−1.02
Taiwan	−0.06	−0.54	2.07	−1.54
Ceylon	−0.79	−0.56	0.62	−1.50
Indonesia	−1.77	0.41	0.16	−1.17
Pakistan	−2.05	−1.01	0.60	−0.85
Egypt	−0.46	−1.01	1.07	0.54
Algeria	−1.00	0.53	−1.50	−0.61
Mauritius	−0.37	−0.02	1.45	−0.72
Lebanon	0.07	−0.36	0.49	0.11
		Western Community		
Mean	1.15	−0.31	0.14	−0.28
Standard Deviation	0.45	0.38	1.24	0.88
Denmark	1.73	−0.84	0.59	−1.05
Sweden	1.55	−0.41	−0.16	−0.13
Norway	1.29	−0.33	−0.16	−1.05
United Kingdom	1.78	−0.63	0.70	−0.92
United States	1.90	−1.11	−0.87	0.54
Switzerland	1.37	−0.81	1.00	−0.21
West Germany	1.51	−0.00	1.11	0.18
Finland	0.93	−0.01	−0.50	−0.82
Canada	1.47	−0.93	−1.33	−0.01
Netherlands	1.34	0.00	1.85	0.08
France	1.18	−0.11	0.55	0.32
Iceland	1.01	−0.19	−2.27	−1.00
New Zealand	1.57	−0.37	−1.30	−1.39
Australia	1.74	−0.56	−2.86	−1.39

TABLE 2.3—(Cont.)

Countries' Factor Scores on Sociocultural Dimensions

	Factor 1 Economic Development	Factor 2 Communism	Factor 3 Intensive Agriculture	Factor 5 Catholic Culture
Belgium	1.26	−0.29	1.87	0.56
Austria	1.10	0.29	0.80	0.50
Luxembourg	1.31	0.14	0.87	0.51
Cyprus	0.40	−0.39	−0.02	−0.44
Ireland	0.77	−0.52	0.21	0.52
Argentina	0.79	−0.72	−1.88	−0.87
Japan	0.77	−0.12	1.13	−1.79
Greece	0.18	−0.32	0.44	−0.24
Italy	0.75	0.57	1.02	1.28
Israel	1.24	0.19	0.27	−1.43
Malta	0.64	−0.37	−1.54	1.09
Trinidad	0.58	−0.11	0.44	−1.03
		Latin America		
Mean	−0.66	−0.40	−0.55	1.20
Standard Deviation	0.38	0.27	0.66	0.30
Colombia	−0.58	−0.28	−0.91	1.83
Honduras	−1.09	−0.45	−0.54	1.42
Nicaragua	−0.76	−0.08	−0.48	0.97
Ecuador	−0.74	−0.34	−0.28	1.21
Guatemala	−1.18	−0.43	0.02	1.32
El Salvador	−0.70	−0.55	0.21	1.47
Dominican Republic	−0.70	−0.25	0.14	1.38
Peru	−0.55	−0.33	−0.97	1.07
Costa Rica	−0.41	−0.37	−0.65	1.29
Mexico	−0.44	−0.70	−0.24	1.28
Brazil	−0.32	−0.83	−0.71	1.12
Bolivia	−1.10	−0.06	−1.94	0.85
Paraguay	−0.75	−0.52	−0.94	0.98
Panama	−0.41	−0.61	−0.37	1.19
Philippines	−1.18	−0.82	0.65	0.44
Venezuela	0.35	0.19	−1.74	1.38
	Semi-Developed Latins			
Mean	0.23	−0.47	0.24	1.11
Standard Deviation	0.21	0.14	0.95	0.12
Uruguay	0.62	−0.34	−1.54	1.09
Puerto Rico	0.09	−0.40	1.23	1.03
Cuba	0.14	−0.28	−0.16	1.27
Spain	0.39	−0.66	0.78	0.94
Portugal	0.01	−0.60	1.11	1.10
Chile	0.12	−0.56	−0.01	1.27

TABLE 2.3—(Cont.)

Countries' Factor Scores on Sociocultural Dimensions

	Factor 1 Economic Development	Factor 2 Communism	Factor 3 Intensive Agriculture	Factor 5 Catholic Culture
Eastern Europe				
Mean	0.20	2.55	−0.01	0.18
Standard Deviation	0.57	0.21	0.63	0.74
Romania	−0.17	2.72	0.15	0.23
Yugoslavia	−0.22	2.36	0.38	−0.37
Bulgaria	0.11	2.74	0.11	0.14
Poland	0.06	2.17	0.54	0.98
Albania	−0.82	2.76	−0.06	−0.78
Hungary	0.46	2.45	−0.17	1.16
Czechoslovakia	0.71	2.42	0.11	0.43
East Germany	1.02	2.72	0.42	0.72
U.S.S.R.	0.66	2.58	−1.58	−0.92
Unclassifiable				
Haiti	−1.87	0.03	0.68	0.12
Jamaica	−0.21	−0.29	0.53	−0.84
Guyana	0.15	−0.26	−1.17	−0.92
South Africa	−0.04	−0.47	−1.44	−0.86
China	−1.83	2.48	−0.14	−0.69

plicate communication, there is much to be said for simply labeling the factors X, Y, and Z. Otherwise one risks the fallacy of misplaced concreteness: for example, the argument that the factor scores must somehow be wrong because Argentina is *really* more Catholic than Uruguay, not less so. "Catholic culture" is a useful and descriptive label, but still an imperfect one for the underlying dimension being measured. The factor scores themselves of course do not enter into the actual Q-analysis.

These factor scores have been standardized with a mean of zero over the entire world and a standard deviation of unity. At the head of each grouping in Table 2.3 we give the mean and standard deviation of each set of factor scores for the group. The smaller the standard deviation the greater the group's homogeneity on that dimension. Thus we can easily see the profile of the "Afro-Asian" group: very underdeveloped, moderately noncommunist, decidedly not Catholic in culture, and in which population densities and agricultural patterns may vary rather widely.

Although abstractly Turkey might have been considered a candidate for a European grouping, actually it fits the Afro-Asian profile almost perfectly. And Lebanon, as the wealthiest Middle Eastern country in our sample, and with a population that is one-half Christian, barely makes the cluster. Several other countries which might have been expected to group with the other Asian states do not. Japan and Israel both load more highly on the dimension that identifies the "Western Community" than on the Afro-Asian one—each is economically much more developed (by three and four times the standard deviation from the mean respectively) than the typical Asian nation. And the Philippines, predominantly Roman Catholic in religion and heavily influenced by the colonial rule of Spain and the United States, is on these dimensions more like a Latin American than an Asian country. China, listed with the unclassifiables at the end, is in political ways like her fellow communist states, but is economically much more backward.

The second grouping is best described by some term like "Western Community." Leaving aside for the moment a few countries in the fourth group ("Semi-Developed Latins"), it includes all the states of Western Europe, North America, and Oceania. And in addition to Israel and the European or European-settled nations it includes, fairly far down in the list, Japan and Trinidad. From Table 2.3 we can see that these states vary substantially in the intensive agriculture and Catholic culture dimensions, but are characterized by moderately low communism scores and, uniformly, by a high level of economic development. The presence of Japan is especially noteworthy. On three of the four original dimensions Japan's profile shows quite a close approximation (within a standard deviation of the mean) to the countries of Europe and North America. Japan's economic prosperity has brought her to a per capita income level not far below the other industrial states, and Japan is the only member of the Organization for Economic Cooperation and Development from outside the geographically-defined area of the North Atlantic.[6] Only Japan's very non-Catholic culture keeps her from a more central position in the cluster, and provides a loading, albeit fairly low, on the first factor which in Table 2.2 is identified with Afro-Asia. Greece and Cyprus have some affinity for the Afro-Asia factor, but still come in here toward the bottom. This Western Community of developed industrialized nations makes no distinction between Western Europe and the English-speaking states, or between neutrals and NATO allies. In their modest way, these findings support the advocate of "Atlantic Union" against the Gaullist notion of a Europe "from the Atlantic to the Urals." Along with Guyana (former British Guiana) and Jamaica, South Africa loads about as highly on the first factor as on the second, and is put with the unclassifiables. It is of course precisely the efforts of its white government to keep the country from becoming socially and culturally Afro-Asian that has produced the present political tension.

Although there are some important exclusions, the third cluster, "Latin

[6] The underdeveloped countries increasingly share this perception of Japan as not one of them and frequently exclude her from their deliberations, as at the June 1964 U.N. Conference on Trade and Development (Okita, 1965).

America," includes only Western Hemisphere countries and the Philippines. But several of the twenty republics of Central and South America are missing. Haiti's absence is readily understandable. Its level of economic development is two standard deviations below the Latin American mean, and is actually well under the average even for Asia. It also ranks comparatively low on Catholic culture (Voodoo?), has a higher population density than most Western Hemisphere states, and even rates moderately high on communism. (Perhaps its above-average score on "communism" is typical of certain kinds of non-communist but authoritarian regimes.) Haiti's score does not, of course, approach that of nations which actually have communist governments.[7]

Also missing from this group are all the political units which have, or had until recently, colonial governments. Trinidad, relatively well developed and non-Catholic, fits uneasily at the end of the Western Community listing. Most relevant to the exclusion of Guyana was its score on Catholic culture, eight standard deviations below the Latin American mean. The same is true of Jamaica, which joins Guyana among the unclassifiables. Like the other countries at the bottom of the table, they were left separate because they had two or more loadings above 0.40, the higher of which, when squared, was less than twice the magnitude of the smaller one squared. That is, the proportion of the variance accounted for by the more important factor was less than two times that accounted for by a second. As a result these states cannot be placed unambiguously in a single cluster.

Most commonly in a factor analysis of this sort the factors can with relative ease be used to identify groups of countries. But several countries in this analysis are distinguished by the way in which they load more or less equally on the same two factors, those which above picked out the Latin American and Western Community states. This is illustrated in Figure 2.2, a scattergram with the positions of the countries on the two competing factors plotted between the axes. The vertical axis represents the percentage of variance (100 times the factor loading squared) accounted for by Factor 2, and the horizontal axis the percentage explained by Factor 3. All the countries with loadings of 0.40 or higher on *both* factors are represented, as well as several others for reference.

In some instances one factor accounts for three or more times as much of a country's variance as does the other, and when this happens there is little question as to where the nation should be grouped. This applies, for instance, to Venezuela, which I unhesitatingly assigned to the Latin American cluster. Any country which occupies a position either between the vertical

[7] Asians frequently perceive the identity of their area as distinct from Latin America and Africa in population density as well as underdevelopment (Lakdawala, 1964, p. 80).

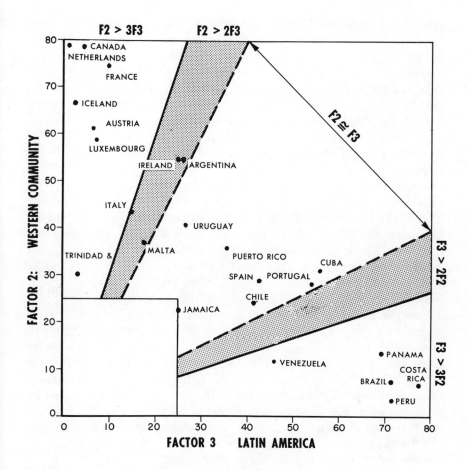

FIGURE 2.2:   Semi-Developed Latins Grouping as Identified by Moderate Loadings on Factors 2 and 3

axis and the sloping solid line to its right, or between the horizontal axis and the sloping solid line above it, has this variance ratio of more than three to one. Although the countries occupying this space are distinctly more marginal than ones lying closer to the axes, it is usually not unreasonable still to assign them as weak members of the group whose factor accounts for more than twice as much variance as any other. Accordingly I did so with Argentina, Ireland, Italy, and Malta, putting them too with the Western Community. And states which have less than 25 per cent of their variance accounted for by either of these factors would fall into the square at the lower left of the diagram, which has been left empty.

But six states go into the area where the percentage of the variance explained by the more powerful factor is less than twice that of the other. They are Portugal and Spain from Europe, Cuba and Puerto Rico from the Caribbean, and Chile and Uruguay from South America. All share much the same Catholic culture as the Latin American states, but their level of economic development is appreciably higher, even though short of the Western Community mean. The presence of the poor Iberian states, bearers of Latin culture to the New World, is instructive if not really surprising. (In a sense the French proverb should be revised to declare, "Latin America begins at the Pyrenées.")[8] The label "Semi-Developed Latins" is awkward and probably the least satisfying, intuitively, of the inductive classifications so far encountered here. We shall, nevertheless, treat this as a separate group even though it is not as distinct from either the Latin Americans or the Western Community as the latter two are from each other. Jamaica is shown on the graph but ought not to be considered part of the cluster. Its case indicates the limitations of a two-dimensional presentation. Had we a third dimension, depth, represented here we would see that Jamaica is kept distinct by a moderately high loading also on the "Afro-Asia" factor.

Finally, we come to the "Eastern European" group, which could with some justice be equated with the communist countries.[9] Communism is of course the most sharply discriminating dimension for this group, but a middle level of economic development and fairly low Catholic culture are also typical features. As with all the other clusters, there is a wide variation in agricultural patterns and the mean of the scores from the "intensive agriculture" factor is neither very high nor very low. On all of them the group is quite homogeneous (with low standard deviations). Yugoslavia is not notably different, by these criteria, from any of the countries under more

[8] The idea that Western civilization is divided between a "liberal" North Atlantic culture and a traditionalist and authoritarian Southern European and Latin American one certainly is not new. Cf. Salvadori (1947, pp. 16-17). Cohen (1963, pp. 128-31) discusses the political and cultural as well as physical similarities between the Old World Mediterranean and the New World Mediterranean (Caribbean).

[9] The data used here antedate the Castro regime in Cuba.

immediate Russian influence. Mainland China, however, is put with the unclassifiables because of its high loading also on the factor identified with Afro-Asia and high *negative* loading on the Western Community factor. And note that China's backward satellite Albania, though in the Eastern Europe group, itself has quite a high loading on the Afro-Asian factor, much higher than that of any other Eastern European state.

There have been a few peculiarities, but despite them we have found that, by purely inductive techniques, using indicators identified with only four cultural dimensions, we can classify, with a high degree of plausibility, the world's polities into socio-cultural "regions." Four factors, which find five groupings, account for 80 per cent of the variance. (Nine factors with eigen values greater than one were rotated, but only the first four accounted for as much as three per cent of the variance.) This occurs without the injection of any *a priori* judgments as to the number of regions which should be found, or what those regions should be. We did not include, as we might have, some explicitly geographical variables (like longitude and latitude) in the analysis. And we have been using the geographic term "region" loosely. For historical reasons regions and sociocultural groupings often more or less agree, but they need not. Yet in four of the five cases the regions which emerged from our analysis do correspond to generally recognizable geographic groupings, and all make substantial cultural sense.

We could not, of course, insist that the groupings coincide perfectly with common usage since, as we found in the previous chapter, there *are* no generally accepted, unambiguous sociocultural criteria for grouping. Nevertheless, where in Table 2.2 there were exceptions to the usual conceptions it was possible to explain them, and in explaining them to add something to our understanding of international comparative politics. For example, Haiti's presence in the Asia group made substantial sense on reflection, as did Japan's absence from Asia. Both of these cases in fact suggest important aspects of the countries' political and social systems.

3

SOME ALTERNATIVE ANALYSES AND THEIR CONSEQUENCES

THE SEARCH FOR TRUTH

THE *INTELLECTUAL CONSTRUCT* OF A REGION AND THE *mathematical technique* of factor analysis share an important property— neither produces Truth: In the opening chapter we made it clear that we expected to find no universally applicable set of regions, for the delineation of a region will vary both with the general type of criterion applied (homogeneity, interdependence, etc.) and with the particular variables (such as those which made up our cultural dimensions) employed. A quest for such an all-purpose region would be as fruitless as the alchemists' search for the universal solvent. Similarly, in words which form virtually a cliche to students of multivariate statistics, in factor analysis you "get out only what you put in." That is to say, the factor pattern which emerges is, like that from any inductive procedure, dependent upon the original choice of variables.

The regions identified in chapter two were derived from a Q-analysis of 29 variables representing four particular dimensions, which themselves come from a larger set of 54 variables with data for a particular point in time which was subject to particular sorts of error in the original compilation of the data. No other set of data would produce precisely the same factor loadings, or quite the same rank order of countries on the various factors, or perhaps even quite the same groupings. These differences are likely to be greatest for those countries which in any given analysis are found at the periphery of a region. We have not found Truth, nor will anyone else. Our aim, of course, is more modest—to find groupings or regions which are reasonably stable and not unduly dependent upon a choice of socio-cultural variables which cannot be justified in terms of existing theories of what is relevant to political integration. Without pretending that our choice cannot be improved by expansion or contraction of the list of indicators, we must then go on to compare our set of groupings with those derived from different types of criteria and attempt to reach some conclusions about the temporal and causal relations between say, regions of high socio-cultural similarity and regions of interdependence. To repeat with emphasis: we are not attempting to make a definitive identification, nor merely to *describe* and engage in a mapping exercise in any case, but in the course of this volume to examine the association of a variety of variables and to discover if there is some systematic pattern of organization among them. But to make exhaustive comparison worthwhile we must first establish the degree to which our results so far have depended upon our particular choice of indicators and method.

Several other investigators have clustered countries on more or less related dimensions. The regions of chapter two coincide rather well with those derived by Brian Berry (1960, 1961a) from examination of countries' scores on an economic development and a demographic scale. Most of Berry's variables were economic, but the similarity of results indicates a degree of cross-method validation. Nevertheless the use in chapter two of more dimensions, and explicitly political and cultural rather than just economic ones, allows much better differentiation than Berry was able to achieve within the limits he set himself. In the original (and largely unknown to geographers and political scientists) study by Raymond Cattell (1950) similar regions were also found, though with more unclassifiable countries and with more countries whose classification it was hard to interpret substantively. The difference there is partly attributable to differences in method (factor analysis used only for finding the cultural dimensions, then a *clustering* method for finding regions), but mostly to the poorer quality of the pre-World War II data with which Cattell was then forced to work.

Two more recent attempts show substantially greater variation. Arthur Banks and Phillip Gregg (1965) performed a Q-factor analysis of all 68 political variables in the *Cross-Polity Survey* (Banks and Textor, 1963). They found five factors or groupings, which they identified as "polyarchic," "centrist," "elitist," "personalist," and "traditional." The five bear no very close resemblance to the groupings of this study; the "centrist" factor, for example, loads such socially and culturally diverse states as Afghanistan, Spain, and Czechoslovakia. Though there are a number of anomalies, the groupings do make a degree of intuitive sense in terms of *political* similarities. This is to be expected from the authors' exclusive choice of explicitly political variables, and it comes as no surprise that they differ from the ones in this book.

Similarly, Rudolph Rummel (see Rummel, Sawyer, Guetzkow, and Tanter, 1967) analyzed a "distance matrix" (a procedure to be discussed below) built from 14 factors in turn derived from 236 original variables.

Except for one grouping made up of the majority of the Latin American states, and another of several of what we called "Anglo-Saxon" countries, there is little similarity to our groupings, and nearly a third of his countries failed to load as high as 0.50 on any factor. But again this is not surprising when one recalls Rummel's different theoretical purpose, the great diversity in his original choice of variables, and the fact that a number of his factors more nearly indexed characteristics of nations like size rather than *socio-cultural attributes* of the sort we have emphasized. (The nature of Rummel's variables and dimensions will be considered in greater detail below.)

ARE THE DIMENSIONS RELIABLE? DIFFERENTIATING WITHIN SUBGROUPS

From this brief reference to other grouping attempts it is apparent that two major questions must be asked. First, to what degree are our regions a peculiar result of the *method* (factor analysis) employed, and would they be substantially different with other but still objective and generally accepted techniques for grouping or clustering? Second, to what degree are our regions the result of a unique set of *variables* or socio-cultural dimensions that differ seriously from those that have been employed in similar studies in the past or that might be selected in future explorations? Let us turn first to the latter problem, with the former treated in the Appendix.

From the infinite list of possible indices of socio-cultural differences among nations, in chapter two we selected 54, which were then reduced to five factors or dimensions. The selection was based upon the availability of data and a rather intuitive sense, grounded in the literature of international integration, of what variables were relevant. But since the selection could not be derived from a complete and a rigorous theory of international relations we could not assert either that all the variables were relevant, or more important perhaps, that of all the possible variables in the universe we had the most relevant ones. On the contrary, we expressed substantial doubt as to the prospects for ever compiling such a list of universally relevant variables precisely because of the differing role that variables play in contrasting socio-political contexts. The most important influences often change over time and place.

Yet we must establish whether the variables we did select do at least combine into stable factors measuring seemingly important dimensions of cultural variation. Two approaches, employed together, commend themselves. First we must discover whether similar dimensions have been found in other studies, and if so whether there are any additional ones that were not turned up among our 54 variables. This will be done by means of a systematic comparison with other factor analyses of cross-national ecological and political data. After comparing the results we can then ask generally how limited or distorted our dimensions are and whether something important perhaps has been overlooked in all the studies.

One possible objection to our five major socio-cultural factors is that although they exist on a *universal* basis, over all countries, they would not necessarily differentiate nations within selected relatively homogeneous subgroups. For instance, though "Catholic culture" may help to distinguish nations within the total international system, no such dimension might appear when only states with a high proportion of Catholics, such as those of Latin America, are analyzed. Given our intention to differentiate among nations throughout the world this objection does not in any case cut to the heart of our approach; nevertheless it will be useful to demonstrate the degree to which our five dimensions do emerge even from the analysis of sub-groups. For this purpose I divided the 82 nations into four relatively homogeneous and contiguous groups much like those in the preceding chapter: Asia and Africa, Latin America (including the colonies), Communist Countries, and Western Community.

Table 3.1 below shows the degree of association between each of the five major factors or dimensions which emerged from our 54 variable analysis of all countries and those found in separate analyses of each of the four "continental" aggregates defined above. Recall that in introducing factor analysis we discussed it in both geometrical and algebraic terms. In algebraic language the factors of an orthogonal analysis were said to be uncorrelated; in geometrical terms they are perpendicular to each other and delineate the dimensions of a factor space. Yrjo Ahmavaara (1954) has developed a technique which can compare two separate factor analyses of different populations by examining the factor loadings of those variables which are common to both studies. This technique can be expressed geometrically as transforming the factors of one study into the factor space of the other. Since each factor can be represented by a straight line, when two factors are given the same mid-point their degree of similarity can be measured by the angle between them, with a very small angle of course representing near identity.

The values in the following tables are the *cosines* between the angles. Only cosines of at least 0.50 are shown. The cosine of an angle may vary between zero and 1.0, with 1.0 representing identity of the lines and zero an angle of 90° or perpendicularity, and the cosines here may be interpreted as indices of agreement or regression coefficients (beta weights) showing the degree of fit between the two factors.[1]

[1] Further exposition and examples of its use can be found in Ahmavaara (1957), and Ahmavaara and Markkanen (1958), with discussion and application to cross-national political research in Namenwirth and Brewer (1966) Rummel (1967), and Rummel, Sawyer, Guetzkow, and Tanter (1967). Harman (1960, pp. 233-38) also develops this method, although he has not applied it in the manner here. On

TABLE 3.1
Indices of Agreement Between Worldwide Dimensions and Dimensions of Continents

	Economic Development	Communism	Intensive Agriculture	Size	Catholic Culture
Asia and Africa					
Factor 1	0.94				
Factor 2				0.94	
Factor 3			0.94		
Factor 4		0.69			
Factor 5					0.91
Latin America					
Factor 1	0.97				
Factor 2				0.62	0.98
Factor 3			0.93		
Factor 4		0.80		−0.53	
Factor 5		0.54			
Western Community					
Factor 1	0.94				−0.52
Factor 2			0.79		0.68
Factor 3				0.90	
Factor 4		0.84			
Communist Countries					
Factor 1	0.98				
Factor 2				0.96	
Factor 3		0.89			
Factor 4					0.56
Factor 5			0.68		

The five "worldwide" factors from chapter two each occupy a column in Table 3.1. All factors from each of the continent analyses which account for at least 5 per cent of the variance and have cosines equal to at least 0.50 with one of the worldwide factors are given in the rows. The numbers in the cells are the cosines.

A factor very closely corresponding to the original economic development dimension is found as the first and largest factor in each of the four conti-

---

pages 256-59 Harman introduces an index for comparing factor scores, as applied by several earlier writers, which is in fact the cosine of the angle between the vectors. Kaiser (1960) developed a similar method. Despite the expositional hazards of introducing yet another methodological discussion into what is intended primarily as a substantive volume, I have done so because the alternative means of comparing factors, correlation of their factor loadings, frequently gives an inaccurate comparison. The major difficulty is that a correlation of loadings might show high similarity between two factors which had a similar pattern but great differences in the absolute value of their loadings.

nental analyses. The cosine in no instance drops below a very striking 0.94. An intensive agriculture or density dimension is also found in each, although the cosines are usually a little lower indicating not quite such a good fit. Size clearly emerges in three of the four continents, but not so unambiguously in the Latin American analysis. Communism is also distinguishable as a reasonably distinct dimension in every case. Examination of the actual factor loadings for each variable in the Western Community analysis (I have not reported the loadings here) shows the reasons for the relatively low index—the factor in question is discernibly political, but is better defined by the size of the governmental activity or welfare state rather than communism. Government revenues and expenditures as a proportion of G.N.P. load very highly on it, as does voting turnout. But the proportionate vote for various parties (communists, socialists, etc.) is little related to it. In Asia and Africa precisely the opposite applies, where there is no distinct dimension of governmental activity but rather one well defined by the party composition of votes. Finally Catholic culture, or at least some sort of religious dimension, appears everywhere and most strongly in Asia and in Latin America. Thus with quite moderate qualification we can conclude that these five dimensions provide useful ways of differentiating among nations even within areas of fairly high cultural homogeneity.

What factors, other than our basic five, emerged in the intra-continental analyses? Not many, in fact. A dimension defined chiefly by high loadings for executive stability and deaths from domestic violence appeared in the Western Community and Communist factor analyses, and one with the former but not the latter emerged also in Asia and Africa. The only other instance of a similar factor emerging in more than one continent analysis is what might be termed a military dimension. With its highest loadings on defense expenditure percentage and military personnel ratios, it appeared in both the Asian and Western Community analyses. But except for two quite idiosyncratic factors in Latin America and one each in the Western Community and Communist aggregates, that exhausts the list.

Dimensions from Other Studies

Another approach to this problem is to compare our basic five factors with those that were found in seven worldwide cross-national studies by other researchers, so as to examine the effect of including different sorts of variables. Table 3.2 is set up like the one before it except that each section now refers to a study by another analyst in which *some* of his variables are similar or identical to ours. It shows each of the factors in the other studies which have cosines equal to at least 0.50 with one of our five factors. The descriptive labels attached to their factors by the other authors are also given, as are the total number of factors extracted in each study.

TABLE 3.2

Indices of Agreement Between Factors From Different Studies

	Economic Develop-ment	Commu-nism	Intensive Agri-culture	Size	Catholic Culture
Robinson: Nine Factors					
2 Religion					−0.87
5 Population Density			−0.90		
6 Size				−0.90	
7 Economic Development	−0.91				
9 Totalitarianism		0.73			
Rummel: Fifteen Factors					
1 Economic Development	0.94			0.90	
2 Power Bases					
3 Political		−0.54			
6 Latin American					0.72
7 Density			0.91		
Berry: Four Factors					
1 Technological Scale	0.88				
2 Demographic Scale		−0.59		0.86	
3 Income and External Relations	0.80				−0.82
4 Large and Small			−0.87		
Gregg and Banks: Eleven Factors					
Factor 1	0.92		0.59	0.56	
Factor 3		0.54			−0.56
Factor 6		−0.55			−0.53
Factor 7			−0.69		
Factor 8				0.71	
Cattell and Gorsuch (1965): Fourteen Factors					
1 Vigorous Development	0.63				
3 Morality-Responsibility					−0.61
5 Size				0.60	
8 Narrowness vs. Enlightened Affluence			−0.70		
11 Medical Development	0.53	−0.62			
Cattell (1951): Twelve Factors					
1 Enlightened Affluence	0.56				
2 Vigorous Order	0.58				
4 Size	0.54	−0.83	0.57	0.78	

TABLE 3.2—(Cont.)

Indices of Agreement Between Factors From Different Studies

	Economic Development	Communism	Intensive Agriculture	Size	Catholic Culture
6 Classical Parochialism					0.50
7 Oriental Pattern					−0.62
8 Metropolitan Laxity			0.62		
Cattell (1949): Twelve Factors					
1 Size				0.50	
3 Enlightened Affluence				0.67	
4 Conservative Patriarchal Solidarity		0.54			
7 Vigorous Order	0.67				
9 Peaceful Progressiveness					0.58
12 Good Internal Morality			−0.53		

The best overall fit is seen between ours and the analysis by Robinson (1965) which analyzed 85 variables, the majority of which (57) are political variables from Banks and Textor (1963) but also include 25 variables coded in part from Russett et al. (1964) and the rest from other materials, including Ginsburg (1961). Thus, while there is some overlap between our study and Robinson's, the greater part of the data are quite different. Furthermore, Robinson found or estimated data for as many as 116 countries, and in addition reduced his data from interval to ordinal (0 to 10) scales. We thus have a useful example of what can result from the analysis of a substantially different set of cross-national data.

Three factors (our economic development, intensive agriculture, and size) have agreement indices of 0.90 or greater with three of Robinson's, to which he has assigned similar labels. Given differences in the "sample" of countries, in scaling, data error, and in the effects of other variables, these three factors can be considered nearly identical. Very close correspondence also is found between our Catholic culture factor and the one Robinson more generically identified as "religion." Even his "totalitarianism" and our "communism" factors are sufficiently similar to produce a cosine indicating an angle less than 45°. This much correspondence gives us substantial confidence in the stability and reliability of our basic socio-cultural dimensions.[2]

[2] The signs in the table should be ignored, since they merely indicate that the factor was *reflected* in one study so that countries with highly positive factor scores on one should be very negative in the other. The size, not the sign, is what should be watched.

The analysis of Rummel, Sawyer, Guetzkow, and Tanter (1967) on the whole supports this conclusion. Their examination of a host of variables (236) produced 15 factors, of which three correspond very closely with ours —our numbers one, three, and four, again, for two of which in fact the correspondence is even closer than with Robinson's.[3] Substantial similarity also appears between our Catholic culture and their "Latin American" factor. The fit between their "political" and our "communist" factors is less good but still respectable. A careful comparison of the two studies shows why the differences occur. Of the six variables which loaded over 0.50 on "communism" in our study, three deal with voting turnout or distribution and were not included by Rummel *et al.* And though Rummel *et al.* had a single measure of government participation in the economy, it dealt only with budgets and not public enterprises—thus for "mixed" and especially communist economies it bears little relation to our *two* indices of government involvement in the economy.

Berry (1960) analyzed 43 variables explicitly collected to measure economic development; it is understandable therefore that he obtained but four factors and that by far the largest part of the variance was accounted for by a "technological scale" which matches our economic development dimension well. But in addition, at least one of his dimensions corresponds well (cosine in the 0.80's) with each of ours.[4] Berry's choice of labels is different, but the influences behind the high cosines can readily be discovered. He called his second factor a "demographic scale" because of the high loadings of such indices as birth rate, infant mortality, and population growth. But moderately high loadings were also achieved by size variables including *total* G.N.P., total energy resources, and total energy consumption. Had Berry included more aggregated (rather than per capita) indices they almost surely would have loaded highly on this factor and he might have chosen another label. By contrast his factor identified as "the large and the small" was so named because it identified countries which on various indices are high or low *per unit area* "by virtue of their size" (Berry, 1961a, p. 116). But what size measures Berry did have (mentioned above) were not high loaders on this factor, and in fact Berry's highest loading is for a density measure. Our interpretation of his factor as related to density rather

---

[3] The comparison here is with the 15 oblique (slightly correlated) factors presented by Rummel *et al.*—which in fact are very similar to their orthogonally rotated analysis.

[4] Reading the table horizontally we see that occasionally *two* or more of our factors have quite high cosines with *one* of those in another study. This is because when the factors of our study are put into the space defined by the factors of another the requirement of orthogonality is relaxed, allowing two of our factors to become correlated with each other if necessary to produce the best fit with one in the other study. The result is that our two factors may straddle the other factor, fitting it between them like the line that bisects the angle between two lines.

than density "by virtue of size" is further supported by the fact that several large dense countries (e.g., India and China) have factor scores much nearer those of the United States, Canada, and the U.S.S.R. than the other end of the scale. Factor number three of Berry was called "contrasts in income and external relations." Our communism and Catholic culture factors result essentially from the fissioning of Berry's factor when a wider variety of cultural and political indices are included. On the list of "income and external relations" factor loadings the communist countries cluster at one end and many Latin American states are at the opposite pole.

In their analysis, Gregg and Banks factored a total of 81 variables, both ecological and political, from Banks and Textor (1963).[5] Though they did not label their factors, it is clear from the table, as well as from the variables which load highly on their first factor (G.N.P. per capita, newspaper circulation, etc.) that they extracted an economic development dimension much like ours. They also have a size factor and an intensive agriculture one, although the cosines between theirs and ours are rather lower. But our Communism and Catholic culture factors both split, each with about equal loadings of around 0.55 on their factors three and six. In Gregg and Banks' study some religious and geographical characteristics load on each dimension: Latin American region, former Spanish colony, and percentage Catholic on factor three; Middle Eastern, percentage Moslem, and religious homogeneity on factor six. There also are a number of political variables correlated with their factor three (governmental stability, presidential system, semi-modern bureaucracy) and one with factor six (political development under tutelage). None of the political variables, however, seems to have much to do with Communism. Certainly there is a resemblance between two of our factors and two of theirs (one largely religious and the other religious-political), but the way in which our two split up prevents us from claiming more than that.

Cattell's three studies (Cattell, 1949, Cattell, Breul, and Hartman, 1951, and Cattell and Gorsuch, 1965) can be considered more or less together. The first two were performed on 72 variables, with the data gathered largely from League of Nations and other pre-war sources. His first analysis included 69 countries; the second was cut to 40 where the data were more complete—mostly fairly advanced industrial states. The effort was undoubtedly hampered by the unreliability and incomparability of the data with which he was forced to work. His 1965 study was able to employ more recent and more accurate data for some variables, but his psychologist's interests and research design demanded the inclusion of a number of indices

---

[5] This study is different from that reported in the text of Gregg and Banks (1965), but is referred to in their footnote 15. I am very grateful to the authors for having provided me with the factor matrix.

whose data or operationalization remains shaky (e.g., deaths from various diseases, suicides, clashes with other countries). Even so, and allowing for the relatively few indices which are essentially the same in his studies and ours, we still find that each of our dimensions is fairly closely related to at least one of Cattell's in each of his analyses.[6] The cosines are only moderate (between the 0.50's and the low 0.80's) but that much correspondence is enough, with that found for the work of Robinson, Rummel, and Berry, to support strongly our belief in the essential reliability of our five factors.

The reliability is most clearly established for the *economic development, size,* and *intensive agriculture* dimensions. The frequency of a *Catholic culture* factor is also rather high, as it achieves cosines in the 0.80's with factors in two studies and in the 0.70's in a third. One could claim, however, that in many of the seven studies with which we have compared ours it is a more generalized religious factor than a specifically Catholic culture one. The weakest correspondence is between our *communism* factor and those in other analyses, but even here there is to be found one cosine in the 0.80's and another in the 0.70's. Again, perhaps a more general political factor would find better correspondence.

SINS OF OMISSION

Should we be working with more generalized dimensions? Despite the seeming parochialism of a Catholic culture factor, I think the answer for that one is no. The alternatives are either too parochial themselves, or obviously highly correlated with something else. Percentage Christian, as a variable, is well tapped by the economic development and Catholic culture variables (see Table 2.1). Another Eastern religion (such as percentage Buddhist, had we included it) would have had near-zero values for over 90 per cent of our countries. Possibly a better result would have derived from the inclusion of variables which might have correlated enough with percentage Moslem to produce an "Islam" dimension, since that variable is tapped only imperfectly by the first and fifth factors of our study. But in fact it cannot produce even as broad (multi-variate) a dimension as our Catholic culture because there are so few variables, other than geographic ones (which we have explicitly excluded from this phase of the analysis) which correlate highly with it. Of the 236 variables in the Rummel *et al.* (1967) study, only a very few had correlations above 0.50 with percentage Moslem.

Some might also question our communism factor, wishing instead for

[6] The number of variables in each comparison is: Robinson, 25; Rummel, *et al.*, 36; Berry, 12; Gregg and Banks, 13; Cattell (1949 and 1951), 9; Cattell and Gorsuch (1965), 12.

a broader political dimension, perhaps a factor that would distinguish more effectively among the non-communist states since the factor score distribution on the "communism" dimension is essentially bimodal. I did consider adding one or more variables to try to tap a democracy or "polyarchy" dimension, but was unable to devise an adequate index.[7] A quite different approach would have been to resort to judgmental or *expert coding* variables, but the procedure would have been so different from the insistence on *"hard,"* objective indicators elsewhere in this volume that I decided against that too. Any index or dimension which equated the non-democratic states— the totalitarian states of Eastern Europe and the traditional oligarchies of Asia and the Middle East—would be profoundly disturbing to a democrat and to a Marxist equally. In any case, with the communism dimension we are tapping with some success the most pervasive political dimension in the world today—and a political dimension which has greater impact on the organization of a nation's economy and society than any other. Finally, we have actually had rather good success, in the clustering, in distinguishing the democratic states from the others. In the clusters a few democratic nations in Asia and Latin America do not differ notably from their authoritarian neighbors, but some (e.g., Japan, Israel) do and the Western Community group pulls out the democracies rather nicely. Rather than search for some additional indicator to do the job mechanically, the reader who is concerned about this matter might better simply use the factor results as guides to thought and imagination, not rigid categories.

The major question remaining is whether any important dimensions have been entirely omitted. To return to other analyses, not surprisingly the largest number of dimensions was extracted by Rummel *et al.* (1967) from their 236-variable study. Our 54 variables were concerned exclusively with the social, economic, political and cultural attributes of national systems—but not yet with their *physical* characteristics or spatial location, their *behavior* in international politics and organization, nor their *interdependence* with specific countries or areas. Approximately one-third of Rummel *et al.'s* variables are of the latter types. Thus it was to be expected that they would find more dimensions, though not necessarily one that we would want to adopt for our rather different, and in some ways more limited, purposes. Six of the minor Rummel *et al.* factors were composed of

[7] One possibility would have been "percentage of votes cast for largest party." Yet while non-democracy might be well measured by this variable at the extremes (over say, 90 per cent, and zero where there are no elections) it is almost useless in between, where one has little basis for calling a multi-party system with 45 per cent of the vote for the largest party either more or less democratic than a state where the largest party gets 55 per cent of the vote. Most students of politics conclude that democracy or polyarchy is actually a multi-dimensional concept and cannot be measured by any single index. For an ingenious attempt to operationalize various aspects see Neubauer (1967).

such diverse variables that they defied the authors' efforts at appropriate description, and so they left the factors unlabelled. Of those they did name, we earlier found that five more or less corresponded with our five. The others they identified as "foreign conflict," "domestic conflict," "ethnic-linguistic homogeneity," and "trade to G.N.P. ratio."

Gregg and Banks (1965) found a number of distinct political dimensions, as was only to be expected from a study where three-fourths of the variables were explicitly political. Robinson (1965) also found two political factors, which he identified as tapping stability and elitism, in addition to a demographic (population growth rate and age distribution) factor and one he left unnamed. Cattell found a number of other factors in each of his studies, but despite his imaginative labels it is hard to be sure just what is the meaning of many of the dimensions. Berry (1960) had one less factor in his study than we did.[8]

From this it would appear that the most important dimension ignored by our five factors is probably a political one, dealing either with the stability or conflict aspects of national polities, or with the role of elites and leadership. Yet these attributes have been only imperfectly defined and identified in the literature of political science; to attempt to include them in this analysis would perhaps be sailing beyond the limits of our existing navigational charts. Certainly the role of such attributes in the process of international integration is far from clear. Any social scientist, and especially an anthropologist, could suggest many others. Cultural traits like family structure, linguistics, and personality types all may have some relevance. But just to mention them shows how this job can never be complete. Future research can doubtless refine the work of the last two chapters, but for the present we must turn to mining the ore of several quite different lodes.

[8] In an attempt to measure political development Adelman and Morris (1965) performed a factor analysis on data for 74 less-developed countries. In addition to an economic development factor they found three political factors, which seemed to measure democracy-authoritarianism, stability, and leadership characteristics. Because the "sample" is of underdeveloped states rather than worldwide, and because too few of their variables were similar to ours, however, a systematic comparison of factors was impossible. See also Adelman and Morris, 1966.

*APPENDIX

DIFFERENT METHODS: HIERARCHICAL CLUSTERING

The other problem was whether our regions were primarily artifacts of our choice of analytical method. We can establish with a high degree of confidence that they are not, and that other methods would produce similar results.

Of the host of other methods available, the most appropriate seemed to be a hierarchical grouping technique whose intellectual ancestors include the analysis of variance.[9] It begins with each of the 82 countries treated as a separate unit and finds the two which are most similar, using to measure similarity an index of "distance" derived from several uncorrelated (orthogonal) indices. Here I used the factor scores from Table 2.3. The distance between two countries on each factor is simply the difference between the two countries' factor scores, and the combined distance for the four dimensions is the square root of the squared differences on each of the four factors summed.[10] With this index we get a measure of the "cultural distance" between each pair of countries. Countries like the United States and China, which differ widely on all four factors, will be far apart; states like Costa Rica and Honduras, which are very similar on three of the four, will be much closer. Each of the dimensions is weighted equally. At each step of the program either an additional country is added to an existing group, or two previous groups are merged, always according to the criterion that the new combination be that which will add least to the previous total of summed distances. It continues until all countries are together in a single group.

In addition to its central employment of the criterion of minimizing within-group variation, which is just what we mean by homogeneity, the major advantage of this technique is its use of the hierarchical principle. That feature acknowledges a key element in any regionalizing scheme, and permits us to see precisely how a large group is built up from subsets and individuals. Its chief disadvantage is that within-group variation is minimized *at any given stage* with the limitation that a group, once formed, cannot later be decomposed. By treating previously formed groups as given it cannot allow for the possibility that splitting up tentatively formed groups and rebuilding them in different combinations might well produce even less within-group variation. Both the virtues and faults of the technique will be obvious in Table 3.3.

* Some readers may prefer to omit this technical section on the first reading.
[9] The program used was *MESA 502-Grouping*, written by B. Choppin from a method described by Ward and Hook (1963). Computations were performed at the University of Chicago Computing Center. A similar procedure is described by Sawyer and Nosanchuk (1960).

[10]

$$D_{ij} = \sqrt{\sum_{p=1}^{k} (X_{ip} - X_{jp})^2}$$

where i and j are two nations, x_p the factor scores on factor p, and there are k factors. For a similar formulation and use see Stone (1960). This and related notions of distance have been employed for some time, as may be seen in Sokal and Sneath (1963, pp. 143ff.), and Osgood, Suci, and Tannenbaum (1957, Ch. 3).

TABLE 3.3

Five Socio-Cultural Groups Formed by Hierarchical Procedure

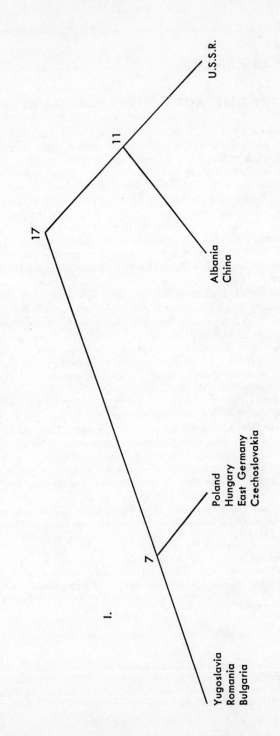

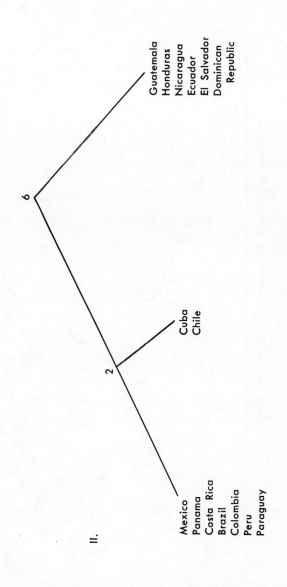

TABLE 3.3—(Cont.)

Five Socio-Cultural Groups Formed by Hierarchical Procedure

II.

Mexico
Panama
Costa Rica
Brazil
Colombia
Peru
Paraguay

2

Cuba
Chile

6

Guatemala
Honduras
Nicaragua
Ecuador
El Salvador
Dominican
  Republic

TABLE 3.3—(Cont.)

Five Socio-Cultural Groups Formed by Hierarchical Procedure

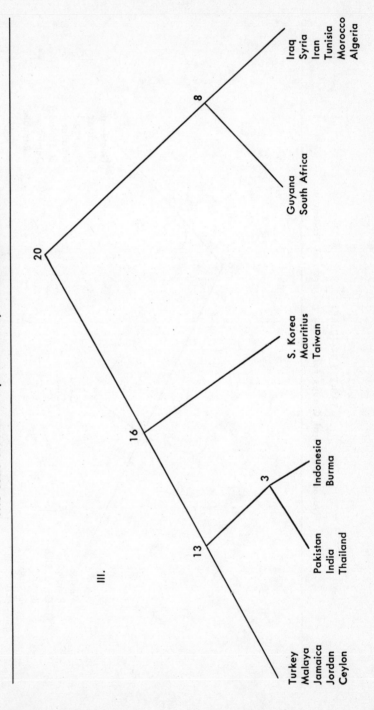

TABLE 3.3—(Cont.)

Five Socio-Cultural Groups Formed by Hierarchical Procedure

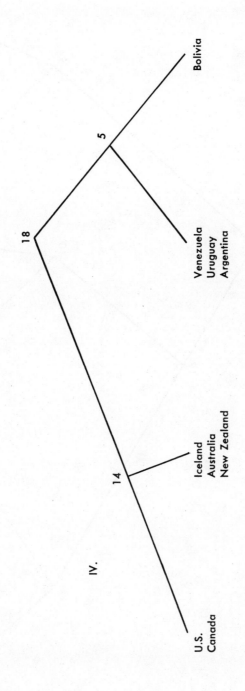

TABLE 3.3—(Cont.)

Five Socio-Cultural Groups Formed by Hierarchical Procedure

The table shows hierarchically how the data were reduced to given groups. I stopped at five clusters as a basis for comparison with the previous factor analysis, but without that guideline one might well cease at more or fewer groupings—and knowing the proper point at which to decide one has the correct number of groups is not simple. For the table I have carried the analysis back a total of 21 steps to show the hierarchy; although information exists to carry it back as far as the beginning with 82 separate "groupings" such a graph would provide more detail than is necessary. The number at each juncture in the graph indicates the step at which the two groups were joined, with the steps numbered from 1 (earliest) to 21 (last).

One group contains almost the same countries as we formerly labelled Eastern Europe, though the sub-groupings, especially of the Balkan states and of Albania and China, set off a bit more vividly some of the information contained in the earlier factor loadings. (It is also tempting, if not at this point fully legitimate, to note the correspondence between the socio-economic subgroups of the communist countries and current political alignments: USSR; China-Albania; relatively independent Romania and Yugoslavia—though not Bulgaria; and the East European states still tied fairly closely to Russia and to each other.) Two of the other groups correspond well with those originally called Afro-Asia and Latin America but there are a few differences. Bolivia and Venezuela are not in this Latin group. Haiti is here with Afro-Asia, as are Jamaica, Guyana, and South Africa. The reasons will be apparent on examination of the remaining groups. But note the high homogeneity of this Latin American cluster, as illustrated by the early point at which the entire group coalesced. Many of the sub-sets of both groups are also interesting, such as the early emergence of Southeast Asian and Arab clusterings under Asia, and of a Caribbean group (plus poor Ecuador) in Latin America. The richer Central American states of Mexico, Panama, and Costa Rica join the complete Latin cluster via another route.

The two remaining groups resemble the Semi-Developed Latin and Western Community clusters only in a rather general way. Some of the Anglo-Saxon countries become joined with a few Latin American nations, but the rest go together in a very large and complex group that also includes Lebanon, Egypt, the Philippines, and Haiti. (All 82 countries were classified somewhere by the time this step in the hierarchical analysis was reached.) Certainly the most puzzling cases are Haiti and Egypt, but on close scrutiny the reason, and the limitation of the method, appears. Returning to Table 2.2 we see that Haiti loaded rather highly on both Afro-Asia and on Latin America. The Philippines also showed moderately high (0.43 and 0.81) loadings on those two factors, so the merging of those two with Egypt (high on Afro-Asia) into a group by this method is not so very inconsistent with the analysis of Chapter 2. Similarly, Portugal, Puerto Rico, and Spain load on both Latin America and Western Community, so their further combination is also somewhat compatible with the Q-analysis results. And from there to the other West Europeans and Semi-Developed Latins is only a matter of several more steps in the hierarchy. But if at 21 Haiti and Egypt could then be removed and shifted into the Afro-Asian cluster the within-group variation in Western Community would be reduced by more than that of "Afro-Asia" was increased. A similar succession of steps accounts for joining some Anglo-Saxons with the richer Latins (plus Bolivia), which results in a rather peculiar group.

Because I used factor scores rather than all the raw variables I could not expect a perfect match with the Q-analysis anyway. But it is still apparent that the irreversibility of grouping decisions in the end makes this program less appropriate for our needs. In principle the program could be modified to remove this restriction, but the number of computations added would be most formidable and cannot yet be performed economically.[11]

A similar procedure, known as Multivariate Analysis of Contingencies (MAC II) has been programmed by James Lingoes (1963). After drafting this chapter I became aware of his procedure and ran my data through it as a check on the above results. The clusterings were very much like those from the Ward and Hook routine, though a couple of the worst anomalies (such as those involving Bolivia and Haiti) did not occur. Since the above demonstration illustrates this class of hierarchical clustering methods we can omit the detailed MAC II results, but they again confirm the basic resemblance of the outputs from different procedures.

Another procedure I tried was to use the matrix of socio-cultural distances described above, convert the distances into proximities with a range of zero to one, and input them into a direct factor analysis as though they were correlation coefficients. Direct factor analysis is a common and accepted procedure which will be employed extensively later in this book. Yet there is reason to think it is not fully appropriate for distances which meet the Euclidean criteria (as these do), in which case it may somewhat distort the configuration and dimensionality. Accordingly I have not published those results here.

One other possibility of great promise is a recent innovation in multidimensional scaling (MDS) methods not affected by the scale, or metric, of the raw data. The basic procedures are nonmetric in that they utilize the rank-order of countries' distances rather than the absolute distances. The scale of measurement is therefore ordinal rather than interval, and is useful under circumstances where one is unsure whether each unit in one's scale is equivalent to every other unit. A number of men have worked on the technique, with the most important breakthrough in computational procedures being that of Roger Shepard (1962a, 1962b). Since then refinements have been introduced by Kruskal (1965a, 1965b) and Lingoes (1964, 1965a, 1965b), drawing on work of their own and that of others, including Coombs (1964) and Louis Guttman, which has been underway for a number of years. The Guttman-Lingoes technique, for example, gives as final output the minimum number of co-ordinates necessary to describe the configuration of points (countries) in space, and the co-ordinates resemble the dimensions of factor analysis.

In most cases where one is unsure that one really has interval data the new non-metric procedures are hypothetically superior. (Though note the cautions of Torgerson (1965).) The margin of superiority may easily be overestimated, however, if two points are not remembered. First, the MDS computer routines currently available are limited at best to a 70 variable capacity, and most of the demonstrations in the literature are concerned with less than half that. Even that number requires much more computer time than a comparable factor analysis—approaching an order of magnitude difference. Of the many clustering attempts performed in this book

[11] Since first writing this it has been pointed out by the most recent work of Brian Berry (1965, 1966) that discriminant function analysis, performed iteratively, provides a means whereby a near-optimal clustering solution, as given by the Ward-Hook techniques, can be made into an optimal one. As such it forms a useful alternative, but two difficulties with it still remain. The decision as to the number of groups or clusters at which to stop is more arbitrary than with factor analysis, and its virtual requirement that every country must belong to *some* group is too restrictive when dealing with truly marginal cases.

only one is on a matrix with fewer than 70 countries, and several exceed 100. It is simply impossible, in the present state of technology, to produce with MDS a full simultaneous analysis of a large matrix that can be compared rigorously with the analysis of a second matrix (as we did in the main text of this chapter). Some compromises are possible, for instance breaking the large matrix into several pieces that can be processed separately, but this is crude and approximate.

Second, the differences in results produced by MDS and factor analysis are often exaggerated, especially if one is concerned not with finding the minimum number of *dimensions* to which a large matrix can be reduced—MDS will almost always provide fewer dimensions than factor analysis—but merely with comprehending the *configuration* of the variables vis-a-vis each other. In virtually all the cases I have seen (one of which is discussed in chapter eight, footnote 9) there has been little difference between the results of the two methods. This is not to say that on occasion one might not find substantial differences. It does require that, to settle the question finally, we have a *large sample* of rigorous comparisons in which all the comparisons are reported, not just those that produce very similar (or different) results as the analyst happens to want to show. Doubtless the MDS procedures will come to play a major role in social science, but the use of factor analysis will also continue for a long time in those cases where the assumption of interval data is not too outrageously violated and where a retreat to mere ordinality would lose valuable information.

We shall return to factor analysis with orthogonal rotation as the key grouping method of this volume, though supplemental use of the others might well occasionally add to our insights. But in making this decision after examining several leading alternatives we can do so with more confidence.[12] Consistent use of the same

[12] There is of course an enormous literature on clustering techniques which we have not discussed. In addition to a few which are essentially variants of the factor analysis methods here employed (e.g., the procedures discussed in Harman, 1960, pp. 128–31, 216–30) there are a number of other inductive procedures. These others, however, seem to suffer from either of two faults. Some, such as the very interesting HIDECS procedure of Alexander (1963), Alexander and Mannheim (1963), and Alexander (1964), and used by Brams (1965b), require an arbitrary transformation of ordinal or interval measures of pair similarity to dichotomous nominal measures which become merely "similar" and "different." Until very recently the same seems to have been true of the most complex and otherwise satisfactory methods of L. L. McQuitty (1964), but now this restriction may have been removed (McQuitty, 1966). Alternatively, techniques such as that introduced by Sawrey, Keller, and Conger (1960) group from an interval distance matrix but need an arbitrary limit for the dissimilarity tolerated in a group, a threshold beyond which a new member will not be added. All three of the procedures explored in this chapter avoid such inflexible requirements. Many other techniques are available if one chooses to test the homogeneity of pre-defined groups rather than to form groups inductively. An example of multiple discriminant function analysis applied to regions of Italy is Casetti (1964). For reviews of other methods see Bonner (1964) on clustering methods and Duncan, Cuzzort and Duncan (1961) and Haggett (1966) on procedures specifically for regional delineation. See also Sokal and Sneath (1963), Regnier (1964), and Ball (1965), who discusses many of the methodological and psychological problems involved in a large number of clustering techniques. The new BCTRY system of Tryon and Bailey (1966) may well prove to be the most efficient means of comparing a large number of procedures, but again there is little reason to expect it to modify seriously our conclusions.

One further variation on our basic method which deserves mention is *oblique*

method will help insure the highest possible degree of comparability from one set of data to the next. Such comparisons are of great importance to this study, and the factor matrices are uniquely suited for rigorous matching via the cosines.

---

rotation of the factor matrix. This procedure allows the factors to become correlated with (oblique to) each other if such correlations provide a better fit to the data. A need for oblique rotation is sometimes especially indicated if there are a large number of variables which load moderately on more than a single factor. I have not tried it on all the factor matrices reported on in this book, but as a check I did do it for two, without producing any important changes in the configuration. MacRae (1966) indicates some circumstances when oblique rotation may be important.

4

POLITICAL ATTITUDES AND UNITED NATIONS VOTING

GENERAL ASSEMBLY VOTING AS A SOURCE OF DATA

IN THE PREVIOUS CHAPTERS WE WERE CONCERNED WITH similarity on a number of socio-cultural attributes, only one of which, that measured by the "communist" dimension, was very political. Yet it also seems relevant to inquire about the similarity of people's *attitudes,* and especially political ones. To measure the attitudes of people at all levels, ideally we would like to have hard data from survey research, with highly comparable questions administered to national samples in every country which interests us. A number of such studies have been completed (e.g., Almond and Verba, 1963; Cantril, 1966; Szalai *et al.* 1966) or are under way (such as those under the direction of Alex Inkeles and Frederick Frey), usually with special attention to attitudes toward the national political system. Rigorous comparative elite studies in several nations, such as those of Free (1959) and that being conducted by Jacob *et al.* (1965), tap attitudes at a higher level of national decision-making systems. Despite the importance and promise of these studies, however, so far they have dealt with far fewer countries than come under scrutiny in this book.

A different approach, and perhaps ultimately one of equal promise, is exemplified by the content analysis made by David McClelland (1961) of children's readers in 41 countries. Though the sample of countries in this case (the product of very extensive research) is much larger than that available to provide comparable material from survey research, it still is smaller than we would wish—it would limit us to precisely half the number of nations we analyzed in the preceding pages. Equally serious is the difficulty involved in validating the data. For his indices McClelland reports "split-half reliability coefficients." That is, for each country the texts to be analyzed were divided randomly into two equal groups. Each group was then separately analyzed for the frequency of certain themes. Thus he had two sets of data, each for the same 41 countries, and could correlate the frequencies in one set with those in the other. The result, especially for his measures of the need for power and need for affiliation, was rather low correlations (r^2 of 0.24 and 0.32, respectively). Where two different analyses of the same country's materials differ so much one must hesitate to use the results as input to the kind of elaborate multi-variate analysis which is basic to this book. And finally, the attitudes, while of great importance to politics, are not strictly political and so would still omit dimensions that seem of direct relevance to political integration.

One other possible option might be to infer the relevant attitudes by some kind of intuitive process. The utilization of coding by experts, as practiced by Fitzgibbon and Johnson (1961) on the characteristics of Latin American nations, or by Klingberg (1941) on the distances separating nations on a number of dimensions, might be applied, with variations, to judge attitudinal similarity. The procedures of Banks and Textor (1963) for coding types of political structures are also relevant. But such techniques, however useful they may be for identifying national attributes, are of very dubious value in the measurement of *attitudes,* since they must rely upon extremely sparse and vaguely defined data bases. Some more direct and objective measure is required.

Given the constraints imposed by both data availability and relevance, the best solution would seem to be an analysis of nations' voting *behavior* in the United Nations General Assembly. Roll-call votes in the General Assembly provide a unique set of data wherein many national governments commit themselves simultaneously and publicly on a wide variety of major issues. The range of issues includes almost everything of major worldwide concern; even policy questions on parochial or regional issues (the intra-bloc relations of Communist states, for instance) can often be inferred from the nations' votes on other issues. The United Nations of course gives no perfect image of broader international politics; due to the one-nation one-vote principle and the fact that it is not a world government with authority to enforce its decisions, power relationships within the Assembly are not the same as in other arenas, such as functional or geographic ones. It might well be argued that because of the majority-rule principle the smaller and poorer states have an incentive to band together in the UN that they do not have elsewhere. Thus the discovery of a "bloc" of underdeveloped countries in the UN does not prove anything about the cohesion of that "bloc" in other contexts. And surely it is a rather long jump to equate the *behavior* of a *government,* with the *attitudes* of its *populace.* Governments are not always representative of their peoples' wishes, and especially so in the case of weak states whose regimes may find themselves under substantial environmental pressures in the international arena.

Yet the distance can nevertheless be exaggerated. Totalitarian governments have powerful means for restructuring their subjects' desires, and at the same time can seldom be utterly unresponsive to them. As we shall see in the following chapter, there is a striking degree of continuity in governments' basic voting positions over time, despite changes in personnel, party, and even regime—indicating a basic similarity between the interests of the politically relevant strata of a country and its government of the day. As for environmental pressures, they limit but do not freeze the movements of national governments. Just as a state in the United States may have both a Republican and a Democratic Senator, each building his support on a different subset of national as well as local interest groups, governments in international politics have some choice as to the style in which they will respond to environmental influences. Even if the image of world politics and national attitudes conveyed by actions in the General Assembly is warped and distorted, voting behavior there remains one of our best sources of replicable information on the policies of its over 100 members. And if there is a gap between elite attitudes as manifested in the Assembly and mass attitudes at home, the former is as relevant as the latter to any consideration of the prospects for the political integration of two nations. Without "a state of mind or disposition to be cohesive, to act together, to be committed to mutual programs," (Jacob and Teune, 1964, p. 10) at the governmental level there can be no long-term political integration. Thus we shall employ data on voting *behavior* as a surrogate for information on *attitudes,* which are what we really would like to measure but are unable to get at directly. In so doing we recognize that voting behavior is largely, but by no means totally, a function of attitudes, and that the jump to elite attitudes is shorter than to mass beliefs.

We shall analyze roll-call votes taken in the 18th Session of the General Assembly, which commenced in the autumn of 1963. Due to the United States vs. Russia and France controversy over dues, there was only a single recorded vote in the 19th (1964) Session, so these 1963 votes were the most recent data available at time of writing, and would not have been superseded before the *Official Records* of the 20th Session were published sometime in 1967. Our data consist of *all* 66 roll-call votes, both plenary and committee, except those which are virtually unanimous (defined here as more than 90 per cent of those voting taking one side—usually in favor; no country was recorded as affirmative as much as 85 per cent of the time either). This restriction is necessary because the product moment correlation coefficient is seriously distorted by a distribution more lopsided than 90–10. The omission might result in hiding any very small group that was virtually always with the majority or consistently in the minority, but is not likely to be important because typically such very lopsided votes account for less than 10 per cent of all those in a session. In practice the only group whose cohesion and isolation might be understated is the handful of states (Portugal, Spain, South Africa, France, Belgium, sometimes the United Kingdom) which is so out of step with the Assembly majority on African colonial issues. As we shall see below, Portugal and Spain do actually cluster together anyway, and South Africa is not even included in this analysis because of its high absenteeism. (This example, however, constitutes a warning against proc-essing the data too mechanically without a careful inspection of the *Records.*)

On every vote each state was coded either 2 (affirmative) 1 (abstain) or 0 (negative). Absenteeism is rather frequent in the Assembly, however, and posed something of a problem. In a few cases a country, though absent, later officially indicated its position. I recorded it as if it had so voted. Also, in some cases an absence is clearly intended to demonstrate opposition to the resolution, or a conviction that the Assembly is overstepping the bounds of its authority in considering the issue. The United Kingdom found itself in such a position over several votes on Southern Rhodesia in the 18th Session. In those cases I recorded the absence as a negative vote. Both of these procedures are in conformity with the practice of earlier researches (Lijphart, 1963, Alker and Russett, 1965).

The remaining absences are in general concentrated on a few countries, often those with small delegations. While it would sometimes be possible to estimate an absent nation's voting position from the votes of other states in its geographical area or caucusing group, in our inductive search for voting groups such a procedure would prejudice the results and not be admissible. Instead I chose to equate an absence with abstention. In many instances an absence does in fact mean abstention, but by no means always, and when it does not, the result is to incorporate a degree of imprecision in the analysis. The average absenteeism for the Assembly is about 12 per cent, and for the vast majority of states less than 25 per cent. Since the equation of absence with abstain actually assigns a state to a middle position on our three-point scale, and since it is sometimes the correct interpretation anyway, this treat-ment of absences will not seriously distort the voting position of all countries with 25 per cent or fewer absences—their scores on the factors below are not affected by more than about 8 per cent. For those countries (11 in the 18th Session) with greater absenteeism the distortion is potentially more serious, and in Table 4.3 (pp. 69–71) below they are marked with a † symbol to indicate that their positions should be treated with some caution. Four other states (Dominican Republic, Honduras, Luxembourg, and South Africa) were absent more than 40 per cent of the time and so were excluded entirely from the analysis. Kenya and Zanzibar, admitted well after the Session was under way, were also omitted.

BASIC ISSUES IN THE 1963 GENERAL ASSEMBLY

Before proceeding to the identification of groups of countries it is appropriate, and analogous to the procedure of chapter two, first to delineate the major issues around which conflict centered in the 18th Session. (By their nature non-unanimous votes pick out issue areas of conflict rather than areas of consensus, but votes on which high consensus existed would hardly give us a basis for distinguishing *differences* among countries.) We first, therefore, examine the results of a factor analysis employing every one of the 66 roll-calls as a variable. Table 4.1 shown on pp. 64–65 presents the rotated factor matrix with the loadings of each roll-call on each of the major factors. In all, nine factors with eigen values (i.e., the sum of the squared loadings) greater than unity were extracted, accounting for 78 per cent of the total variance. Four of those, however, were highly idiosyncratic factors accounting for no more than 4 per cent of the variance apiece and having no roll-calls with a loading as high as 0.70. Only the first five are presented, accounting for 66 per cent of the total variance. All primary loadings of 0.40 or higher are given. Each vote has a brief substantive label, preceded by a code as to where it occurred (Plenary Session, 2nd Committee, etc.). Some issues required more than one vote.

By and large the issues voted upon in the Assembly during the Session closely resemble those that prevailed in earlier years. A previous study (Alker and Russett, 1965) showed that three major issue dimensions or "super-issues" could be identified in each of four different Sessions spread over virtually the entire history of the United Nations. They were characterized as "cold war," "colonial self-determination," and "supranationalism" issues, and among them they regularly accounted for more than half the total variance in all roll-call voting. Two other super-issues, concerned with problems of intervention in southern Africa and of Palestine, were found in three of the four Sessions. The four or five factors appearing in any Session always accounted for between 59 and 70 per cent of the total variance in that session.

Most prominent among the concerns of the Assembly in 1963 was a factor we can clearly identify with cold war issues, accounting for 21 per cent of the variance and characterized by votes on such specific matters as the seating of Communist China and the role of the United Nations in Korea— both topics which have long characterized the cold war issue in the Assembly. A new matter, in form at least, concerned a resolution about extended participation in general multilateral treaties concluded under the League of Nations. A disagreement arose over whether all nations should be eligible, or merely those which were members of the United Nations and its specialized

TABLE 4.1
Major Issues Before the General Assembly in 1963–64

Factor 1 Cold War 21%		Factor 2 Intervention in Africa 19%		Factor 3 Supra-nationalism 18%	
P – Participation in Multilateral Treaties	0.89	P – Southern Rhodesia	−0.89	P – Compostion of Security Council and ECOSOC	0.86
P – Participation in Multilateral Treaties	0.88	4 – Southern Rhodesia	−0.86	P – UN in Congo	0.86
6 – Participation in Multilateral Treaties	0.82	P – Portugese Territory	−0.85	P – Composition of Security Council and ECOSOC	0.85
6 – Participation in Multilateral Treaties	0.81	4 – South West Africa	−0.85	SP – Composition of Security Council	0.85
1 – Unification of Korea	0.80	4 – Southern Rhodesia	−0.85	SP – Composition of ECOSOC	0.84
6 – Fact-Finding for Peaceful Settlement	0.78	4 – South West Africa	−0.83	5 – UN in Congo	0.84
P – Fact-Finding for Peaceful Settlement	−0.78	P – South West Africa	−0.82	P – UNEF	0.83
P – Seat Communist China	0.76	4 – Portugese Territory	−0.82	P – UNEF	0.79
P – Fact-Finding for Peaceful Settlement	−0.74	P – Southern Rhodesia	−0.76	5 – UNEF	0.79
*1 – Unification of Korea	−0.71	4 – Southern Rhodesia	−0.75	5 – UNEF	0.77
*P – Unification of Korea	0.70	4 – South West Africa	−0.71	5 – Personnel of Secretariat	0.61
3 – Elimination of Racial Discrimination	−0.69	SP – Apartheid	−0.69	P – Denuclearize Latin America	0.59
6 – Fact-Finding for Peaceful Settlement	−0.68	4 – South West Africa	0.67	*P – Unification of Korea	0.56
3 – Elimination of Racial Dis-crimination	0.62	*P – Conference to Prohibit Nuclear Weapons	−0.65	*1 – Unification of Korea	0.56
*1 – Unification of Korea	−0.61	*P – Apartheid Procedural	−0.65	*1 – Unification of Korea	0.54
*5 – Personnel of Secretariat	0.59	1 – Prohibit Nuclear Weapons	−0.62	P – Electric Voting Equipment for UN Bodies	0.51
		*P – Social Change and Economic Development	0.50	1 – Denuclearize Latin America	0.50
		4 – Portugese Territory	−0.50	P – Expand ECOSOC	0.48
		*4 – Aden	0.44	P – Electric Voting	0.48
		3 – Elimination of Racial Dis-crimination	−0.43	3 – Elimination of Racial Discrimination	0.47
				*5 – Personnel of Secretariat	−0.46
				*3 – Elimination of Racial Discrimination	−0.46
				*P – Social Change	

TABLE 4.1—(Cont.)

Major Issues Before the General Assembly in 1963–64

Factor 1 Cold War 21%		Factor 2 Intervention in Africa 19%	Factor 3 Supra- nationalism 18%	
*4 – Aden	0.58	*SP – Procedure on Refugee Resolution 0.43	and Economic Development	0.43
*3 – Elimination of Racial Discrim- ination	0.58		3 – Elimination of Racial Discrim- ination	0.43
3 – Elimination of Racial Discrim- ination	0.57			
*1 – Prohibit Nuclear Weapons	0.55			
*P – Conference to Prohibit Nuclear Weapons	0.50			
*P – Apartheid— Procedural	0.49			
3 – Elimination of Racial Discrim- ination	0.49			
*SP – Procedure on Refugee Resolution	0.47			

Factor 4 Palestine 4%		Factor 5 Self- Determination 4%	Other
SP – Palestine Refugees	0.88	3 – Independence for Colonial Peoples 0.85	3 – Commission on Human Rights
P – Palestine Refugees	0.88		2 – Economic Development
P – Accept 4th Commit- tee Draft on S.W. Africa	0.49	3 – Independence for Colonial Peoples 0.81	4 – Information on Non-Self-Governing Territories

* Loads moderately on two factors

CODE:
   P—Plenary Session
   SP—Special Political Committee
   1–6—Committee Number

agencies. Since the latter formula would exclude mainland China and East Germany, but include West Germany (which is a member of several specialized agencies) it is not surprising that the issue was perceived and voted upon in much the same way as the more familiar cold war issues. Another set of roll-calls loading highly on this super-issue came from the discussion of item A/5671, a resolution on "Consideration of Principles of International Law Concerning Friendly Relations and Cooperation Among States." One section called for the establishment of an international center of inquiry and fact-finding for the peaceful settlement of disputes; the Soviet Union and its allies opposed the measure on the grounds that the Security Council alone was responsible for the maintenance of international peace and security.[1]

A second super-issue, accounting for 19 per cent of the variance, concerned such familiar problems as (Southern) Rhodesia, South West Africa, and "territories under Portuguese administration." These issues formerly turned up on the self-determination factor or on the southern Africa one; here the super-issue can quite clearly be identified as southern Africa. With the dismemberment of the great overseas empires there are hardly any other concrete colonialism questions. A similar though less thorough convergence occurred in 1961 (Alker, 1964, Table 2). What remains of any separate self-determination issue may perhaps be found in a small factor identified in only two roll-calls and accounting for but 4 per cent of the variance. A section on granting independence to colonial peoples and countries was inserted in the "Draft Declaration on the Elimination of All Forms of Racial Discrimination." The United Kingdom and some Western Europeans tried to have the section deleted, with the argument that it was irrelevant to the Declaration.

The other major super-issue, accounting for 18 per cent of the variance, is related to what has for previous years been called supranationalism, composed of votes affecting the retention or expansion of the Organization's powers, especially its peace-keeping forces. As in earlier years, votes on the United Nations' role in the Congo and UNEF in the Middle East loaded highly on it, as did a number of roll-calls about the proposed expansion and new composition of ECOSOC and the Security Council. Finally, there was a factor composed primarily of two votes on the status of Palestine refugees and accounting for 4 per cent of the variance.

Thus the basic issues in the 18th Session are familiar ones. How familiar can be seen by examining Table 4.2, which gives the percentage of the total

[1] More detailed information on the resolutions can be found in the "Summary of Activities" of the General Assembly in *International Organization* (1964, pp. 313–467), and of course in the *Official Records* themselves. *International Conciliation* (1963) discusses the issues prior to their consideration by the Assembly.

TABLE 4.2

The Continuity of Issues in the General Assembly

Factor	Percentage of Variance Accounted for in				
	1947	1952	1957	1961	1963
Cold War	31	9	23	15	21
Self-Determination		24	23	32	4
Intervention in Africa	6	10	10	—	19
Supranationalism	10	12	7	12	18
Palestine	11	10	—	11	4
Total 5 "Super-Issues"	59	64	62	70	66

Source for 1947–61: Alker and Russett, 1965, chs. 3–6; "important" roll calls only. Percentages do not always add to total because of rounding.

variance accounted for by each of the five major issue dimensions or super-issues. Clearly then the attitudes underlying our groupings in 1963 will not be transitory concerns of only temporary significance, but ones on which governments operating in the international system have long been at odds.

GROUPINGS IN THE 1963 GENERAL ASSEMBLY SESSION

As in chapter two, in order to identify groups of countries that vote together we need a technique which is inductive, given to a means of presentation which is readily interpretable, which shows gradations in agreement among nations, and which reliably identifies all the groupings. Again factor analysis meets these requirements.

In chapter two we were faced with 54 socio-economic variables, gathered in a wide-ranging but somewhat eclectic manner wherein one of the criteria for selection was simply the availability of relatively reliable data. We had a "sample" of variables drawn in a far from random manner from an infinite universe, and wanted to pick out only those related to interpretable dimensions which bore some relation to theories of regionalization and integration. So we used the R-analysis to discard some variables.

But here the situation is different. We can deal with the universe of roll-call votes (except for the nearly unanimous ones) before the Assembly in the 1963–1964 Session. Under those circumstances we can properly use all the information contained in those roll-calls, because we want to know how nations group together on *all* issues which are voted upon in the Assembly, not just on the major super-issues accounting for two-thirds of the variance. No roll-call can be ruled out as irrelevant. In this Q-analysis we used all 66 votes.[2] Table 4.3 gives the rotated factor matrix,[3] and Figure 4.1 maps the results.

I have labelled the first grouping "Western Community" in an attempt to indicate the predominance of European and European-settled states among those with high loadings. Western Community in this context must be interpreted as a cultural and not just a geographical phenomenon, including the Old Commonwealth. The strength of this relationship is indicated by the fact that of 35 UN members either physically located in Europe or whose population is predominantly of European origin (Argentina, Australia, Canada, Costa Rica, Cyprus, New Zealand, Uruguay, and United States), 22 have loadings of 0.50 or greater on the second factor. This works out to a fairly low correlation coefficient of 0.35. Each of the top 15 loadings, however, is held by such a country.

Note also the high loadings of Japan and Nationalist China (Taiwan) on this factor. Japan's basic foreign policy has become quite well integrated with those of her North Atlantic associates in recent years. Nationalist China is of course heavily dependent upon United States military and diplomatic support. This leads to another observation about this factor: among those with 0.50 or higher loadings are 33 of the 38 UN members who have a formal military alliance with the United States (including the United States itself and counting Iran). Such a close association produces a correlation of 0.76. France is by far the lowest of all NATO allies on this factor, with also a strong *negative* loading on the Afro-Asian factor (number three). More detailed analysis of this group's characteristics, and a systematic comparison of the UN groupings with those obtained in chapter two, will be postponed until later in the book.

The second cluster is named "Brazzaville Africans," though the name is far from perfect and a number of non-African states load on the second factor. The six highest loadings, and 14 above 0.50 in all, are possessed by countries which were members of the former Brazzaville caucusing group, of whom all but Congo (Leopoldville) were ex-French colonies. Both the Brazzaville and Casablanca groupings had been formally dissolved by the 1963 Session, ostensibly in the interest of promoting African unity, but the essential differences in voting patterns seem still to persist. Note also the high

[2] An application of Q-analysis to the Kansas State legislature can be found in Grumm (1963). In his pioneer study of voting blocs in the United States Congress, however, David Truman (1959, p. 329) noted the difficulty of finding blocs in a large matrix and suggested that factor analysis might be superior to his own method. Alternative techniques for identifying voting groups are reviewed in an article which earlier presented some of the substantive findings of this chapter (Russett, 1966). A clustering analysis of this session, done independently by Robert Keohane (1966) using a version of Lijphart's agreement index, produced very similar results.

[3] All 15 factors with eigen values greater than one were rotated. Nine factors which had no more than one loading as high as 0.50 are omitted from the table.

TABLE 4.3

United Nations Groupings in 1963

	Factor 1 23%	Factor 2 17%	Factor 3 16%	Factor 4 11%	Factor 5 4%	Factor 6 2%
			Western Community			
Denmark	0.90	0.12	−0.02	−0.27	−0.01	−0.17
Norway	0.89	0.10	−0.03	−0.23	−0.11	−0.04
Sweden	0.89	0.09	−0.03	−0.25	−0.12	−0.09
Finland	0.88	0.06	0.03	−0.22	−0.04	−0.10
Austria	0.87	0.20	0.00	−0.17	−0.10	−0.01
Ireland	0.86	0.15	−0.08	−0.25	0.16	−0.03
Turkey	0.83	0.18	−0.10	−0.33	−0.04	0.23
Australia	0.82	0.10	−0.15	−0.38	0.01	0.10
Belgium	0.82	0.13	−0.15	−0.44	−0.07	0.15
New Zealand	0.82	0.17	−0.14	−0.27	0.07	0.05
Iceland	0.82	0.14	−0.05	−0.22	0.14	−0.20
United States	0.81	0.07	0.23	−0.27	0.09	0.23
Italy	0.81	0.12	−0.12	−0.37	0.14	0.11
Canada	0.80	0.09	−0.15	−0.44	−0.02	0.17
Netherlands	0.80	0.05	−0.11	−0.46	0.03	0.09
Japan	0.76	0.23	−0.11	−0.33	0.31	0.06
China (Taiwan)	0.75	0.40	−0.01	−0.11	0.07	0.09
United Kingdom	0.72	−0.16	−0.22	−0.46	0.07	0.09
Greece	0.71	0.23	−0.21	−0.29	−0.03	0.15
Iran	0.61	0.38	−0.01	−0.04	0.33	−0.04
†El Salvador	0.59	0.36	0.00	−0.29	0.29	0.34
France	0.59	0.01	−0.48	−0.02	−0.23	0.27
			Brazzaville Africans			
Chad	0.12	0.87	0.17	0.01	−0.03	0.06
Cameroun	0.20	0.79	0.29	−0.08	−0.08	−0.06
†Gabon	0.20	0.79	0.23	0.08	0.06	0.04
Central Afr. Rep.	0.17	0.78	0.03	0.01	−0.09	0.10
Niger	0.02	0.78	0.34	−0.03	0.04	0.14
Congo (B)	0.07	0.77	0.28	0.08	−0.09	−0.00
Rwanda	0.23	0.76	0.16	−0.09	0.05	−0.20
†Haiti	0.16	0.74	−0.06	0.00	0.01	0.10
Ivory Coast	0.08	0.73	0.35	−0.04	0.27	−0.04
Upper Volta	−0.09	0.73	0.37	0.05	−0.12	−0.06
Congo (L)	0.22	0.72	0.22	0.01	0.01	−0.17
Dahomey	0.07	0.70	0.32	−0.03	0.05	−0.11
†Bolivia	0.37	0.68	0.10	−0.15	0.14	0.01
Senegal	0.12	0.68	0.26	0.19	0.19	0.15
Uruguay	0.35	0.68	0.11	0.08	0.23	0.04
Madagascar	0.39	0.62	0.05	−0.14	0.32	−0.09
Sierra Leone	0.05	0.62	0.41	−0.01	−0.02	−0.09
Liberia	0.41	0.62	0.09	−0.14	0.32	−0.17
Togo	0.09	0.62	0.49	−0.02	0.23	−0.01

TABLE 4.3—(Cont.)

United Nations Grouping in 1963

	Factor 1 23%	Factor 2 17%	Factor 3 16%	Factor 4 11%	Factor 5 4%	Factor 6 2%
		Latin America				
Venezuela	0.70	0.52	−0.01	−0.07	0.13	−0.02
Argentina	0.70	0.49	−0.04	−0.10	0.12	0.09
Guatemala	0.65	0.52	0.07	−0.17	0.09	−0.05
Panama	0.63	0.51	0.05	0.08	0.09	0.05
Colombia	0.62	0.52	0.15	0.08	0.16	0.09
Ecuador	0.62	0.50	−0.05	−0.06	0.32	0.05
Costa Rica	0.61	0.61	0.09	0.11	0.11	0.05
Mexico	0.61	0.52	0.11	0.01	0.39	−0.07
Thailand	0.60	0.52	0.05	−0.02	0.15	0.14
Jamaica	0.59	0.51	0.03	0.06	0.32	−0.19
Chile	0.58	0.52	0.28	−0.08	0.18	0.05
Brazil	0.56	0.43	0.01	−0.04	0.10	0.05
Peru	0.56	0.49	0.03	0.02	0.17	0.34
Malaysia	0.55	0.55	0.21	0.06	0.43	0.03
†Nicaragua	0.55	0.38	0.09	−0.32	0.02	0.17
Paraguay	0.53	0.47	0.00	−0.20	0.19	0.18
Cyprus	0.52	0.71	0.04	−0.06	0.08	0.01
Pakistan	0.50	0.51	0.21	0.01	0.09	−0.09
Philippines	0.49	0.63	0.09	−0.05	0.26	0.03
Israel	0.43	0.53	−0.04	−0.18	0.04	−0.31
		Afro-Asians				
Ghana	−0.09	0.14	0.88	0.17	−0.11	−0.04
Afghanistan	−0.15	0.15	0.84	0.23	−0.00	0.06
Indonesia	−0.17	0.08	0.82	0.13	−0.19	0.12
Egypt	−0.09	0.07	0.82	0.30	0.06	0.06
Syria	−0.05	0.09	0.82	0.30	0.04	0.07
Ethiopia	−0.02	0.11	0.82	0.18	0.00	−0.14
Yugoslavia	−0.18	0.15	0.80	0.29	−0.03	0.02
India	0.12	0.19	0.75	0.02	0.31	−0.07
Algeria	−0.22	0.16	0.74	−0.40	0.09	0.02
Nigeria	0.01	0.26	0.74	−0.13	0.04	0.25
Iraq	−0.24	0.15	0.73	0.30	0.25	−0.04
Tunisia	−0.02	0.25	0.73	0.13	−0.01	−0.07
†Burma	0.05	0.13	0.72	0.24	−0.06	0.08
Cambodia	−0.13	0.13	0.72	0.31	0.03	−0.03
Tanganyika	−0.18	0.33	0.67	0.22	0.10	−0.16
Guinea	−0.13	0.29	0.67	0.32	0.09	0.05
Mali	−0.25	0.09	0.65	−0.42	0.27	−0.11
Ceylon	0.02	0.19	0.65	0.21	0.05	−0.02
Sudan	0.00	0.24	0.60	0.24	0.05	−0.09
Morocco	−0.15	0.13	0.58	0.35	0.40	−0.06
†Somalia	−0.04	0.22	0.55	0.11	0.08	0.27
†Uganda	−0.02	0.32	0.55	0.27	0.06	0.03
†Yemen	−0.02	0.24	0.53	0.32	0.04	−0.13

TABLE 4.3—(Cont.)

United Nations Groupings in 1963

	Factor 1 23%	Factor 2 17%	Factor 3 16%	Factor 4 11%	Factor 5 4%	Factor 6 2%
			Communists			
Czechoslovakia	−0.42	−0.04	0.28	0.85	−0.02	−0.02
U.S.S.R.	−0.42	−0.04	0.28	0.85	−0.02	−0.02
Bulgaria	−0.41	−0.05	0.29	0.85	−0.03	−0.02
Byelorussia	−0.42	−0.05	0.29	0.85	0.07	−0.06
Poland	−0.42	−0.05	0.29	0.85	0.07	−0.06
Cuba	−0.36	0.00	0.28	0.85	−0.07	−0.02
Romania	−0.39	−0.05	0.32	0.84	−0.02	0.02
Ukraine	−0.45	−0.02	0.28	0.83	−0.04	−0.03
Hungary	−0.40	−0.07	0.27	0.83	0.16	−0.08
Mongolia	−0.42	−0.06	0.29	0.82	0.16	−0.10
Albania	−0.27	0.01	0.49	0.59	−0.05	−0.07
			Conservative Arabs			
Lebanon	0.09	0.16	0.46	0.08	0.66	0.10
Jordan	0.17	0.34	0.46	0.25	0.58	−0.03
Libya	0.21	0.44	0.45	0.01	0.54	−0.05
Mauritania	0.08	0.53	0.38	0.18	0.49	0.00
Kuwait	0.14	0.29	0.58	0.24	0.47	−0.06
			Iberia			
Portugal	0.23	−0.25	−0.06	−0.44	−0.08	0.68
Spain	0.52	0.13	−0.11	−0.26	0.09	0.66
			Unclassifiable			
Burundi	0.14	0.30	0.48	0.19	−0.09	−0.17
†Laos	0.26	0.19	0.40	0.07	0.27	0.04
Nepal	0.14	0.36	0.47	−0.06	0.04	−0.01
†Saudi Arabia	0.22	0.14	0.39	0.32	0.18	0.15
Trinidad	0.42	0.41	0.18	0.06	0.07	−0.03

† More than 25% absenteeism (but less than 40%); absent equated with abstain.

loadings of Haiti (Negro, very underdeveloped) and of several Asian and Latin American states. Previous studies have noted that the Brazzaville states tend to be less anti-Western on cold war issues than the Afro-Asian "neutralists," but more so, and especially on colonial questions, than the typical Latin American state. This second factor then picks out, in addition to the Brazzaville Africans, both several of the more pro-Western Asians (Philippines and Pakistan, plus Israel) and a number of Latin Americans

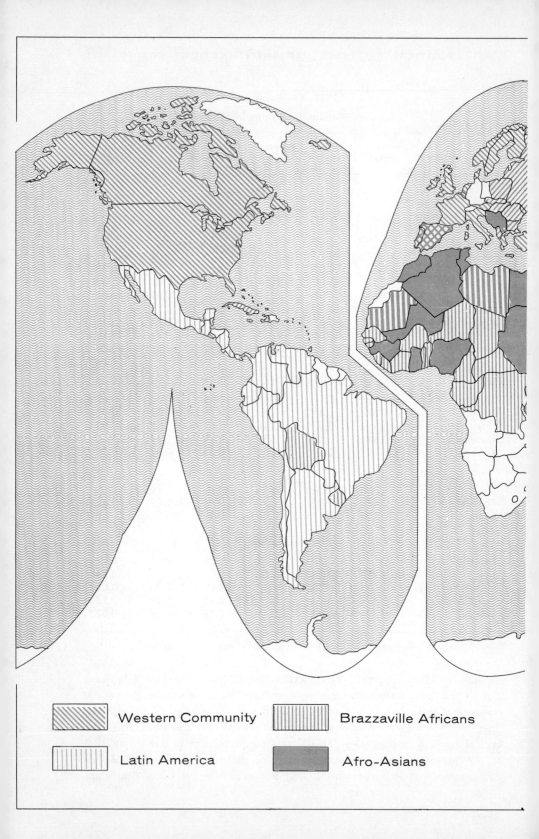

Western Community Brazzaville Africans

Latin America Afro-Asians

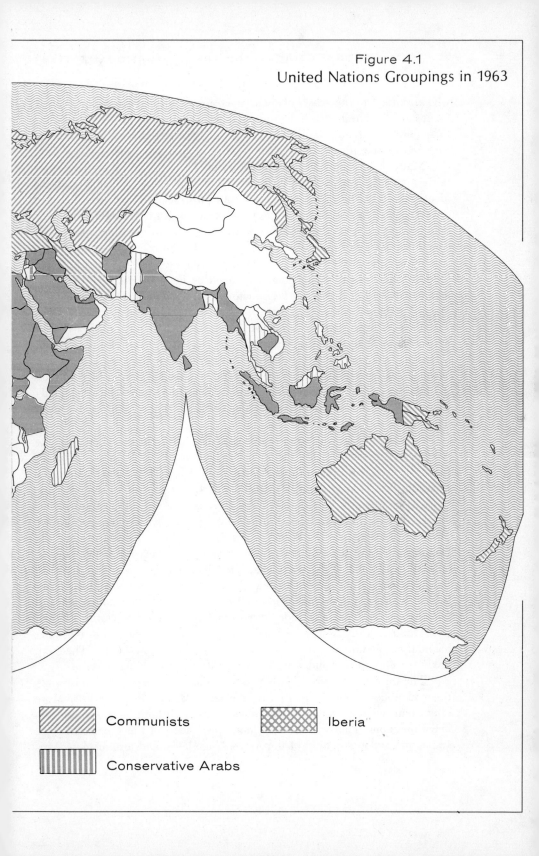

Figure 4.1
United Nations Groupings in 1963

Communists

Iberia

Conservative Arabs

who are rather to the "east" of their caucusing group (Uruguay and Bolivia, for instance). The first two factors together account for 40 per cent of the total roll-call variance, and indicate most of the states that can generally be expected to take the Western position on most cold war issues.

Many of the countries loading either on Factors 1 and 2 actually show fairly high loadings on *both* factors, so that they cannot unequivocally be identified with either. The majority of states with loadings between 0.50 and 0.70 on either factor share this property. Once again it is useful to make a scattergram and plot the positions of the countries in question on the two competing factors. Figure 4.2 is a graph like Figure 2.2, where the vertical axis represents the percentage of variance accounted for by Factor 2, and the horizontal axis the percentage explained by Factor 1. All countries with loadings of 0.40 or higher on *both* factors are represented, as well as several others for reference.

There is little question about what to do with Uruguay and Bolivia, for whom Factor 2 accounts for almost 50 per cent of the variance and Factor 1 less than 15 per cent. It also seems appropriate to think of Liberia and Madagascar with the Brazzaville countries. And for any state which has less than 25 per cent of its variance accounted for by any factor (e.g., Trinidad) we have little choice but to term it unclassifiable. The square in the lower left marks out this area of the diagram.

But for the countries where the percentage of variance explained by the most powerful factor is only about twice that of the next most important factor, or even less, a separate grouping is called for. This is clearly so in the situation illustrated in the above figure, where no less than 18 states occupy the area between the two dashed lines. Here we must speak of another voting group, which we can label "Latin America." Twelve of these nations are physically located in the Western Hemisphere. With Honduras and the Dominican Republic excluded from our analysis for excessive absenteeism, only Haiti, Bolivia, Uruguay, Cuba, Trinidad, (in the lower left box) El Salvador, Argentina, and Nicaragua do not fall into this area. And the latter two are extremely marginal. These 20 countries (including Argentina and Nicaragua) can best be considered as comprising a separate cluster of their own, though with policies related to the first two and with indistinct boundaries. A number of pro-Western Asian states—Malaysia, Thailand, Pakistan, Philippines, and Israel—have quite similar voting patterns.

The third factor quite clearly picks out those Asians and Africans sometimes identified in world politics by the term Afro-Asian neutralists. More often than not they vote with the Soviet Union on both cold war and colonial questions. They include such long-time leaders of this group as Egypt, India, and Indonesia, most of the Arabs, Yugoslavia, and a number of Afri-

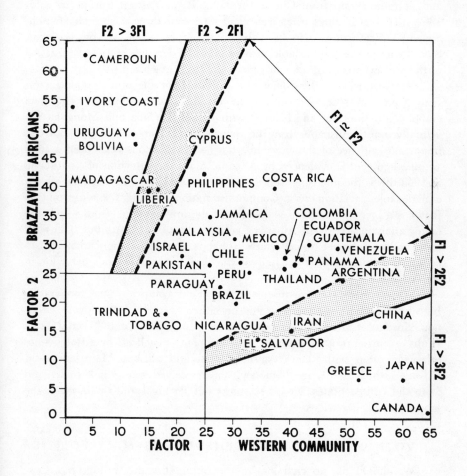

FIGURE 4.2: Latin American Grouping as Identified by Moderate Loadings on Factors 1 and 2.

can states, especially (but not only) those with rather leftist governments and which belonged to the former Casablanca caucusing group. And while except for Yugoslavia these are non-Communist governments, of 24 UN members outside of the Sino-Soviet group known to have received economic and/or military aid from China, the U.S.S.R. or Eastern Europe by mid-1962, 19 have loadings of at least 0.50 on factor three. Using all 96 non-Soviet bloc governments in this table, and simple receipt or non-receipt of Sino-Soviet aid as the variable, this produces a correlation (r) of 0.72. All of the top seven countries on this factor received much aid.

Not surprisingly, the Soviet bloc accounts for the other major factor. Only Communist states load heavily on this factor—though Yugoslavia emphatically does not and belongs with Factor 3. Cuba and Mongolia are virtually indistinguishable from the European members of the bloc. But one important evidence of the crack in what had in previous years been a solid voting alignment is evidenced by Albania. Since the defection of Yugoslavia in 1948 this is the first time that any study of the United Nations has shown a noticeable deviation by a Communist nation. Albania's loading on the factor is a mere 0.59, and if we return to the original votes from which the factor analysis is derived, Albania's voting pattern correlates but 0.75 with those of other Soviet "bloc" states. That is, voting by the U.S.S.R. "accounts for" little more than half of the variance in Albania's behavior in the Assembly.

Finally there are two minor groups. Four countries have moderately high loadings both on Factor 5 and on either Factor 2 or Factor 3: Lebanon, Jordan, Libya, Mauritania, and Kuwait. The name "Conservative Arabs" seems appropriate, for in cold-war politics each of these states votes relatively often with the Western powers, and all but Mauritania and Kuwait (which hardly needs money) have received substantial foreign aid from the United States. Factor six picks out Portugal and Spain only; the label "Iberia" is obvious.

VOTING GROUPS AND GENERAL ASSEMBLY POLITICS

We should like to characterize the different voting groups more explicitly in terms of their positions on the major political issues before the Assembly. The factor scores that can be computed from the R-analysis (looking for clusters of issues) provide an opportunity to do so. As in the first factor analysis of chapter two, every country has a factor score on each of the super-issues, and these scores serve as summary indices of national behavior. We are not here sufficiently interested in the voting behavior of particular states for it to be worthwhile to list the factor scores for all 107 countries. But on a gross level we can find the general orientation of each group by correlating the factor scores with the same nations' factor loadings from the Q–analysis. Table 4.4 below gives the correlation of states' factor scores on the three most important issue dimensions (cold war, intervention in Africa, and supranationalism) with their loadings on the six major factors from the Q–analysis.

TABLE 4.4

Correlation of Q-Analysis Loadings with Super-Issue Factor Scores

Factor Identified With:	Cold War	Inter-vention in Africa	Supra-national-ism
Western Community	0.79	−0.33	0.38
Brazzaville Africans	0.47	0.45	0.36
Afro-Asians	−0.82	0.43	0.17
Communists	−0.56	0.45	−0.64
Conservative Arabs	0.11	0.26	0.16
Iberia	0.10	−0.74	−0.06

From this we can quickly obtain a thumbnail sketch to characterize the behavior of the groups of countries. The Afro-Asians, for example, are quite pro-Soviet on cold war issues and anti-colonial about the problems of southern Africa.[4] But they generally favor initiatives, such as those concerning the role of ONUC in the Congo and expanding the Security Council and ECOSOC, which comprise the supranationalism dimension and which the Soviet Union vigorously opposed in 1963. It is on these issues that they oppose the Communists and on which Yugoslavia (fairly favorable to strengthening the UN in these contexts) is distinguishable from the other Communist states of Eastern Europe. Similarly, the Brazzaville countries more or less share the Afro-Asians positions on southern Africa and supranationalism but are rather pro-Western on cold war questions. The Western Community countries generally vote in favor of those supra-na-tionalist initiatives that actually come to a roll-call, and while moderately unsympathetic with the Assembly's basic position on intervention in Africa are nowhere near as isolated as are the lonely Iberians.

[4] The fact that the Asians and Africans correlate more highly than do the Communists with the "cold war" factor indicates that the latter is a slightly misleading label. There are some roll-call votes, such as those about the role of the UN in re-unifying and rehabilitating Korea, or establishing a fact-finding commission for the peaceful settlement of disputes, which have substantial "superanational" loadings and overtones. On these votes the Afro-Asians and Communists often part company, at least to the degree of an abstention. Putting a descriptive label on a factor is always a somewhat tentative exercise, so, as in chapter two, we initially enclose the labels in quotation marks.

is tempting to refer to the major groups by more explicitly political ____. The Brazzaville Africans, for instance, are not well named since they include Latin Americans, Asians, and other Africans as well. Possibly one might want to call them simply "pro-Western underdeveloped states." But we must ascetically refrain from plucking that apple. A word like pro-Western demands a unidimensional set of issues which does not exist. Each group's substantive position can be spotted only with reference to all *three* of the major issue dimensions. Imagine a cube defined by three axes—left to right: cold war, with the West at the left and the Communists on the right; vertical: intervention in Africa, with the colonial powers at the top and the ex-colonies at the bottom; depth: supranationalism with those favoring a stronger UN at the front and their opponents behind. These three axes can be thought of as dividing the whole cube into eight subcubes, and each of the major groups falls into a different subcube. The Western Community states belong in the upper left front cube, and the Communists are more or less polar opposites in the lower right rear segment. But the other two groups do *not* fall between the two poles; rather they are off to one side or the other of the shortest-distance-between-two-points lines. The Afro-Asians are lower right but front, and the Brazzaville nations lower front but left. Such a picture implies a pattern of cross-pressures and shifting coalitions that can mitigate international conflict.

In describing the correlations of the issue factor scores with the grouping loadings we of course are only ascertaining the *typical* voting position of a group, especially of those countries loading heavily on the R–factor. Any individual member may differ from the group pattern, as for example the United States is appreciably more supranationalist than are most states with equally high loadings on the Western Community factor. Except for establishing very general limits from the group, the behavior of a particular country can be determined only by a check of its factor scores.

In the Q–analysis we found that an inductive procedure identified six factors, and through them seven voting groups, in the General Assembly. The six factors together accounted for 73 per cent of all the countries' variance. Thus the UN political process is relatively structured and subject to description by a small number of alignments. Yet the groups resemble only to a limited degree those which would be discovered from a list of caucusing groups alone. Of our inductively-derived groups only the Communists closely resemble a geographical or caucusing group in terms both of who was included and who excluded.[5]

[5] The not always mutually exclusive caucusing groups in 1963 were: Benelux; British Commonwealth, Afro-Asian, including Cyprus and Turkey and with an African subgroup; Arab; Latin American, including Trinidad but not Jamaica; Communist, excluding Yugoslavia; and Scandinavian.

In contrast to the mere evidence of caucusing groups our analysis reveals:

1. The members of the Scandinavian caucusing group do indeed agree almost entirely among themselves in the Session, but Ireland and Austria differ from them in no significant way.

2. Analysis of the Latin American caucusing group or a geographically defined Latin America would find a moderate element of cohesion, but entirely miss the very high similarity of Israel and several pro-Western Asians to the Latin voting pattern.

3. If the examination were based on caucusing groups extant in 1963 it would also not uncover the great consensus remaining within the officially disbanded Brazzaville and Casablanca groups.

4. The convergence of interest among the Western Community countries would not be uncovered by examining any formal caucusing group.

And though we have often used geographic *labels,* most of the groups are broader than geography. While the majority of the countries loading on the Brazzaville factor for instance are indeed African, it includes underdeveloped states from other areas, nations which are pro-Western on cold war but not other issues.

The use of an inductive procedure also permits us to make some more general statements about politics in the Assembly. A simplified East-West-Neutral categorization which has characterized so much journalistic and even scholarly analysis of the world organization is utterly misleading. In terms of states' behavior, five major groups (on four factors) emerge, in addition to two small groups and a few marginal countries. It should be emphasized that the identification of these groups depends upon their final behavior in the vote, not upon tacit or explicit bargaining among diverse log-rolling coalitions which may exchange promises of support before the vote. It might be supposed, for instance, that one set of countries might offer its support to another on a cold war issue, in response to the other's votes on a self-determination roll-call. While this kind of bargaining undoubtedly does occur, an analysis of voting patterns alone would not find it since both sets of countries would *vote* identically, whatever their reasons for so doing. But a number of groups in the General Assembly do retain their distinctiveness in the actual voting. However one interprets the consequences for the stability or efficacy of the political process, the Assembly is not bipolarized, tightly or even loosely.

5

THE STABILITY OF UN VOTING GROUPS

ORGANIZATIONAL AND ENVIRONMENTAL CHANGE

SINCE ITS INCEPTION THE UNITED NATIONS HAS MORE than doubled its membership. All areas of the world have been represented among the new entrants, but fully 80 per cent have come from the former colonies of Asia and Africa. The world organization itself has gone through periods of substantial internal change. After the early efforts to achieve agreement in the Security Council fell victim to Soviet-American conflicts and the veto, there followed in the early 1950's a Western attempt to channel the major decisions of the UN through the veto-less General Assembly. The Uniting for Peace Resolution of the Korean War best exemplified this effort. Later, in the face of new admissions, effort was shifted to the Secretariat, which seemed better able to carry out flexible diplomacy than could the much-enlarged Assembly. This period in turn came to an end with the death of Secretary-General Hammarskjold and the partially successful Soviet attempts to restrict his successor's freedom of movement. Coupled with Russian and French refusal to pay the peace-keeping costs assessed by the Assembly majority, diplomats' efforts returned once more to trying to achieve a limited consensus in the Security Council. After all the major organs had been tried it became clear again, as it had been when the Charter was drafted, that major action by the UN required agreement or at least abstention by all the great powers.[1]

Equally great changes were occurring in the international environment, as all students of world politics are aware. The European powers lost virtually their entire colonial empires, as countries with a combined population of over one billion achieved sovereignty. Europe recovered from World War II and went on to unprecedented prosperity; the European states in both the major alliance systems began to exhibit increasing independence of the bloc leaders. Nuclear weapons, at first concentrated solely in the hands of the

[1] For useful interpretations of the world body's evolution see Bloomfield (1961), Haas (1962), Jackson (1961), and Wilcox (1964).

United States, first diffused to the Soviet Union to reinforce the existing polarization of military power and then, more recently, spread to other countries and weakened that bipolarity.

In the face of these major and well-known developments in both the structure of the United Nations and the political environment in which it operates, one might naturally expect substantial shifts in the number and type of voting groups in the General Assembly. A reasonable hypothesis might call for an increase in the number of groups and also for substantial changes in the composition of some blocs. But this hypothesis is on the whole disconfirmed by an examination of the evidence, as we shall demonstrate in the remainder of this chapter. We shall examine analyses for two previous sessions in order to identify what changes did occur and provide some of the bases necessary for an attempted causal analysis later in the book. In identifying a basic stability, despite changes in the specific matters brought before the Assembly, we shall incidentally be validating the results of the preceding chapter.

Another Q–analysis, comparable in every respect to that exhibited in chapter four, was performed on roll-call votes in the 12th Session of the General Assembly (1957–1958). The Assembly's membership was smaller then, with only 81 countries included in the analysis. (One other, South Africa, was excluded because it boycotted most of the meetings in protest against the Assembly's consideration of what South Africa considered its internal problems.) The number of roll-calls, however, was much larger— 183—but that does not in any way determine the number of groupings of countries that emerge. In the analysis a total of 11 factors with eigen values greater than one were found and rotated. Except for three that had but a single loading above 0.50, Table 5.1 following presents the countries' loadings on those factors (eight in all). For ease in reading, however, the format of this table varies somewhat from that used in the previous chapter. All low loadings are omitted, and in general only countries' loadings of 0.50 or greater are shown. An exception is made for those nations which had loadings of 0.40 or greater on two different factors, and where the squared loading on one of these factors was less than twice that on the other. It is important to preserve that information, but except *possibly* for the four states which load on both Factors 1 and 6 there are not enough cases to warrant separate clusters. All such countries are marked with an asterisk in the table. Because of the simplicity of the structure we are able simply to give each factor a regional name. As before, states which were absent between 25 and 40 per cent of the time are indicated with a dagger, and their groupings should be interpreted with some caution.

The picture obtained of Assembly politics in 1957 essentially resembles that for 1963, but there are some differences. Most notable is the size and

TABLE 5.1

United Nations Groupings, 1957

Factor 1 West 33%		Factor 2 Afro-Asians 14%		Factor 3 Pro-West Asians 7%		Factor 4 Communists 13%	
Norway	0.88	Ceylon	0.86	†Lebanon		Albania	0.82
Austria	0.85	India	0.84	Greece		Bulgaria	0.82
United		Burma	0.83	Haiti		Byelorussia	0.81
States	0.85	Sudan	0.80	*Tunisia		Romania	0.81
Cuba	0.84	Indonesia	0.78	Iraq		Ukraine	0.81
Chile	0.84	Morocco	0.73	*Guatemala		Hungary	0.80
Denmark	0.84	Yemen	0.72	*Philippines		U.S.S.R.	0.78
Turkey	0.84	Afghanistan	0.71	Liberia		Czechoslo-	
†Peru	0.82	Yugoslavia	0.70	†*Jordan		vakia	0.77
Canada	0.82	Egypt	0.67	*Ethiopia		Poland	0.75
Brazil	0.82	Syria	0.65				
Spain	0.81	Saudi					
Luxembourg	0.81	Arabia	0.63				
Nicaragua	0.81	Ghana	0.62				
Honduras	0.80	Nepal	0.61				
Dominican		*Tunisia	0.54				
Rep.	0.80	*Ethiopia	0.54				
Iceland	0.80	*Mexico	0.48				
Belgium	0.80						
Colombia	0.80						
Italy	0.79						
New							
Zealand	0.79						
Netherlands	0.79						
Australia	0.79						
Taiwan	0.79						
France	0.79						
Sweden	0.79						
United							
Kingdom	0.79						
Portugal	0.78						
Israel	0.74						
Ireland	0.74						
Argentina	0.69						
*Venezuela	0.68						
Japan	0.66						
Paraguay	0.66						
*Ecuador	0.65						
Finland	0.62						
*Pakistan	0.61						
*Thailand	0.60						
*Philippines	0.54						
*Panama	0.54						
*Costa Rica	0.50						

TABLE 5.1—(Cont.)

United Nations Groupings, 1957

Factor 5 Southeast Asia 3%		Factor 6 Latin America 4%		Factor 7 Conservative Arabs 2%		Factor 8 Leftist Latins 2%	
Malaya	0.61	El Salvador	0.69	†Libya	0.57	†Bolivia	0.62
*Pakistan	0.59	Uruguay	0.66	†*Jordan	0.54	*Guatemala	0.54
*Thailand	0.49	*Costa Rica	0.64			*Mexico	0.47
		*Panama	0.54				
		*Ecuador	0.52				
		*Venezuela	0.48				

No Group

Cambodia
†Laos
Iran

* Two loadings above 0.40 with the larger r² less than twice the smaller.
† 25% or more votes absent (and therefore estimated = abstain), not more than 40% absent. South Africa deleted for greater than 40% absenteeism.

comprehensiveness of the first factor, which seems best labelled simply "West." It includes all the geographically North Atlantic countries plus Australia and New Zealand, and in addition two-thirds of the Latin American states and five generally pro-Western Asians. As we shall determine more systematically below, this factor bears a very strong resemblance to the one called Western Community for 1963, except that it is somewhat more inclusive.

Factor two, accounting for quite a bit less of the variance than its predecessor, very clearly identifies the "Afro-Asians" and is much like the factor of the same name in 1963. Again such states as India, Indonesia, Burma, Egypt, Ghana, and Afghanistan most typically represent it. The third factor, however, does not correspond much to anything in 1963 except for a vague resemblance to the "Brazzaville Africans" (allowing for the fact that the members of the actual Brazzaville *caucusing* group did not even belong to the UN in 1957). Loading on it are a few Latin Americans, Greece, some Asians like the Philippines with a military alliance with the United States, and a few other Afro-Asians such as Lebanon and Liberia. As can be discerned from the factor scores presented in Alker and Russett (1965, pp. 299–307) these are states which were "west" of the Afro-Asians on cold war issues but not as much so as most of the states on the West factor, and fairly strongly anti-colonial on self-determination issues. The label "Pro-Western Asians" is probably as good as any.

Factor four of course picks out the Communist states, and except for the absence of Cuba, the solidarity of Albania, and the exclusion of Mongolia from the Assembly in 1957 it is virtually identical with the Communist group of 1963. Factor six has been named "Latin America," although it is obviously a subset of the Latin states, including but a third of them. Despite the existence of this factor, the evidence for a separate "Latin American" group of substantial size is weaker than it was in 1963 when the group could be identified through its members' high loadings on each of two distinct factors. I have called Factor seven "Conservative Arabs" because of its close resemblance to the factor of the same name in 1963 (each loading both Jordan and Libya). Several other Arab states that might in some sense be called conservative or pro-Western are of course found under Factor three. The other two small factors can be dismissed fairly briefly; one corresponds to SEATO allies Pakistan and Thailand, plus Malaya. I have labelled it "Southeast Asia," but imperfectly so since it does not include Burma, Indonesia, or the Philippines. The other includes the rather leftist Latin American regimes of Guatemala, Bolivia, and Mexico; "Leftist Latins" may do for a name.

Thus a total of four major factors and four smaller ones, accounting among them for 78 per cent of all the variance, is required to present an adequate picture of the groupings in the 1957 Assembly. This is more than the four major and two minor factors in the 1963 session, even allowing for the fact that in 1963 an additional group (Latin American) of some size could be found by picking it out from two factors. Though there are a number of countries with moderately high loadings on two separate factors in 1957, this characteristic is not particularly concentrated and no group of any substantial size (more than three or four states) could be identified that way.

Table 5.2 presents the pattern for the Seventh General Assembly Session, beginning in 1952. Like the Twelfth Session, I chose the Seventh because the issue dimensions had been thoroughly analyzed in an earlier publication (Alker and Russett, 1965). The Assembly was still smaller, with 60 members. After the omission of Iceland, Panama, and Paraguay for high absenteeism only 57 remain. A total of 87 "non-unanimous" plenary and committee roll-calls were analyzed, and six factors with eigen values greater than unity were found and rotated. Four of those after rotation met our customary criterion of having more than one loading equal to at least 0.50.

The first and largest factor this time is the Afro-Asian one which, allowing for the smaller representation of non-Western countries in the 1952 Assembly, is remarkably similar to groups in the other two Sessions. *Most* typical, however, are the Arab countries rather than such cold-war non-aligned states as India and Burma which loaded most highly on the

TABLE 5.2
United Nations Groupings, 1952

Factor 1 Afro-Asians 24%		Factor 2 Western Community 22%		Factor 3 Latin America 18%		Factor 4 Communists 8%	
Iraq	0.86	New		†Costa Rica	0.83	U.S.S.R.	0.77
Saudi		Zealand	0.88	Ecuador	0.79	Ukraine	0.77
Arabia	0.86	United		Cuba	0.78	Byelorussia	0.77
Syria	0.34	Kingdom	0.86	Colombia	0.78	Czechoslo-	
Egypt	0.84	Netherlands	0.84	Brazil	0.75	vakia	0.77
Yemen	0.83	Australia	0.84	†Nicaragua	0.75	Poland	0.76
Afghanistan	0.82	Denmark	0.84	Chile	0.74		
Indonesia	0.80	Norway	0.83	Dominican			
Iran	0.80	France	0.82	Rep.	0.73		
Ethiopia	0.78	Canada	0.81	Uruguay	0.73		
Pakistan	0.77	Sweden	0.80	Peru	0.72		
Yugoslavia	0.76	United		Venezuela	0.71		
†Lebanon	0.75	States	0.79	Honduras	0.65		
Guatemala	0.70	Luxembourg	0.79	*Argentina	0.61		
India	0.70	Belgium	0.79	*Israel	0.59		
*Mexico	0.67	South Africa	0.78	*Haiti	0.59		
*Bolivia	0.66	†Turkey	0.64	*El Salvador	0.54		
Liberia	0.64	Greece	0.58	*Bolivia	0.53		
Philippines	0.61	*Israel	0.47	*Mexico	0.50		
*El Salvador	0.61						
Burma	0.58						
*Argentina	0.44			No Group			
*Haiti	0.42			Taiwan			
				Thailand			

* Two loadings above 0.40, with the larger r² less than twice the smaller.
† 25% or more votes absent (and therefore estimated = abstain), not more than 40% absent. Iceland, Panama, Paraguay deleted for greater than 40% absenteeism.

Afro-Asian factor in 1957. The 1952 and 1963 factors are in this way rather more similar to each other than to the one intervening in 1957.

Factor two, called Western Community, is also familiar and closely re-sembles a factor in each of the other two years, allowing for the increase in Assembly membership which brought in Austria, Ireland, Finland, Italy, Portugal, and Spain only in 1956. The major difference lies in the absence of *any* Latin American or Asian state from this group. Even Nationalist China does not load highly here (or on any of the other four factors). The Latin Americans remain distinctly by themselves on Factor 3. Substantively the Latins stayed with the United States and its other allies on cold war issues but as a group were as anti-colonial as anyone on self-determination matters

(Alker and Russett, 1965, pp. 299–307). It might be desirable here to consider the five Latin Americans that load on both Factors 1 and 3 as constituting a separate cluster, possibly labelled "Neutralist Latins" for want of a better term. The Soviet Bloc, though not large in 1952 when many of the European Communist states were still outside the UN, was as tight and distinct as ever. But even then Yugoslavia voted like an Afro-Asian country rather than like a Russian satellite.

Four factors therefore account for 72 per cent of all the roll-call variance and provide quite an adequate picture of countries' groupings in the Assembly. Again, no significant group falls between any two factors.

CONTINUITY AND CHANGE IN VOTING GROUPS

Thus in each of the three years four major factors emerge from the analysis, accounting among themselves in each case for at least two-thirds of all the variance. While there are in the later years several smaller factors, and in 1963 a fifth major group (Latin American) which can be identified only as being between two factors, the stability is striking. It is all the more remarkable when one recalls how the Assembly has grown and changed in its membership. (Almost half of its 1963 members were colonies before 1946. In 1952 a majority of the UN members were allied militarily to the United States; by 1963 only a minority was allied to *either* bloc. Despite inflation and economic growth in most of the world, the admission of poor non-Western states meant that the average per capita income of member states *dropped* over the period.)

Many many observers have talked about the new multipolar system in the world, the emergence of unaligned powers, and even the fragmentation of the underdeveloped areas into rival coalitions. But in terms of voting groups in the General Assembly we find no such trend. A real multi-group system was there from the first year examined, but despite a near-doubling in the size of the Assembly the number of major factors did not expand. A few minor ones were added, but actually more (four) in the 1957 Assembly than in the larger 1963 body (two). American observers may quite recently have become aware of something other than an East-West cold war pattern in UN voting alignments, but that says more about the belated perspicacity of the viewers than about changes in the world of international politics. The expansion of Assembly membership (from 57 to 107 for purposes of this analysis) has in fact outpaced the differentiation of new voting groups.

We can more systematically compare the factors themselves employing the method introduced in chapter three. By inputting the factor loadings for all countries represented in both of two Sessions we can match each of the factors in one Session with each of those in the other, using as the measure of agreement the cosine of the angle formed between them in the space of our geometrical representation. Table 5.3 below shows the results of the comparison of the three Sessions with each other, tracing back the lineage of each 1963 factor. Each factor is labelled to indicate the cluster of countries which loaded highly on it. Because we are of necessity comparing factors rather than clusters, the Latin American group of 1963 cannot be identified directly here, but we can trace its ancestry even so. For simplicity only cosines equal to or greater than 0.50 are shown in the table, and factors which had no cosine that high with any other factor are therefore omitted entirely.[2]

As was apparent even from the less precise comparisons made previously, the basic identity of three major groups over time is very clear. For

TABLE 5.3
The Lineage of 1963 Factors:
Cosines Between Them and the Factors of Earlier Years

The overall product moment correlations among the studies are:

1952–1957 = 0.92
1957–1963 = 0.89
1952–1963 = 0.91

[2] The three comparisons (1963 with 1957, 1963 with 1952, and 1957 with 1952) are of course not *fully* comparable, since each is based on a different universe of countries—those who actually took part in the Assemblies in the two Sessions being compared.

the Afro-Asian, Communist, and Western Community (or West) factors the cosines from one analysis to the next are in all but two cases over 0.90; even the two exceptions are well above 0.70. In their essential respects these three groups correspond to the widely-held image of a political world split along an East-Neutral-West division. (Finding these three groups, however, does not tell us whether the Afro-Asians are *neutral between* the other two blocs or merely *separate* on another dimension.) But it is by no means a complete picture, for these three factors together in no analysis account for more than 60 per cent of all the variance.

In every Session there was also a more or less distinguishable Latin American group. Most obvious in 1952, it was smaller and in part merged with the Western Community countries in 1957, and between two factors in 1963. Whatever the label (Brazzaville and/or Latin America) there is substantial continuity over the entire period; one or more groups of states are on the whole fairly pro-Western on cold war matters but distinctly unsympathetic to the European powers on most colonial self-determination issues. Originally only a Latin American group, and rather fragmented in 1957, it has been succeeded by the Brazzaville factor which has come to include many Asians and Africans as well. In the later years another and much smaller group (Conservative Arabs and/or the pro-Western Asian groups) stands more nearly in a middle position on both cold war and self-determination questions. During 1952 no group of this sort was differentiated. Most such states (Libya, Jordan, Malaysia) were not even members, and those who were (e.g., Lebanon) showed an affinity for either the Western Community or the Afro-Asian factor. The emergence of these countries from the Western Community and Afro-Asian clusters represents one of the greatest changes in the Assembly over the period.

At the bottom of the table we give an indicator of the overall similarity between each paired comparison of the factor matrices. The correlations are uniformly high, in the high 0.80's or low 0.90's. Squaring them, we find that about four-fifths of the variation in one year's voting pattern can be predicted by knowing, for the same states, what that pattern looked like in one of the other years. It is not notably lower for the entire 11-year span than for either of the shorter periods. This is an impressive continuity, though to evaluate it more fully will require closer examination of the nature and location of countries that do shift, and a comparison with the degree of stability shown in international groupings formed according to other criteria.

NATIONAL POLICY: SYSTEM vs. SUBSYSTEM DETERMINANTS

Among students of international politics there has long been a major controversy over the degree of flexibility and choice available to foreign-policy makers. In the language of general systems theory, the debate turns on whether the international system itself, characteristics of the national system, or subsystems within the national system, exert the most influence on the behavior of the nation-state. One side holds that the basic goals of states are relatively fixed and unchanging, that states essentially pursue the same aims for long historical periods. There are many distinct schools of thought on this side, however. Some argue for the objectivity and immutability of national interests. Others couch the argument in terms of the determining power of particular types of international systems—bipolar, balance of power, etc. In yet another context the case may be made that though ministers may come and ministers may go the civil service stays forever. But different analysts, taking up the debate on the side of subsystem determinants, emphasize variations in national policies over time, variations which they may ascribe to personality differences between one chief executive and another, to changes in the parties or groups at the helm, or to such major changes in the national political system as might be produced by revolution or a coup d'etat.[3]

The data here in chapter five bear heavily on this debate. To a very substantial degree our finding of a basic continuity in the number and membership of the major groupings supports those who hold that the international system or, at most, aggregated characteristics of national systems, account for most of the variance in national foreign policy behavior on important matters. (The phrase "important matters" is worth stressing. Undoubtedly presidents and premiers are less restricted by international pressures on issues that are considered relatively trivial by the major powers. Most UN voting concerns quite serious conflicts—e.g., cold war, colonialism, the powers of the UN itself—even though the particular roll-call vote itself may be about a seemingly trivial aspect of the conflict. The great lengths to which the United States government sometimes goes in order to insure the votes of wavering states on some of these issues certainly suggests that it cares about the outcome.) The point can be documented more thoroughly, however, by another output of the same analysis which gives us the cosines for comparing the factors in two different years.

Table 5.4, following, gives an index (d^2) which shows the degree to which a given country's position in one year varies from that in another. When the factors of one study are rotated into the factor space of another, each factor in the first can be located, in terms of cosines, with regard to every factor in the second. From the knowledge of a particular country's loadings on the factors in the second study, and the cosines between the

[3] For a useful analytical statement of this problem, see Singer (1961).

TABLE 5.4

Major Changes in National Voting Alignments, 1952–1963

	1952–1957	1957–1963	1952–1963
Cuba	0.12	_2.16_	_1.14_
Guatemala	0.09	0.24	_0.44_
Iran	0.13	0.14	_0.41_
Uruguay	0.12	0.19	_0.34_
Pakistan	0.09	0.07	_0.30_
Greece	_0.79_	_0.69_	0.02
Portugal	—	_0.61_	—
Colombia	0.07	0.16	_0.28_
Yemen	0.17	0.06	_0.24_
Mean for all Countries	0.11	0.16	0.13

factors of each, one can "predict" what that country's loadings on the factors of the first study would be. By then comparing the *predicted* loading on each factor of study one with the *actual* loading thereon, one has a measure of the "error" involved in predicting a country's voting position in one year from its position in another year. The sum of these squared errors or differences, d^2, represents the total variation across all factors. The prediction, naturally, is in terms of a country's relation to other states. If the entire Assembly should change its position on an issue no difference would show up in this analysis, but if a particular state changes its position while others remain relatively constant, we will find that easily. The analysis is designed to discover, in effect, which states swap allies. A nation which votes with the Latin Americans on most issues one year and with the Communists in another will have a very high d^2.

There is, of course, a case that fits this description: Cuba. In principle the value of a country's d^2 over four factors could go as high as 4.00, but to do so it would require a most unusual configuration of loadings in the early year. (Its total variance would have to be fully accounted for by the four factors, and the loadings would have to be plus or minus 0.50 on each.) In the real world the shift represented by Cuba is about as great as one could expect to find. Certainly on purely intuitive grounds one can discover no comparable international shift of alignments in the postwar period. Therefore we can use the Cuban experience as a benchmark by which to judge the magnitude of other nations' changes. For example, for 1952–1963, the figure 0.23 would indicate a move approximately one-fifth as great as Cuba's. Table 5.4 shows all countries which made shifts more than one-fifth as great as Cuba's, and those indices are underlined (d^2 greater than 0.23

for 1952–1963 or 0.43 for 1957–1963). Only one substantial shift occurred in 1952–1957, and that too is listed and underlined.[4]

Most important, we find no other instance of a net change over the eleven years that even approaches the Cuban experience. Following it at some distance, the greatest net shifts are by Iran and Guatemala. Both have moved perceptibly west—Iran following the ouster of Premier Mossadegh and the country's later adherence to the CENTO Treaty, and Guatemala a cumulative consequence of the overthrow of the pro-Communist Arbenz regime in 1954.[5] The only other changes greater than "one-fifth of a Cuba" were the westward shift of Pakistan over the period, moving from a fairly strong Afro-Asian orientation to a rather tenuous voting alliance with the Western Community; Uruguay's gradual adoption of a more anti-colonial position than is typical of Latin American states; and the results of prolonged civil war in Colombia and Yemen.

Greece's position changed drastically (almost one-third of a Cuba) from 1952 to 1957, when it shifted from a fairly strong Western position to alignment with the Pro-West Asians. But it moved dramatically back to the Western Community camp in 1963, for a negligible *net* shift over the entire span. The movement perhaps escaped notice by most American observers because it was due primarily to Greek attitudes on *colonial* questions and especially Cyprus—matters which, compared to the cold war, were of little salience to the United States. Finally, in recent years Portugal's colonial problems have caused her to become increasingly isolated from her Western allies. No other important variations occurred even between the two close years (1952–1957 or 1957–1963).

The very striking aspect of this table is that in three brief paragraphs we have been able to mention all the major changes in the voting alignments of more than 80 nations. Substantial shifts are most rare, and the greatest occurred only after a society-shattering revolution and a polar switch in military alliance. A major change of regime had some discernible effect in a few of the cases in the above sentences, but whatever the *domestic* consequences, such important revolutions as those in Iraq (1958) and Argentina (1955) have not had great impact on their nations' *international* alignments. Iraq withdrew from the Baghdad Pact and bought arms from the Soviet Union, but did not otherwise alter its policies so very greatly. *Even the most publicized change of regime in recent years, the rise of Gaullism and of*

---

[4] Again, one cannot simply add (or subtract) column one and column two to get the net shift (column three) because each of the three comparisons is derived from a somewhat different universe of countries. In addition, the comparison is made by rotating the factor space of the year with the larger number of factors into the year with the smaller. Thus the 1957–63 comparison involves a six-factor space whereas the other two are merely for a four-factor space. It is therefore appropriate only to compare d^2 down one column, not across rows. The statement "Cuba's 1957–63 change was twice as great as its overall 1952–63 movement" would be misleading.

[5] One way or another the C.I.A. seems to have been involved in the major shifts!

Republic number five, did not affect France's international alignment more than marginally. Seen through the perhaps microscopic eye of American reporting, France's new independent policy seemed to make a great difference in Western Europe and in French relations with the Communist states. But on the basic alignments that have characterized behavior in the United Nations over the past decade and a half Paris has not deviated significantly. It remains as it has been: anti-Communist on the critical cold war issues,[6] sympathetic with its fellow colonial and ex-colonial powers, and resistant to efforts to strengthen the world organization's feeble powers to coerce its members.

Though they may often share similar values, such as wealth and national unity, not all states pursue the same specific goals. Or one nation may achieve its values by proscribing the independence or wealth of another. But they do not seek those goals in a volatile or capricious manner. In the foreign affairs of the 1950's and early 1960's nations did not readily change their basic strategies, and their elites, whether from preference or because of internal and external systemic pressures, did not quickly alter their international alignments. Given the continuity we found despite changes of regime, one is strongly inclined to discount the role of most internal (subsystem) pressures—they account for little of the variance. "The national interest" may be neither objectively defined nor immutable, but short of utter domestic upheaval the men who most powerfully control national foreign policies have held rather constant preferences and/or perceptions of alternatives. Governments rose and fell without great change in states' positions on the central super-issues of world politics.

In building a "pre-theory" of foreign policy making, James Rosenau (1966) has made a useful distinction among influences at five levels of the decision-making process:

1) idiosyncratic variables, particular to the individual decision-maker,
2) variables peculiar to the decision-maker's rôle,
3) variables peculiar to the governmental structure,
4) societal variables, and
5) systemic variables.

He then constructs a tentative classificatory scheme for various types of states (developed and underdeveloped, small and large, etc.), and suggests some hypotheses about the relative influence of each type of variable for different kinds of countries. Such a double set of distinctions might be useful here, but even without it we can offer some general conclusions about the explanatory power of different variables. On these major issues in the

[6] France's recent conversion to advocacy of UN membership for Communist China would modify this statement only slightly.

United Nations, the importance of *idiosyncratic* and *rôle* variables is slight—changes in the person or even party of the major decision-makers made little difference in nations' alignments. Occasionally—but not often—changes in the type of *governmental* system had a discernible effect, but the only very substantial shifts coincided with governmental changes that ran deeper, affecting the basic distribution of values in the *society*; i.e., Guatemala, Iran, and most notably, Cuba. Because the international system itself did not change greatly in any clearly measurable pattern, we cannot weigh the relative effect of societal *vs.* systemic influences, but surely either or both of them appear to be more important than the others. Probably the *system* sets forth a very limited menu, from which a nation may make a selection which is largely a function of its pattern of social organization. Thus the international system itself does permit an underdeveloped country a certain degree of choice in its orientation. It may accept foreign aid from the West (usually but not exclusively from the United States), from the Soviet area, from both (e.g., Egypt) or substantially from neither (e.g., Burma). This choice of patron of course coincides with, and in turn further restricts, the nation's basic orientation in world politics. But barring a change in regime that shakes society as well as government, later variations in this orientation are usually marginal or limited in scope.

Whether the stability noted above is typical of a longer historical epoch is, of course, another question, and one to which the answer must be negative. The *early* post-World War II years were marked by many realignments that would have rivaled Cuba's in the above table. All of Eastern Europe was changed from fascist or, in a couple of cases democratic, regimes, to alignment with the Soviet Union. For Yugoslavia this was only temporary, and was followed by a foreign policy that, in the UN, looks like some Afro-Asians'. China too went Communist, and Taiwan, which for the first few UN sessions behaved like an anti-colonial Asian, became a mere appendage to the Western Alliance. And Germany and Japan receded as independent power centers. But most of these too were essentially social, not just political, revolutions.

In short, what we have had in the last two decades is the calm *after* the storm, an era of stability following great realignment. Historically there have been similar periods after great wars, including the Napoleonic War, the Franco-Prussian conflict, and World War I. And in each case these periods of stability lasted only a couple of decades. According to a simple cyclical theory, then, we are due to witness another era of flux, when the international system will offer more, and perhaps less divergent, choices to national policy-makers than they were presented with during the height of the Cold War. But there is more to international politics than the simple ebb and flow of a tide or cycle. Before speculating further, let us look at other elements in the structure of the international system.

6

THE NETWORK OF INTERNATIONAL ORGANIZATIONS

INSTITUTIONS AND THEORIES OF INTEGRATION

WE HAVE SEEN HOW NATIONS ARE RELATED IN TERMS OF the common possession of certain attributes such as socio-economic characteristics, and have examined United Nations voting behavior in order to infer how their elites share similar political attitudes. In addition, states often share common formal bonds, in the shape of intergovernmental or, less frequently, supranational institutions. These institutions may be virtually universal in membership, limited to a particular geographic area, or restricted in membership yet including states sharing a common interest but with otherwise widely varying characteristics. An example of the latter would be the International Tin Council, composed of industrial and underdeveloped states, consumers and producers, scattered over the globe.

International organizations can originate for a variety of purposes, among them: to stabilize commodity prices among major producers; to foster trade among member states; to facilitate international communications, like mail or telecommunications; to promote technical cooperation; to improve health conditions; to deal with some other specific ad hoc problem like refugees; to provide for joint military defense; for explicitly political reasons, including the promotion of further political integration; or for a variety of these purposes. In doing so they may directly affect some of the other conditions for integration that have been or will be the subject of analyses in this book: socio-economic homogeneity, similarity of major political attitudes, and international transactions such as trade. They may also affect those conditions far less directly, in the way that an organization designed to foster technical cooperation may have the effect of promoting more trade among member states. And of course an institution's very success in dealing with a particular function may create new problems that can be solved only with a new organization or an expansion of the old one's functions. The manner in which the creation of a free-trade area leads to the coordination of national fiscal and welfare policies is a case in point.

This is of course precisely the argument made by the functionalist school; i.e., an institution which works effectively in one area will create needs either for the broadening of that institution or for the creation of new ones.[1] Note, however, that there is no unilateral causal relationship stated in this argument. An institution may give rise to new relationships which may in turn require new institutions, in a feedback situation, but the need may also arise independently without being a consequence of institutional development. For example, technological advances such as the airplane resulted in the need for such functional institutions as the I.C.A.O. to be established.

There has long been confusion and disagreement in the functionalist and other literature as regards the precise meaning of international *integration*. Some writers prefer to limit its use to instances where formal organizations exist. Haas (1957), for example, set as an ideal-type for heuristic purposes a federal or other centralized political system, and Etzioni (1965, p. 300) limits the term to cases of "the development of a center of decision-making identification, and control of force." While many authors do indeed use some sort of *structural* definition calling for institutions with powers superior to those of the member states, such a focus is too narrow for the purposes of this analysis. A structural definition, even as an ideal-type, too easily implies that integration is a smooth continuum, and that amalgamation (with supranational institutions) requires merely the same conditions, only in greater volume, than pluralistic integration (among still-independent states). Whether the continuum idea is accurate remains an empirical question yet to be properly investigated. Here we shall avoid any definition in terms of institutions, for we are more concerned with the *behavioral* behavioral of integration. Deutsch et al. (1957) defined integration as the probability that conflicts would be resolved without violence; the ideal-type for them would be when the states concerned ceased to prepare for war against each other. Similarly, North, Koch, and Zinnes (1960) offer several criteria for measuring integration, one of which is the probability of violence.[2]

My own choice is for a behavior measure, but not one limited to the presence or absence of violence. Elsewhere (Russett, 1963) I have suggested that states be considered more *integrated* the higher the ratio of capabilities to loads or burdens in their relationship. *Responsiveness* is the behavioral

---

[1] The classic statement of this position is by David Mitrany (1946), with the most ambitious critique, restatement, and testing that of Ernst Haas (1964). See also Sewell (1965).

[2] Despite his emphasis on the need for certain institutions, Haas' definition of political integration also is not structural, but concerned with the process whereby behavior is changed: "the process whereby political actors in several distinct national settings are persuaded to shift their loyalties, expectations, and political activities toward a new centre." (Haas, 1957, p. 16).

consequence of that ratio, and in turn states' responsiveness to one another can be defined as the probability that the requests or demands of one will be met favorably. It must be quite clear that the idea of responsiveness does not insist that for a state to be considered "responsive" it must always give in to the demands of the other. If so, the demanding state would be acting in a manner highly unresponsive to the needs of its jelly-fish partner. Between nations as between individuals in primary groups, interests will not always coincide, and the interaction of the partners will insure that some conflicts of interest become salient. When this happens there must be explicit or tacit negotiation, resulting perhaps in compromise, an exchange of concessions on one issue for some on another, or an "upgrading of common interests" (Haas, 1961) to a new solution. Sometimes two governments' interests will be nearly identical, sometimes they will merely converge on the same goal for different reasons. But very often they will indeed conflict, and it is a relationship or pattern of behavior, the ability to work out that conflict with a minimum of violence and without one party always making the important concessions, that marks the *condition* of successful political integration.[3] In research the absence of violence is relatively easy to measure, and for that reason attractive. Even so, it is surely no indicator whatever of integration if violence is prevented merely by repression or deterrence, or on the other hand if it is avoided just because the parties are irrelevant to each other and have nothing to fight over. In chapter twelve we shall look at some data on the frequency of war between different countries and consider this aspect in more detail.

Though one can postulate an ideal-type for behavior as well as for any other definition, at which one could say that nations had reached the state of perfect integration, we of course have nothing of the sort among the many nations represented in this study. We expect only to compare the achievements of various areas and to be able to look at elements in the process by which nations become *more or less* integrated. As the study progresses we shall be examining several points in time to see whether certain conditions (e.g., institutional bonds) follow or precede others (such as similarity of political attitudes on major foreign policy questions).

We do not limit our concern for integration to cases where supranational institutions exist. If we did so we would have hardly any examples in the political units under study; the nearest would be the organizations tying together the nations of the European Common Market, and even they would pass only a weak test of supranationality. Nor, as was indicated, do we limit it to instances of common institutions, even weak intergovern-

---

[3] This is close to what Etzioni (1965, p. 300) means by harmonization. Economists sometimes define integration as the absence of discrimination within an area. (Balassa, 1961, p. 1)

mental ones. The analysis of this chapter, which will identify states joined together by a number of intergovernmental organizations, is intended merely to map areas where *one* of the apparent conditions—common institutions—for integration is present. Of course any reader who wishes to interpret the results as integration in the structural sense is free to do so.

We shall look at the accumulation of capabilities which are largely channels for the communication of information. Information is essential to continued responsiveness; without information, rational behavior is impossible. Information is not always dependent upon current communication, since it may be stored from previous experience. Tacit communication requires different kinds of channels than does the explicit variety, but channels (for observing the other's behavior) must still exist. Stored information is of little use in dealing with changes in the environment. Without adequate communication the adjustment of conflict must become haphazard and accidental. As Quincy Wright (1955, p. 299) emphasized, "Considering all its aspects, communication can be studied as central in all the social sciences. . . . The study of communication is more fundamental than the study of power or of trade because it is the condition for both." Richard Meier (1961, p. 113) has discussed the role of information in avoiding or settling conflicts in the international system:

> A large continuous flow of information makes it possible to mobilize the requisite experience and data quickly. . . . It may also bring the anticipated crisis to the attention of the decision-makers sooner than would otherwise occur. Large flows of information . . . make it possible to reduce the chances of blundering into international conflicts.[4]

Even for those who prefer to employ a behavioral measure of integration, institutions remain highly relevant. Organizations surely do not guarantee the non-violent resolution of conflict, but empirically they nevertheless have been of great assistance. Of course one can point to many instances like the American Civil War, or the Anglo-Irish conflicts of the 19th and early 20th Centuries, to confirm the insufficiency of a common government to resolve conflict. Common institutions, erected by force or in the absence of other essential preconditions for successful amalgamation, can bring burdens and make salient many conflicts of interest that would otherwise not arise. Two of the major disputes among the American states in the 1850's for instance—slavery and the tariff—would have been much less relevant to the relations between separate nations. It was only their inability to work out a mutually agreeable common policy that led to

---

[4] The piece by Meier was brought to my attention by the excellent exposition in Brams (1965b).

war. England and Ireland might well have lived in peace as separate and sovereign neighbors. Furthermore, amalgamation may result in a situation where too much of the political elite's attention is concentrated on the problems of the new large unit and too little is left for the concerns of the component sub-units. Particular groups within some of the member states may feel that their interests are being neglected at the expense of people in other member states. French farmers, for instance, might at some point decide that the Common Market was to blame for their economic difficulties, and their wrath could put serious strain both on the Common Market as a whole and on France itself. Delegation of power to a higher and wider level can produce conflicts that could otherwise have been prevented. The existence of a common government with the power to execute decisions against some members' will may result in very severe stress and a sense of coercion. The American War Between the States was the bloodiest and most bitter conflict of the entire century between Waterloo and Sarajevo.

But to argue that political institutions do not make a *sufficient* condition for integration, or even that a premature effort to impose powerful institutions may lower the level of integration previously achieved, is *not* to say that institutions are *unnecessary*. The impressive degree of Anglo-American integration achieved during World War II was dependent upon the operation of a large number of intergovernmental (though not supranational) organizations (Russett, 1963, ch. 10). Where serious conflicts of interest exist between nations that can affect each others' destinies, some institutional structures must exist to facilitate negotiation, compromise, and coordination to produce common or compatible policies. Institutions provide important capabilities for attention and communication. An institution can be described as essentially a set of channels for processing information, solving problems, and transmitting communications. Along with less formal channels, they are vital capabilities in any effort to produce a high level of responsiveness between political units, even though by themselves they cannot guarantee the non-violent resolution of conflict. Leon Lindberg (1963, p. 9) and Chadwick Alger (1961, 1965) also mention some of the latent effects of institutions on the overall system.[5] Participants in intergovernmental organizations may develop new perspectives and personal friendships which, if these people also are active in national governments, they may carry back with them. Since most of these men are highly educated and play significant roles in the political process of their home countries, in time the effect of their experience may become considerable. An analogy here is to members of the United States Senate who develop a certain loyalty to the "Club" and will defend its interests in a conflict with the

[5] Note the emphasis in the sociological literature, exemplified by Merton (1957, pp. 60–64, *passim*), on the latent as well as manifest functions of institutions.

executive branch even on some occasions when on policy grounds they agree more with the executive than with their fellow legislators.

THE INTERPLAY OF THEORY AND METHOD

Even though we do not choose to define integration simply as the creation of particular kinds of institutions, intergovernmental organizations are nevertheless essential in building the conditions for integrative behavior. On the example of the preceding chapters we must, therefore, discover what groups of countries are linked together by especially strong institutional bonds.

An extraordinarily useful source of information for this mapping exercise is the *Yearbook of International Organizations,* published biennially in Brussels. It lists all intergovernmental organizations as well as very many private (non-governmental) international organizations, whether universal, regional, or functional, with their membership and a description of the organizations' activities. Excluding the non-governmental bodies, for 1963 there was a total of 163 intergovernmental organizations, including the United Nations and many of its specialized agencies, which were relatively permanent bodies with permanent membership.[6] Numbered among them were bodies of such diverse purpose and importance as the European Coal and Steel Community; Euratom and the other institutions of the Six; the African Telecommunications Union; the Central Treaty Organization; the Council of Europe; the Interamerican Children's Institute; the International Institute of Refrigeration; the International Union for the Protection of Literary and Artistic Works; the League of Arab States; the Permanent Court of Arbitration; and the Warsaw Treaty Organization. Their membership varied from three to 113.

It is possible to construct a matrix with both a row and a column for each of 115 states in the period 1961–1962.[7] By examining the membership lists of the various organizations one can fill into every cell the number of organizations to which both the row country and the column country belong. The actual values range from a high of 76 for France and Netherlands to zero for many pairs of countries, one of which is the United States and the People's Republic of China. If each joint organizational membership is weighted

[6] This definition deliberately excludes an organization like UNICEF, whose members are simply the members of an Executive Board the national composition of which changes annually.

[7] Only sovereign states in 1962 are included, with the exception of soon-to-be independent Kenya, which is represented also in several other analyses of the book. The date on which different organizations reported to the *Yearbook* varies over the period 1961–62. Padelford (1956) presented a now somewhat dated bibliography on regional organizations; some useful documents were collected by Lawson (1962).

equally, through a simple normalization procedure (dividing the number of common memberships in each cell by the largest number of any cell in the table—$\frac{Mij}{M\,max}$) we convert the table into a symmetrical matrix of *proximities,* where the largest value (France-Netherlands) is 1.0 and the smallest is zero. I then submitted the matrix of proximities to a *direct factor analysis,* without first computing the correlations. The proximities thus were input at the stage where the factoring procedure would, in the more familiar variants, operate on correlation coefficients. Direct factor analysis is a fairly common procedure, and can be applied to any kind of matrix. Some examples are the applications by Berry (1960, 1961a) and MacRae and Meldrum (1960).[8] Actually the data here present a special case in that they resemble those of a sociometric matrix, where each country "chooses" (joins an organization with) another country a given number of times. Both MacRae (1960) and Wright and Evitts (1961) have used direct factor analysis for this purpose, except that in their instances the matrices were not symmetrical (A might choose B more often than B chose A), which introduced additional complications that we shall discuss in chapter eight. But here, with a square (same number of countries in the rows as in the columns) symmetrical matrix that is logically equivalent to any other n by n matrix, such as one containing correlations, the procedure is quite straightforward. We normalize the values to a range of zero to one (the same as positive correlation coefficients) merely to keep the loadings interpretable according to the magnitudes with which most readers are familiar.[9]

It may be worthwhile to detail a number of aspects of this factor analysis which have important consequences for the pattern that emerges in the output data. Factor analysis is not simply a black box that magically transforms raw input into "the" appropriate results. It is a mathematical procedure which incorporates a particular theory about the relationship among

[8] In his important new methodological work Paul Horst (1965, p. 258) describes the earlier emphasis on the correlation matrix as "unfortunate," and urges more factoring directly on the data matrix. Nosanchuk (1963) shows the superiority of direct factor analysis over some alternative techniques for tasks of the sort considered here.

[9] If one were performing a direct factor analysis on a symmetric matrix that met the requirements of Euclidean geometry, the correct procedure would be to apply a vector model, transforming each "distance" (1 minus the proximity) into its scalar product. (Torgerson, 1958, pp. 251–259, Ross and Cliff, 1964). This matrix, however, fails one of the Euclidean requirements, the law of triangular inequality. According to that law, $Dij \leq Dik + Djk$, where i, j, and k are nations and D is the distance. But there is no reason why it should apply to a matrix of common memberships, and empirically in this case it does not. Thus the "distance" between Britain and Australia is low because of their common memberships in Commonwealth organizations; that between France and Britain is low by virtue of their European and Atlantic memberships, but the "distance" between France (not Commonwealth) and Australia (not Atlantic) is high, greater than the sum of the other two. Hence we merely apply direct factor analysis to the untransformed proximities.

variables, and at several points there are available some choices as to the precise procedures to be followed. Each of these choices is a *theoretical* one in which the decision taken will affect the groupings, and he who uses factor analysis (or any complex computer technique) without understanding the theoretical consequences of his decisions risks producing results that are not appropriate to the questions he thinks he is asking.

One such aspect is the choice of direct factor analysis rather than correlating each column of proximities with every other column, as is the more common method. The result of the latter procedure, however, would have been to give as factors those countries with similar *patterns* of proximities, not necessarily countries which were bound by many institutional ties. For example, a nation linked only to three others, by one institution each, would have the same loading on the appropriate factor as would a country which was bound only to those same three, but by ten institutions in each case.

Another such aspect, which concerns the form of the raw data rather than the factor analysis itself, is the assumption that the marginal utility of every new international organization membership is constant; for instance the political effects of moving from 70 to 71 common memberships are the same as moving from 2 to 3. A less obvious matter involves the decision about what to insert in the diagonals of the input matrix; that is, how to treat a country's self-choice. In factor analysis the most common alternatives are either unities or a value equal to the squared multiple correlations of all the other cells in that row, a sum which is frequently less than unity. In opting for unities we are building into the analysis the assumption that countries with only a few common memberships (e.g., East Germany) are quite isolated—the difference between the self-choice and most other entries in the row will be very great. Had we inserted something equivalent to squared multiple correlations, or communalities, we would have been saying, in effect, that the political effect of a country's ties to one state is dependent *only* upon their number relative to those with another, and its link with its closest partner would be not too much lower than the value assigned to its self-link.

In matrices of the size examined here the communality problem is really not an important one, and in the actual computations has only a minimal effect. Some allowance for the *total* number of ties is made in another feature of the technique. Before rotation the sum of the squared factor loadings for each country is normed to equal unity. Thus a nation with widely dispersed organizational memberships will have a number of *moderate* loadings, while another state, with its common memberships concentrated on a few countries, will have a *high* loading on only one or two factors, even though the maximum number of memberships in common may be the same for both states. An example here is the fact that the United States has about as many common memberships with Mexico as does Argentina, but, because of the United States' links also with the North Atlantic and other countries, its loading on the "Latin American" factor below is not as high as Argentina's.

As a result, these procedures allow us to distinguish three general patterns:

1) *isolated* countries, with high loadings on no factor large enough to report. These states, with a very limited number of institutional bonds are, by this definition, only narrowly involved in international politics and are, probably, heavily dependent on those few bonds for contact with other nations;

2) *regionally involved* countries, with many organizational ties to a particular group of states, and high loadings on a single factor; and

3) *globally involved* countries, with substantial numbers of co-memberships in various parts of the world and moderate loadings on two or more factors. These last, with wide involvements and hence broad perspectives, include two of the major powers (United States and United Kingdom) but are mainly smaller states. In one sense they are the cross-pressured states with wide-flung interests, whose existence prevents the world from becoming deeply fissioned into virtually exclusive aggregates, and which contribute a potential for mitigating inter-regional conflict. We will develop this kind of theoretical argument more fully in the later chapters.

One further assumption in this procedure is our treatment not only of the marginal utility of a new membership as constant, but the assumption that membership in any particular organization is equivalent to membership in any other. The European Common Market counts for no more than the International Office of Epizootics. Obviously they are not of equivalent political importance, however much faith one wants to put in the functionalist argument. But the difficulty here is a common one, how to devise any kind of weighting scheme for different organizations that would not be purely arbitrary and subject to immediate challenge. On balance it seems better to leave them unweighted, especially as those institutions having the greatest political significance actually are most often multiple rather than solitary. The EEC, for example, has precisely the same national membership as six other institutions listed as part of the European Community: the European Coal and Steel Community, the European Parliament, Euratom, the Court of Justice, the Economic and Social Committee, and the European Investment Bank. Since each of these organizations is listed separately in the *Yearbook* for 1962–1963 (Union of International Associations, 1963), the European Community takes on something nearer the relative importance we would want to attach to it, and any further attempt at weighting becomes inadvisable.

COMMON MEMBERSHIP GROUPINGS IN 1962

Table 6.1 below presents the major factors derived from a direct factor analysis performed according to the procedures described in chapter two. Since the vast majority of states have far fewer than half as many common memberships as France and Netherlands (76), however, most of the proximities were well below 0.50. In analyzing the following table it has thus been necessary to relax our former standards and treat as interesting (report) loadings as low as 0.30. But of the 13 factors with eigen values greater than one we show only those seven which have at least three loadings of

TABLE 6.1
International Organization Groupings in 1962

Factor 1 Western Europe 11%		Factor 2 Latin America 9%		Factor 3 Former French Africa 5%		Factor 4 Asia 4%	
France	0.90	Mexico	0.68	Chad	0.55	Thailand	0.55
Netherlands	0.89	Ecuador	0.67	Mauretania	0.55	India	0.53
Italy	0.88	Argentina	0.66	Central Afr.		Pakistan	0.49
Belgium	0.86	Brazil	0.66	Rep.	0.53	Philippines	0.47
West		Chile	0.66	Congo (B)	0.53	Burma	0.46
Germany	0.86	Colombia	0.66	Niger	0.53	*Ceylon	0.46
Denmark	0.76	Nicaragua	0.65	Senegal	0.53	*Australia	0.45
*United		Costa Rica	0.64	Upper Volta	0.53	*Malaysia	0.45
Kingdom	0.75	Guatemala	0.64	Cameroun	0.51	South	
Norway	0.73	Paraguay	0.63	Ivory Coast	0.50	Vietnam	0.45
Austria	0.71	Peru	0.63	Dahomey	0.49	Indonesia	0.44
Spain	0.70	Honduras	0.62	Gabon	0.48	*Japan	0.43
Switzerland	0.70	Panama	0.62	Madagascar	0.47	Cambodia	0.41
Sweden	0.69	Bolivia	0.60	Mali	0.40	South Korea	0.39
Greece	0.66	El Salvador	0.60	Togo	0.39	Laos	0.35
Luxembourg	0.65	Venezuela	0.60	Congo (L)	0.35	*United	
Turkey	0.62	*United				Kingdom	0.33
Portugal	0.58	States	0.59				
Finland	0.51	Uruguay	0.58				
Yugoslavia	0.50	Dominican					
Ireland	0.45	Rep.	0.57				
Iceland	0.38	Haiti	0.56				
*United		Cuba	0.45				
States	0.37						
*Poland	0.36						
Canada	0.35						
Israel	0.35						
*Japan	0.35						
*Egypt	0.32						
*Australia	0.31						

TABLE 6.1—(Cont.)

Factor 5 Eastern Europe 3%		Factor 6 Arabs 3%		Factor 7 Former British Africa 3%		Unclassified
Bulgaria	0.59	Syria	0.53	Uganda	0.55	Afghanistan
Hungary	0.58	*Egypt	0.50	Tanganyika	0.51	China
Czecho-		Morocco	0.50	Kenya	0.49	Cyprus
slovakia	0.57	Libya	0.46	Sierra		East Germany
Romania	0.57	Lebanon	0.45	Leone	0.45	Ethiopia
USSR	0.53	Tunisia	0.44	Ghana	0.42	Guinea
*Poland	0.50	Iraq	0.41	Jamaica	0.37	Liberia
Albania	0.40	Sudan	0.41	Nigeria	0.34	Mongolia
		*Israel	0.38	*Malaysia	0.33	Nepal
		Algeria	0.37	*Ceylon	0.32	New Zealand
		Jordan	0.36			Somalia
		Saudi				South Africa
		Arabia	0.35			Taiwan
		Kuwait	0.35			Trinidad
		Iran	0.30			Yemen

* Appears on two or more factors.

0.40 or higher.[10] Figure 6.1 is the customary map with ambiguous states grouped according to their highest loadings.

The first factor includes all but one of the countries of Western Europe, and is centered most strongly on the nations of the Common Market. Five of the "Six" lead the list, and even tiny Luxembourg, which does not always feel a need to join some of the limited-function organizations, is not far down the list. The Scandinavian states, the United Kingdom, Austria, Switzerland, Greece, Spain, and Turkey also are high on the factor. Once we move outside the institutions of the Six a cold war neutral is about as likely to be high on the list as is a Western ally from the geographic fringes of the continent. Further down on the factor are Portugal, Yugoslavia, and remote Iceland. Only at the very bottom do we find any nations not physically located on or adjacent to the European continent: the United States, Israel, Canada, Japan, Australia and Egypt. These make the factor look more like the Western Community of previous chapters, but the loadings of the non-Europeans are quite low. All but Canada have higher correlations with some other factor.

[10] The decision on the cutting point for reporting correlations is of course arbitrary; I simply have selected that level which seems to portray non-trivial relationships. Equally arbitrary is the decision to rotate only factors with eigen values (sums of squared loadings) exceeding unity. In direct factor analysis the latter criterion means less than in the more usual methods. However it is the last factors, which in fact we have not tried to interpret, that are most likely to be distorted by an inappropriate choice of rotation criterion.

Japan's presence is a bit startling, and must be attributed to its success in working with the other industrialized states in a variety of organizations, especially those with economic goals. This finding is, nevertheless, in harmony with the preceding chapters, which found Japan grouping with its Western associates on political and social indicators. Egypt's presence here is traceable largely to her membership in a number of Mediterranean-wide organizations. Poland shows up as the only one of the Soviet-area states of Eastern Europe to retain in 1962 a substantial number of the institutional ties it has historically had with its neighbors to the west. Newly-independent Cyprus, however, had not in 1962 yet worked its way into many European organizations. It is the *only* non-Communist European state to be absent from the cluster.

Next comes a grouping headed, for obvious reasons, "Latin America." In fact it is perfectly coterminous with the 1962 membership of the Organization of American States and most of the other inter-American agencies, except that Cuba's expulsion is only partially recorded by her moderate loading at the bottom of the group. French-speaking Haiti is next lowest. Canada, which has avoided membership in most of these institutions, is absent along with the other two nations of the Western Hemisphere, Trinidad and Jamaica. But it includes the United States. Despite its correlation with the Western Europe factor the most numerous United States institutional ties are Panamerican, as can be seen by the fact that its *squared* loading with Factor 1 is well under half its squared loading on the second factor.

Next, and just about as clear-cut, is the group of French-speaking African states. It numbers all the former French African territories except Guinea, which declared its independence from the French Union several years before the others did so. Of those who stayed temporarily, Mali, with its leftist government, has associated itself least closely with the others. The French-speaking elite of former Belgian Congo, however, has brought its country somewhat into this web of common memberships.

A fourth and equally large group is identified by Factor 4, and is readily identified with the "Asia" label. Among its members are the majority, but by no means all, of the non-Communist states of east and south Asia. Some of the physically isolated Asian nations such as Afghanistan and Nepal are missing. So too are Iran and politically isolated Taiwan. Japan, which also was numbered with the Europeans, is present here too, but Turkey, despite its geographical location in Asia Minor, is not. Of all the states that are physically outside the Asian continent and its immediate offshore islands only Australia and Britain are found with the group. Australia's loading, however, is quite high, indicating the degree to which the Australian government has chosen to join with its Asian neighbors in quite a number of functional organizations. New Zealand has remained more aloof.

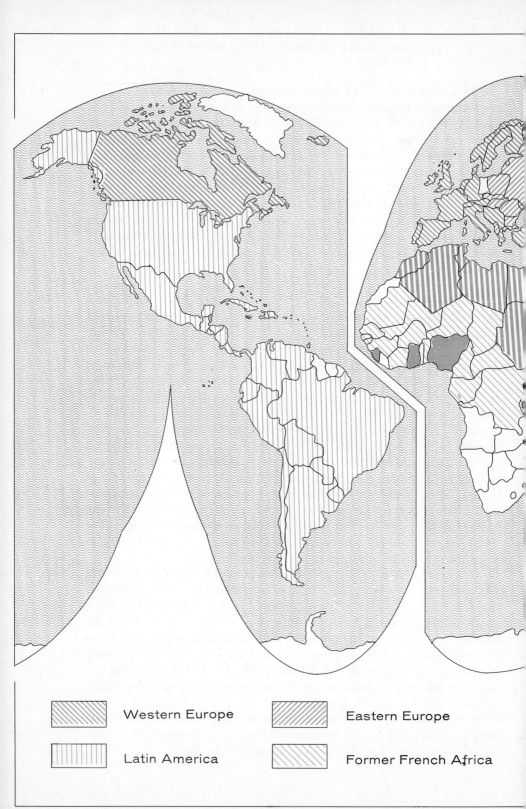

Western Europe

Eastern Europe

Latin America

Former French Africa

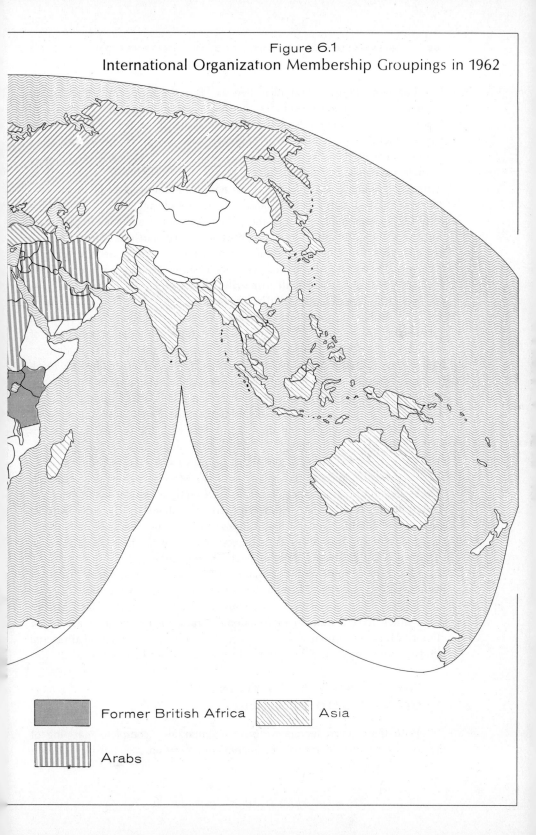

Figure 6.1
International Organization Membership Groupings in 1962

Former British Africa   Asia

Arabs

The next group is best identified as "Eastern European" rather than "communist" because it excludes the Asian communist states. China and Mongolia are not members of the Warsaw Pact, China is also not a signatory of COMECON, and both countries are absent from several other European-oriented institutions. East Germany is also rather isolated: with a single exception it, like mainland China, belongs only to organizations composed predominantly of communist nations, and not to all of them. Two other communist states are also absent from the cluster; Yugoslavia, which withdrew or was expelled from the Soviet-dominated agencies in the early postwar years, and Cuba, whose Soviet-style government was still too new to be included at the time these data were gathered. In any case it would not even now be very tightly linked with these states because so many of the agencies in question deal with primarily European affairs. Albania is present, but rather more tenuously than the others.

The Arab states also form a distinctive cluster of their own. Common membership in most of the universal organizations, plus the development of various local ones like the Arab Postal Union and the Arab Development Bank bring virtually all of them together. While not especially powerful, these agencies are fairly numerous. All the Arabs belong to most of them, though Kuwait, which received its independence only in the middle of 1961, had not yet joined many when this edition of the *Yearbook* went to press. Yemen remained outside even more and is left with the unclassifiable states at the end. The Sudan, though it has quite a large black minority, is governed largely by its Arab majority and belongs to as many of these institutions as does the average nation in the area. Most surprising, of course, is Israel's loading on this factor. Israel is not exactly a charter member of the Arab League, but it is a member of virtually all of the broader Middle Eastern and Mediterranean organizations which include, but not exclusively, the Arab nations. Iran also has its highest loading with these countries even though it is not Arabic; Turkey is strictly European.

One other major group remains. It is composed of Great Britain's former African colonies: Uganda, Kenya, Tanganyika, Ghana, Sierra Leone, and Nigeria. The strongest correlations are found with the East African states which have a number of functional arrangements, but it is a broader cluster. Malaysia, Jamaica and Ceylon show distinct if weak institutional ties with some of their fellow non-white Commonwealth countries.

THE STRENGTH AND ORIGIN OF INSTITUTIONAL GROUPINGS

With these seven factors we have a remarkably complete mapping of the world's pattern of intergovernmental organization membership. Only a score of nations cannot be put pretty unequivocally with one of them. And that score is composed overwhelmingly of countries like Cyprus, Trinidad, and Somalia which were still new and had not yet fully established their institutional links with others, and such real pariahs of international politics as East Germany, the two Chinas, and South Africa. Any analysis that finds the latter polities to be isolated establishes a strong case for its credibility. Ethiopia, Liberia, New Zealand, and a few others simply have in general held themselves aloof from all but the universal organizations.

Some of these groups are more closely united than others. One of the primary virtues of this application of direct factor analysis is the way in which, for the countries most strongly correlated with each factor, the squared factor loadings are related inversely and more or less linearly to the distances among them. Thus France, Italy, Belgium, and the Netherlands have proximity scores of almost 1.00, corresponding to more than 70 institutional memberships in common. Their loadings on the factor identified with "Western Europe" are by far the highest loadings in the entire table, nearly 0.90, giving an r^2 of about 0.80. Mexico, Ecuador, and the other states at the top of the "Latin America" group typically have proximities around 0.58, corresponding to around 44 common memberships. In Latin America quite a substantial number of regional organizations exist for a variety of public health, communications, and economic purposes. These countries' factor loadings, when squared, come to about 0.45. Similarly, the most closely bound "Eastern Europeans" are typically linked together by about 28 common memberships, and Kenya-Uganda-Tanganyika of the British Africans by hardly more than 20.[11]

Once we have established this relationship it is a simple matter to compare the strength of the bonds among each group. The European Six have by far the most numerous institutional ties of any group of countries in the world, nearly twice as many as the most closely linked Latin Americans, and almost three times as many as among the Communist states. In other ways the countries of Eastern Europe may be tightly organized, but their bonds are not manifested in a proliferation of intergovernmental organizations like that in the West. Nevertheless, institutional ties are more numerous for them than for any of the remaining four major regional groupings, which are weaker. Western Europe's organizational strength is well-known, but the numerous linkages in Latin America and Eastern Europe, solidly in second and third place, respectively, are less widely appreciated.

We shall examine the relation of these groups to those defined by other

[11] This relationship is somewhat weakened when a country is associated with more than one regional group. The United States, for example, is no more "distant" organizationally from the highest Latin Americans than they are from themselves, even though its loading on the factor is several points lower.

criteria much more thoroughly in the concluding chapters of this volume, but even at this point the strong resemblance of the clusters to geographically-defined ones bears special comment. The Latin American instance is the most striking one, but it is followed not far behind by the group for Asia, and, if we allow for the political effects of the Iron Curtain, the Eastern and Western Europe clusters as well. "Arab" virtually equals Middle East here, and once more if we allow for the division of a continent by politics, in this case by the colonial past, the two African groups complete the geopolitical picture. In the African instance it will be most instructive to see whether, as the effects of foreign rule fade, the distinctions between the former French and the former British groups fade. The emergence of a single Africa-wide cluster would seem to be the most likely outcome, though further subdivision, possibly into geographically defined East and West African groups, cannot be ruled out.

It is easy to explain why geography plays such an important role in determining the way in which countries aggregate into intergovernmental organizations. Mere proximity brings a common interest in many problems which do not stop at national borders and require cooperative solutions. Mail and telecommunications must pass through one state to reach another. Disease and drought do not respect boundaries. If several states share similar climatic conditions they probably raise similar crops and stand to gain by working out international marketing and price stabilization agreements. Unless neighbors' political relations are unusually bad they will almost surely trade fairly heavily with each other, often giving rise to economic organizations. And though neighbors may frequently fight, they also often have a common interest in political or military arrangements that can offer them joint protection against intervention from outside. All these are logical and intuitively satisfying reasons, in hindsight, for explaining the powerful effect that geography so obviously has had on the groupings found in this chapter. But the ease of that explanation now is not quite enough to permit a knowing "I told you so" in the face of the very strong relationship before us here.

7

INSTITUTIONAL CONTINUITY AND GROWTH IN THE POSTWAR ERA

ORGANIZATIONAL NODES IN 1951

THE NETWORK OF INTERNATIONAL ORGANIZATIONS WAS in 1951 much weaker than it was to become a decade later. In retrospect one of the most important developments in world politics of the 1950's may well have been the proliferation of intergovernmental institutions. Whereas we had a total of 163 organizations to analyze in 1962, at the beginning of the period there were only 107, making an increase of more than 50 per cent over the span.[1] The most visible and best known manifestation of this trend was of course in Western Europe, with the growth of the Common Market and related institutions like EURATOM. In 1962 the largest number of common memberships was held by France and the Netherlands, who belonged to 76 organizations with each other. But the 1951 high, for pre-Common Market days, was between France and the United Kingdom with 42 common memberships. While this surely illustrates the growing strength of the "Six," these developments were by no means limited to Europe. Quite a number of regional organizations have sprung up in Latin America and more recently among the new states of Africa. Other ex-colonial nations have also formed new international organizations, not necessarily limited to rigidly defined geographical areas. In addition the Communist states, especially those of Eastern Europe, have set up several institutions. Yet as we shall see, the pattern of organizational membership changed little over this span. With quite remarkable stability, the same countries cluster together in both periods, especially at those nodes where the linkages are most dense.

I performed an analysis just like that in the previous chapter, this time using data for 1951 from the *Yearbook* for that date (Union of International Associations, 1952). For that time too, seven clusters of countries appeared, bearing quite a close resemblance to those discovered for the later

[1] I have not counted several organizations which, even though listed with the IGO's in the 1951 *Yearbook*, seem actually to be private associations (NGO's).

TABLE 7.1

International Organization Groupings in 1951

Factor 1 Western Europe 13%		Factor 2 Latin America 13%		Factor 3 Middle East 4%		Factor 4 Old Common- wealth 4%	
France	0.87	Mexico	0.70	Iran	0.51	*Australia	0.60
*Netherlands	0.83	Peru	0.67	Iraq	0.48	*Canada	0.55
Belgium	0.81	Brazil	0.66	*Pakistan	0.45	New	
Italy	0.76	Nicaragua	0.66	Egypt	0.44	Zealand	0.53
*United		Dominican		*India	0.41	South Africa	0.47
Kingdom	0.74	Rep.	0.66	Lebanon	0.38	*United	
Denmark	0.67	Venezuela	0.65	*Finland	0.36	Kingdom	0.44
Portugal	0.65	Guatemala	0.65	*Turkey	0.35	*United	
Norway	0.62	Panama	0.64	Syria	0.32	States	0.38
Sweden	0.61	Bolivia	0.63	Thailand	0.32	*Japan	0.34
Luxembourg	0.61	Paraguay	0.63	*Philippines	0.31	*India	0.33
Switzerland	0.61	*United		Taiwan	0.30		
Greece	0.59	States	0.63				
West		Uruguay	0.63				
Germany	0.57	Cuba	0.63				
Austria	0.54	Colombia	0.63				
Spain	0.51	Costa Rica	0.63				
*Turkey	0.47	Chile	0.61				
Ireland	0.42	Ecuador	0.61				
*Yugoslavia	0.42	Haiti	0.58				
*Finland	0.40	Argentina	0.58				
*United		El Salvador	0.57				
States	0.40	Honduras	0.55				
*Australia	0.37						
*Hungary	0.36						
*Czechoslo-							
vakia	0.35						
*Canada	0.34						
*Romania	0.34						
*Poland	0.33						
Iceland	0.32						

year. Table 7.1 shows those with three or more loadings greater than 0.40, plus one that, though just short of this criterion, nevertheless had quite a number of loadings in the 0.30's. Four other rotated factors did not meet the test and are omitted.

The initial two factors are virtually identical with the first two that emerged for 1962. Again we have to read very far down the "Western Europe" listing to find a country that is not physically located in Europe—

TABLE 7.1

International Organization Groupings in 1951

Factor 5 Eastern Europe 3%		Factor 6 Southeast Asia 2%		Factor 7 Arabia 2%		Unclassified
Bulgaria	0.57	Burma	0.58	Saudi Arabia	0.55	Albania
*Romania	0.52	Indonesia	0.48	Afghanistan	0.44	China
*Hungary	0.49	*Netherlands	0.36	Jordan	0.43	East Germany
*Poland	0.44	*Philippines	0.33	Liberia	0.31	Ethiopia
*Czechoslo-		Ceylon	0.31			Israel
vakia	0.44	*Pakistan	0.31			Nepal
USSR	0.41	*Paraguay	0.30			South Korea
*Yugoslavia	0.40	*United				Yemen
*Japan	0.31	Kingdom	0.30			

* Appears on two or more factors.

the United States checks in with a loading of 0.40, and is followed then by Australia and Canada. Even in 1951 the heart of this cluster could be found in the states that later became identified as the Six, though West Germany, still recovering her position and not yet restored to full sovereignty, has a much more moderate loading than do the others. For much the same reasons Austria too is rather far down the list. And by a combination of her own choice and others' exclusion Spain was appreciably more peripheral than she was to be a decade later, after limited liberalization at home and a relaxation of the democracies' ostracism. Portugal's bonds with the rest of Europe were appreciably stronger than Spain's in 1951, but the two countries' positions were reversed by 1962. The United Kingdom was then in the fifth position; only later was it dropped down by tighter continental unity and the integration of Bonn with the other Six. By 1962 Britain had also fallen below Denmark, which continued to lead Scandinavia in its association with EEC countries.[2] In the previous chapter we found that Israel was moderately but visibly associated with Western Europe; as a new nation in 1951 these ties had not yet appeared.

Some quite interesting aspects of this column concern the communist countries. Yugoslavia then looked about evenly balanced between Western and Eastern Europe, mostly because many of her links with the Soviet bloc were moribund but not severed by permanent expulsion or withdrawal. Four members of the Soviet bloc retained, in 1951, substantial ties with their Western neighbors, though by 1962 the loadings of all but Poland had

[2] Etzioni (1965, pp. 196–228) discusses some of the bonds that pull Denmark toward the Continent and away from the rest of Scandinavia.

dropped below 0.30. This certainly was not because the Soviet bloc was more loosely controlled during the Stalinist period. Rather it is because very many of the Europe-wide organizations of the early postwar years were actually remnants of institutions set up in previous decades, when the Soviet Union was the world's only communist state. Despite their changes of government after World War II the East European nations kept most of those memberships even though they often did not take part actively in the organizations' work. For the most part the memberships were still retained in 1962; the difference in loadings stems from the failure of these states to participate in any *new* institution-building. With the rise of so many new agencies in Europe during the 1950's, the mere *retention* of earlier ties left the Eastern European states comparatively much more cut off. In this sense the division of Europe between East and West is traceable less to the simple erection of the Iron Curtain than to the organizational ties that were constructed on either side of it in subsequent years. The Curtain may have become a little more permeable in recent times, but the contrast between it and the conductivity of the media both behind and in front of it is striking.

"Latin America" also looks very much alike in the two different years, again consisting exclusively of the 21 republics of the Western Hemisphere. As later, the United States bonds with Pan America were more numerous than with Western Europe. Argentina, Chile, Ecuador, and one or two other South American countries are rather lower in the list in 1951 than in 1962, indicating that recent events have tended to strengthen the bonds between the southern part of the hemisphere and the Central American and Caribbean states. But equally important is the rise of El Salvador and Honduras since 1951, a development traceable directly to the substantial successes achieved within Central America itself. Note too that, as in the later year, almost all of the loadings on the Latin America factor are higher than for any other except Western Europe; the institutional bonds there were appreciably more numerous than elsewhere. They multiplied more rapidly in Europe than in Latin America over the 1950's, however. In 1951 the highest loading on Factor 1 was 0.87 compared with 0.70 on Factor 2, but in 1962 the difference was between 0.90 and 0.68. In both cases the absolute number of organizations increased, but developments on the European continent substantially exceeded those anywhere else, including the New World.

Factor 3 is labelled, with only partial accuracy, "Middle East." It bears a resemblance to the "Arab" grouping of 1962, but except for the Arab League itself most of the institutions of that area have been set up since 1951. Iran, which was at the very bottom of the Arab group for 1962, leads this one. Other non-Arab but more or less Middle Eastern nations are Pakistan, Turkey, and, by a generous definition, India. Taiwan, Thailand, and the Philippines help broaden it to.a somewhat wider Asian grouping. Finland's presence is most surprising; largely it stems from Finland's membership in a number of organizations which spread across non-Communist Europe and Asia. But it points out graphically a danger of over-interpreting the low loadings, especially in this table. As was stated above, the maximum number of common memberships in this matrix is less than 60 per cent as high as in the 1962 matrix. Loadings of around 0.35 and below hence are at best based on fewer than 15 common memberships, and are thus subject to great influence by only a few organizations with uncommon membership patterns. Such loadings should *not* be considered as indicating numerous or strong institutional ties.

The fifth and sixth factors are also familiar from the 1962 analysis, especially the one identified with Eastern Europe. As in the more recent year East Germany and China are isolated—to the degree that they belonged to *no* intergovernmental organization listed in the *Yearbook*. (Possibly our decision to code simply "China" and "Germany" as Nationalist China and West Germany slightly overstated that isolation, but it is unlikely. In virtually every instance it was clear from the context or the other membership that the Communist states were not meant.) Rather more surprising is the 1951 absence of Albania, which was tied, albeit rather weakly, to the rest of the bloc in 1962.

"Southeast Asia" is again a slightly free interpretation for the cluster, but not by much. The Netherlands and United Kingdom show low loadings on the factor because of their economic and colonial interests in the geographic area. Paraguay, a curious anomaly, barely slips over our arbitrary threshold on the basis of a couple of functional organizations dealing with the problems of tropical countries. A small seventh factor is called "Arabia" for the lack of anything better. The bonds among the otherwise quite isolated members were not numerous, less than ten in fact, and most of them were more or less universal organizations including many other states.

The only clustering without a geographical orientation is the fourth, labeled "Old Commonwealth." It shows up clearly here, with all the white dominions together with the mother country and, just below her, that renegade former colony whose defection provided the belated impetus for a liberal policy toward transplanted Englishmen. As the oldest of the non-white colonies, India's presence at the bottom is not really unexpected, though Japan's may be. It is due largely to a few organizations like the International North Pacific Fisheries Commission and the International Whaling Commission which include the United States, Britain, and Canada. (The U.S.S.R. also belongs to these agencies, which is the primary reason why Japan also shows a low loading on Factor 5. Both exhibit, in an unexpected way, the influence of geography.) On reflection, one of the more curious aspects of the 1962 table was the absence of any British Commonwealth grouping other than the one identified with the former British colonies of Africa. Actually there are not too many Commonwealth-wide organizations. By 1962 most of the old dominions were tied in, at least to a modest extent, with organizations including quite a number of the North Atlantic states. South Africa of course had by then withdrawn from the Commonwealth, and severed many of her old ties without weaving new ones. For the Commonwealth as a specific unit few new institutional bonds have arisen since the end of World War II, to the point that by our rather gross inductive method it was not identifiable as a distinct group in the 1960's. It had been diluted by more geographic patterns of institutions.

INSTITUTIONAL DEVELOPMENT IN THE 1950's: MORE OF THE SAME

The absolute number of organizational ties among nations has increased substantially. As we mentioned briefly above, the number of common memberships for the closest Western European countries jumped from 42 to 76 between 1951 and 1962. The increase elsewhere is less dramatic but still significant, from 25 to 42 for the several most closely tied Latin American states, and from about 14 to 28 for the Communist nations of Eastern Europe. Thus the bonds within each of the major groupings have become appreciably more numerous. And a major implication of such strengthening is that the passage of time has seen the proliferation of institutional ties within the *pre-existing* groupings, *not* the formation of *new* clusters or *shifts* by some countries from one node to another. For a more rigorous look at continuity and change over the 11-year span we shall now employ again the formal technique for factor comparison that was used to match the voting clusters from different United Nations sessions in chapter five. Table 7.2 following gives all the cosines above 0.50 for the angles of the international organization factors in 1962 when rotated into the space of the 1951 factors. The loadings of all 77 countries appearing in the earlier study were matched with their loadings in the later one.

In many cases the basic pattern is unchanged to a degree that is quite astonishing. The Western European and Latin American countries are in almost exactly the same alignments as they were earlier. The countries in Eastern Europe have changed their orientations only very slightly, most of the apparent shift being merely a faster relative growth in the ties with each other than with the states of Western Europe, which have increased very little.

Two of the 1962 clusters represent the conjunction of smaller clusters and individual countries from the earlier period, the development of wider institutions. The Asia grouping of 1962 is revealed as essentially a broadened

TABLE 7.2

The Continuity of International Organization Groupings

1951		1962
Western Europe ——————— 0.99 ——————————→		Western Europe
Latin America ——————— 0.99 ——————————→		Latin America
Eastern Europe ——————— 0.96 ——————————→		Eastern Europe
Southeast Asia ——————— 0.79 ——————————→		Asia
Middle East ——————— 0.74 —		
Arabia ——————— 0.59 —		⇉ Arabs
Old Commonwealth ——————— 0.78 ——————————→		Former British Africa

The overall product-moment correlation between the two studies is 0.93.

version of Southeast Asia in 1951. Asian nations like India, Japan, and South Korea, which were included in the 1951 analysis but did not then load very highly on the Southeast Asia factor, come into the Asia cluster of 1962. These, with substantially higher loadings also for the Philippines, Pakistan, Thailand, and Ceylon, largely account for the fact that the index of agreement between the two factors is only 0.79. Although not given in the table, the Asia group also shows some modest continuity (0.44) with the Old Commonwealth of earlier years. Both India and Japan loaded appreciably on the Old Commonwealth factor in 1951; their presence in the heart of the Asia cluster in 1962, along with Australia, is primarily responsible for the relationship between Asia and the Old Commonwealth of 1951.

The Arab grouping of 1962, you will recall, was notable for its inclusion of all the Arab states except Yemen, and the exclusion of all non-Arabs except, at the very bottom, Iran and Israel. This cluster is one that emerged clearly only in recent years, with the merging of what in 1951 were given separately as Middle East and a minor grouping, imperfectly labelled Arabia.[3] Nearly all the non-Arab Asians and other anomalies of the 1951 groupings were dropped out by 1962, leaving a cluster composed almost solely of states with predominately Arabic cultures. Despite the political setbacks of President Nasser and others, Arab unity did make some progress over the decade.

Of the two apparently new groupings of 1962, only one actually has a substantial ancestry from the previous analysis. Former French Africa has no counterpart in the earlier year, obviously because none of the countries

[3] Because of its extreme isolation, incidentally, this grouping forms an exception to the earlier statement that clusters based on few organizational memberships would have, for their leading members, lower loadings than clusters based upon a larger number of institutions. Despite Saudi Arabia's loading of .55 at its head, this factor does result from substantially fewer, but concentrated, common memberships.

that loaded on the factor in 1962 were sovereign a decade before; France itself was the only one of the French Union states included.[4] The situation is a little different for Former British Africa, which seems to correspond moderately to the Old Commonwealth cluster, with an index of agreement as high as 0.78. This *is* surprising, and to some extent deceptive. In the first place, it is not a continuity based on the *African* states. From that continent only the Republic (then Union) of South Africa was included in the 1951 analysis as an independent nation, and it emphatically does not cluster with the new states of Africa in the 1960's. The comparison over the span of the decade is of necessity based on non-African countries. It so happens that quite a number of British and former British states from outside Africa do have moderate loadings on the Former British Africa factor in 1962. Except for Ceylon none of these showed up on the listing we presented in chapter six, because they all are in the 0.20's, below the threshold employed for cutting off "insignificant" loadings. These countries are Australia, Canada, India, New Zealand, Pakistan, and the United Kingdom itself. All these Commonwealth countries with loadings in the 0.20's, however, loaded fairly highly on the Old Commonwealth factor in 1951. This Former British Africa factor of 1962, then, is the pale successor of the Commonwealth grouping that showed up so clearly in the 1951 analysis.

The Commonwealth remains, but barely, as a source of institutional contacts among the majority of its members. It has largely been superseded by regional ties among subgroups of its membership—in the North Atlantic, in Asia, and in Africa. Present-day British subjects who would tie their nation's fate to the hope of forging new bonds among the nations of their former Empire might be less enthusiastic for the task after a close look at its magnitude. The current links among regional subgroups of the Commonwealth are now immeasurably stronger than over the whole, and the trend is toward ever more of the same. The organizational bonds of Britain herself with the Commonwealth do not distantly approach the number which tie her to Western Europe. With the decline of the global Commonwealth, geographic regionalization triumphs once again.

As in chapter five we can present a table listing the countries with the greatest indices of change, or d^2. Since Cuba's organizational membership pattern did not shift greatly, however, we have no simple benchmark as before. To be sure of finding all the important changes we shall list and discuss those states with d^2 at least twice as big as the average d^2 for all 77 countries, which is a mere 0.05.

[4] Actually the index of agreement between the "Former French Africa" factor and two 1951 factors does equal or exceed .50, but since no country with a loading as high as .25 on "Former French Africa" is available for both analyses the apparent agreement is spurious and not reported.

TABLE 7.3

Countries, With d^2, Which Shifted Orientation in
International Organizations Most, 1951–1962

Japan	0.28
Burma	0.15
Saudi Arabia	0.15
South Africa	0.15
Liberia	0.14
U.S.S.R.	0.13
Iran	0.12
Paraguay	0.12
South Korea	0.12
Finland	0.10
Israel	0.10
West Germany	0.10
Mean for All Countries	0.05

By far the greatest change occurred for Japan, with its recovery of full sovereignty, an extension of ties beyond the North Pacific, and substantially greater involvement with both the countries of Western Europe and of Asia. With regard to Asia, this apparent shift is less a new development for the Japanese than a return to something resembling their former ties and influence. Their fairly close association with the Europeans, however, has less precedent and is potentially of great importance to the western community. Burma and South Africa, each in different ways and for different reasons, have become isolated both from their geographical regions and from the international community as a whole. The South African story, of an increasingly anachronistic racial policy, of expulsions and hasty withdrawals to anticipate expulsion, is well known. Burma's situation may be a little less familiar to some Western observers, and is voluntary rather than a product of compulsion. The recent military governments of Burma have expelled foreigners and restricted tourism, cut off foreign aid, ceased participation in several international organizations concerned with development, and have failed to join some of the new ones. While most of the actions have been directed primarily at Westerners, some of Burma's regional ties have suffered too. In addition, several of the new Southeast Asian organizations have been associated with SEATO: Burma's abstention from this anti-Communist alliance has also contributed to its shift downward on the Asia (or Southeast Asia) factor.

A few of the shifts are less real than apparent. Liberia, Paraguay, and Finland all show up with moderately high d^2. In every instance these were countries in 1951 that had loadings in the 0.30 range on factors where they did not seem to fit, due to the sparsity of their memberships in general and their association with a very few worldwide or special function institutions. All of these anomalies disappeared in 1962 when the overall level of memberships was higher, and especially when Finland and Paraguay were better tied into their appropriate continental nets. Liberia, left behind in the new institution-forming, loaded appreciably on no group in 1962.

As Arab unity grew and the network of Middle Eastern organizations took on a more distinctly Arabic coloration, Saudi Arabia moved in and Iran dropped from the top of the factor to a loading of only 0.30. On the other hand two former isolates, Israel and South Korea, had by 1962 begun to penetrate the network of international organizations and ceased to be lacking in some of the normal global and even regional ties. South Korea had moved into Asia, and Israel into networks that involved Western European and Middle Eastern nations. The Soviet Union also shows up here with a d^2 of some distinction, 0.13. Primarily this indicates a *slight* shift into association with the nations of Western Europe (a 0.22 loading on Factor 1 in 1962, as compared with only 0.04 before), and a greater institutionalization of its bonds with other communist states in Eastern Europe, raising its loading on that factor as well. In some degree it reflects the belated emergence of the U.S.S.R. from its isolation in the interwar period. And at the bottom of this list is West Germany. Like Japan, it too regained its full sovereignty during the decade between our two analyses, and in the course of that time became closely tied to the other nations of Western Europe, especially the Six.

Repeatedly we have referred to the stability of organizational clusterings over this span of the 1950's. An index computed in the course of the factor comparisons documents the point firmly. We noted at the bottom of Table 7.2 that the overall correlation between the two studies was 0.93; knowing only the pattern in 1951 would allow one to predict *86 per cent* of the variance in the same countries' pattern in 1962. This can be compared with correlations of 0.91 for the 1952–1963 UN matching and 0.92 and 0.89 for the two shorter periods marked on either end by 1957.

We shall continue to compute and report these indices as we make other comparisons later in the book. At the moment we have no further examples with which to compare them, but the degree of continuity for intergovernmental organizations does seem impressive, especially when matched against changes in UN voting alignments. Of course we should probably expect to find greater continuity of institutional memberships. Joining an organization is a formal act requiring explicit approval at a number of points in the governmental process. It is usually not done lightly, and once in an organization interests and expectations build up so as to make withdrawal difficult and unlikely. In addition to pressures within a nation's domestic political system, formal treaty requirements often make exit from an intergovernmental organization difficult. Frequently final withdrawal must be preceded by a period of several years' advance notice to the other members. Some institutions, like the European Common Market or the Coal and Steel Community, are deliberately designed so as to make withdrawal unattractive and preferably impossible. And, if the functionalists are right at all, membership in one organization also contributes to the growth of forces that will encourage further membership in groups containing the same states.

Voting with another nation in the UN General Assembly, however, carries none of these formal or domestic commitments. Certainly ties of common interest are forged or reinforced, and some political log-rolling on one roll call may insure that the two nations will, by agreement, vote together on one or more future roll calls. If the issues are not purely trivial or transient, but reflect deeper and continuing international divisions that will continue to come up in slightly changed clothing, then a roll call today is not totally independent of a roll call tomorrow. Sometimes this is formalized with the existence of a caucusing group where there *may* be agreement to form a common front on some issues, but previous analyses have demonstrated that caucusing group membership is not, by itself, a terribly powerful predictor of United Nations voting behavior (Hovet, 1961). Finally, some issues *are* transient and often, in retrospect at least, trivial. A few roll calls, like one on capital punishment in the Twelfth (1957) Session, have no counterpart in other Sessions, and to the extent that occurs the alignments are fleeting.

The major conclusion of chapter five was, nevertheless, that nations' voting alignments in the UN General Assembly had been, over the period 1952 to 1963, remarkably stable. To the degree that they reflected broader political alignments and attitudes, and preferences for political association, they supported the viewpoint of relatively unchanging orientations and goal-seeking behavior in the international system. While we cannot be surprised to discover that international organization membership exhibits even greater stability than voting behavior, the level of continuity achieved still is impressive. The world of the 1950's seems to have been more orderly and predictable than we appreciated at the time.

8

INTERDEPENDENT GROUPINGS IN 1963

TRADE AND POLITICS: THEORETICAL CONSIDERATIONS

AMONG STUDENTS OF INTERNATIONAL INTEGRATION NOT a little confusion exists about the relation between trade and *political* integration. There is an often over-simplified tendency to consider trading patterns as *indicators* of political integration. While this may sometimes be an accurate inference, it leads to too much error if taken as more than a general statement about a fairly weak correlation.

International trade is of course not merely an economic relationship in a world of perfect competition. Models of oligopoly and monopolistic competition are much more appropriate.[1] Buyers do not always purchase from the vendor who offers the lowest price. The United States, for instance, has long paid more than the world market price for sugar from a selected group of countries, and has entirely excluded other nations from the American market. Indians seem to dislike the qualities of American-grown rice, and often prefer their local varieties even at a substantial price differential. Because of structural imperfections in the market, and differences among the goods being offered as more or less substitutable products, price variations become possible. Cultural similarities, at least at a very basic level, affect both of these. Customs, habits, traditions, notions about the goods or the seller, all differentiate two seemingly identical products. A seller who speaks the language and understands the attitudes of his customers has a great advantage over a competitor who does not—he and his product seem

---

[1] The classic analyses of monopolistic (or imperfect) competition are Chamberlin (1933) and Robinson (1933). Stigler (1952) presents a useful discussion of oligopoly and other models. These comments about the *distribution* of international trade do not conflict with the assertion that short-run overall *fluctuations* in trade levels are much more likely to be a result of the business cycle than of broader political and social factors.

more familiar and more trustworthy, and he can tailor his product to appeal in special ways to their needs.

Politics plays an important part in structuring the market. Most obviously, state-imposed tariffs, quotas, or other obstacles to the free market can affect competitors' prices adversely, or close them out of the market altogether. This is not at all uncommon in colonies, but politics is important in other more subtle ways. A merchandiser who is considering whether to extend credit to prospective customers in a colony will be more likely to do so if he knows that officials in the colonial government, of his own nationality, can be depended upon to enforce the terms of the loan. By his resultant willingness to extend credit, or to undercut the rates offered by men not his countrymen, he can obtain sales where they cannot. Or a seller from the mother country may even gain entry to the native market by first selling to the expatriate officials who demand familiar merchandise. (Hence the otherwise inexplicable popularity of lemon "squash" in India.) These are some of the ways in which "trade follows the flag."

Either because of certain minimal cultural ties such as may grow up when enough colonials learn the languages of the metropolitan country, or because of political bonds that alter the conditions of the market, the trade between two political units may become much more substantial than one would "expect." It may become absolutely larger than that between either of the states and any other states without similar bonds, or it may become high relative to some kind of null model expectation. An example of the latter kind of analysis is the null model of Savage and Deutsch, who suggest as an expected value of trade between two countries essentially that the proportion of country i's exports which go to country j will correspond to the mean of the proportion of i's exports in all world exports and j's imports in all world imports.[2] Thus if the United States contributes 26 per cent of all world exports and Britain takes 18 per cent of all world imports, we "expect" Britain to take 22 per cent of American imports. Given the expected values it is then possible to compute a ratio of actual to expected exports, or an index of relative acceptance of one country for another's trade.

In this type of analysis the expected values are those given by a *null* model, not a *predictive* one. The model says nothing about the effect on trading patterns of the international division of labor, or distance, or transportation costs, or political or cultural ties, or governmental restrictions. Instead it is a tool in the search for these factors. It "merely" gives a base

[2] This is a slightly simplified explanation. For the proper formula and discussion of this expected value see Savage and Deutsch (1960), as programmed by Alker (1962). See also Goodman (1963, 1964) and the more general version presented by Brams (1965a). Another null model, which takes into account countries' income as well as total trade, is suggested by Mortara (1960) and the Bank of International Settlements (1958, pp. 149–50).

against which to measure deviations from the null model, deviations which indicate a kind of interdependence, or a lack of it, to be explained by substantive theory. The explanation of a higher than expected value of trade might well be in the realm of cultural factors or political bonds, and in this way trade can serve as an indicator pointing to the existence of such ties.

It *may* even suggest a degree of political integration, but here we are on shakier ground. Empirically we can observe that the indices of relative acceptance for colonies' trade with their metropolitan countries, and vice versa, are regularly quite high. But while a high index frequently points to political bonds, it does not necessarily indicate integration in the sense of responsiveness, as defined in earlier chapters. Much more typically the metropolitan state is *not* highly responsive to the needs of its colony, though the colonial administration may be highly responsive to the needs of the mother country. This exemplifies the kind of one-sided rather than mutual responsiveness that we explicitly ruled out as a case of political integration. To find a pattern of trade that is more likely to be associated with responsiveness we need *another* model, one which relates the value of commerce between two states not to any expected quantity but to the size of the gross national product of each; that is, a measure of the impact that foreign commerce has on their national economies and from there to their political systems. Two kinds of questions can thus be asked. To inquire "How can we *explain* trading patterns?" a null model, pointing out deviations to be accounted for by substantive theory, is appropriate. But to ask "Where are certain political effects of trade likely to occur?" the proper measure is often simply one of the relative size of that trade.

Trade becomes a channel of communication making possible political integration as manifested in responsiveness. People engaged in international trade are exposed to a wide variety of ideas and information that would otherwise never reach them; they must listen to viewpoints that they would otherwise never hear. Commerce can be a means by which the needs of groups in one country become known to those in another. Exporters are likely to develop a generalized interest in the well-being of their markets, an interest that transcends the marketing conditions, narrowly defined, for their products. Despite some abuses we could point to, that interest is unlikely to be limited to economic interests; exporters may become attuned to the needs of the importing country over a range of non-economic matters. The greater the volume and variety of commerce, the less narrow will be the merchandisers' conceptions of their interest. In his study of France's decision to reject the European Defense Community treaty in 1954, Daniel Lerner (1956, p. 220) found that businessmen who conducted no export trade were three times more likely to oppose EDC and to favor maintenance of a French national army than were businessmen whose firms exported over half their production. But in only a very few cases could any of these industrialists be described as having a direct economic interest in the decision. Similarly, in a study of British and American legislators I found a high correlation between trade contacts and responsiveness, over a wide range of issues, to the other country (Russett, 1963, ch. 9). The new attitudes of course result not merely from the communication, but from its interaction with the recipients' pre-dispositions (Bauer, Pool, and Dexter, 1964, pp. 466–68). Jacob and Atherton (1965, p. 326) phrase the relationship like this: "Commerce, as much as any factor, has impressed on nations the advantages of cooperative rather than antagonistic relations."

Where economic interests do exist they may well bias decisions, as an individual acts to further his financial interests. But also, individuals who are already predisposed to a particular decision may try to mobilize available economic interest groups for the support of that decision. That is, economic interests may influence political choice, or they may merely be used to buttress decisions reached on other grounds. There is no need to adopt an economic determinist point of view. *Ceteris paribus,* every political interest group has a power base, or power potential, that is roughly proportional to the share of the national income its members control. The larger the share of country A's national income that is bound up in trade with country B, the larger is this channel of communication between them and the greater the potential influence of country B on policy-making in country A.

The *ceteris paribus* qualifications are doubtless very large, for the relative size of an interest group's economic base is not the only factor influencing its success. It may find converging, opposing, or indifferent interests in other parts of the domestic political system. Other factors include the group's capacity for organization, its previous experience, and its relation to the legislation or administrative action at issue. Supporting or conflicting pressures from the international system are also highly relevant. Amicable and responsive Anglo-American relations are the product not just of a high level of trade, nor even of the other influences on integration that we are measuring in this book—similarity of culture, of political attitudes, and common institutional membership. Foreign policy pressures, and especially the perception of a common threat from the Soviet Union, tell heavily in the same direction. By the same token an increase in East-West trade by itself would hardly guarantee a substantial reduction in Soviet-American tensions. The differences that still separate the two super-powers would remain to dilute the impact of commercial contact.

Surely commercial relations can, like most other transactions, on occasion bring serious ill will and contribute to failures of responsiveness. Many United States bankers bought Latin American states' bonds in the early decades of this century; when a number of these states defaulted the net result of the transaction was not to improve hemisphere relations. Serious conflicts may arise from circumstances where one nation is the world's major exporter of a particular commodity. People in the importing state may feel exploited if the supply is controlled by a monopoly or oligopoly. Even government price supports or production controls, adopted merely to maintain the income of domestic producers rather than to exploit foreign consumers, may nevertheless arouse bitter feelings. More important still is probably the case where one state is the major *importer* of another's goods. In this circumstance the seller is heavily dependent upon good will and the conditions set by the purchaser. The former high level of Cuban-American trade, in which many Cubans felt exploited by the economic power both of their American customers and of United States companies which sold to Cuba or owned utilities and productive facilities in Cuba, surely contributed heavily to Castro's anti-Americanism. Thus one must be very careful to avoid a crude or simple view of the inter-relationship between trade and political integration. While contact and communication are essential to the regular resolution of conflict, of course they also make conflict possible.

The United States-Cuba example actually suggests a refinement in the argument against using deviations from an expected level of trade as an indicator of political integration. In this instance the actual trade was indeed several times higher than would be predicted from the null model. Yet the relative size of the two economies was very different. Cuban-United States trade amounted to over 50 per cent of the Cuban gross national product, but to only 0.2 per cent of that of the United States—hardly a pinprick. While the Cuban political system thus contained very great pressures to be responsive to the needs and demands of the United States, the reciprocal pressures in the United States were trivial and limited to only a few interests. And in a major conflict between the governments the United States for a time was able, by cutting off trade, virtually to cripple the Cuban economy while not hurting itself at all. Much the same situation would apply between the United States and most of its trading partners due to the enormous size of the North American market, and it is especially severe with respect to almost all United States trade with Latin American states. The ratio of actual to expected trade is very high, but so is the disparity between the trading partners' economies and the resultant differential impact of that trade. A similar situation, hardly less severe, operates between a number of European nations and their present or former small and poor colonies. Large states can, if they feel it necessary, simply override the wishes of small ones.

To repeat, trade or other transactions do not give us a *measure* of political integration—there are other and more direct ways of tapping the latter variable. They do, however, give us a measure of some independent variables affecting and often promoting political integration. Whatever the hazards that may remain, it seems likely that under *conditions of relatively equal impact in the two countries concerned,* trade helps induce mutual responsiveness. Thus the measure of trade we employ must be tied *not* to an index of relative acceptance but rather must take into account the ratio of trade between two countries to the national income or G.N.P. of each. We shall consider it to be on balance an influence favoring mutual responsiveness only where that ratio is fairly high in *both* countries. If low in both it is likely to have little political impact in any direction; if high in one only, the result may well be the unilateral kind of responsiveness typical of the colony-colonial power relationship. We want a measure of *inter*dependence, not simply dependence.

By this choice of index we in fact make it impossible for a *very* big country and a *very* little one to be called "interdependent." (The *very* must be emphasized, for as we shall explain below it will take a difference on the order of well over 100 times in national income before "interdependence" would cease to apply at all.) This is appropriate in many political senses, including strategic ones, for a small country can affect a large one only in limited degrees and in circumscribed ways. America's European allies have painfully discovered how difficult it is to modify seriously the United States' policy on matters it considers vital. Even following Europe's resurgence, the relationship between any one state and America is so one-sided that it is hard to call the United States fully interdependent with any other single country. While a European nation can be either a major ally or a serious hindrance to the United States if it chooses, the potential rewards and punishments on either side are very unbalanced. France has found out how hard it is to influence the United States; the British do best but even for them the "special relationship" is part myth.[3]

DISCOVERING TRADING GROUPS: CHOOSERS AND CHOSEN

Previous chapters have identified clusters of countries according to criteria of similarity and of institutional bonds. Our focus here, however, is on clustering as a function of economic interdependence. Looking at virtually all possible pairs of nations and major colonies in the international system of 1963, we shall measure that interdependence on the basis of a ratio between trade (exports plus imports) and gross domestic product (G.D.P.). More specifically, indices of economic interdependence will be computed for

[3] Note the argument by Haas and Schmitter (1964, p. 711) that a certain similarity of size and power between two countries is a precondition for the successful politicization of an economic relationship. Nye (1965, p. 878) disputes this, and Etzioni (1965, pp. 68–69) points out that unions of states of very different sizes have frequently succeeded. To do so, however, requires either an element of coercion by the larger partner, or special efforts to be responsive toward the smaller state's needs. Homans (1950, p. 116) reports that interaction is not associated with friendliness where an authority relation is present in small groups.

every country with each of its trading partners, by dividing the sum of their exports to each other by the G.D.P. of each. Thus, country j's economic impact on country i is equal to $\dfrac{Tij}{GDPi}$, and i's on j is equal to $\dfrac{Tij}{GDPj}$. We therefore produce a matrix of trade to G.D.P. ratios that is square (as before, each country is represented by both a row and by a column) but, for the first time in this volume, *asymmetric,* since $\dfrac{Tij}{GDPi}$ is not equal to $\dfrac{Tij}{GDPj}$.

At the time data were gathered G.D.P. estimates for enough countries were available only for 1962, but the difference between one year and the next is never more than a few per cent.[4] And if the income of all countries grew at the same rate, the effect of using 1962 G.D.P. figures would merely raise all the T/GDP ratios uniformly. Naturally all countries do not show the same growth rate, but with all the other problems involved in estimated G.D.P., and converting estimates from local currency into dollars (*cf.* Russett, *et al.,* 1964, pp. 149–51), this is not an important handicap.[5]

[4] For 68 countries over the period roughly 1950–60, the average annual rate of change in per capita G.D.P. varied from 7.6 per cent to −2.2 per cent, but the standard deviation was only 2.2 per cent (Russett, et al, 1964, p. 160).

[5] The trade data were obtained from the International Monetary Fund's Master Files, and are comparable to those published in the United Nations *Direction of International Trade* series. (The 1954 trade data to be analyzed in the next chapter are from this series—United Nations (1957).) I am very grateful to the Fund for making a data tape available to me. The trade between any two countries is obtained by adding the *export* total for i to j as reported by i to the *exports* from j to i as recorded by j. Sometimes when j is a much smaller country than i or when the volume of i's exports to j is very small relative to its other trade, i simply will not report trade with j separately and will lump it into a regional or world residual category. To correct this situation a special computer program was written. All export cells of i were checked, and when no trade was reported the computer then examined j's reports of *imports*. If some entry was found that figure was then inserted in the list of i's exports to replace the blank. While some factors, chiefly transport costs, may inflate the value of goods when priced at the port of entry rather than the port of exit, this solution introduces an error only on the order of 10 per cent and is far preferable to letting the blanks remain in cases where some trade actually does take place.

Most estimates of gross domestic product at factor costs are from United Nations (1964). Where available I used those UN figures that converted G.D.P. figures in local currency into dollars by means of their calculated parity rates; in the few cases where these were not given I used the UN estimates as they converted them according to prevailing dollar exchange rates. In some instances only gross *national* product figures were given; I converted them to G.D.P. totals according to the ratio of G.D.P. to G.N.P. that prevailed in previous years. Data for Eastern European countries were provided by an economist specializing in Eastern Europe, computed from estimates of G.N.P. in national currencies converted at a purchasing power parity exchange rate. These are the estimates used in a branch of an international organization. The total for U.S.S.R. is from U.S. Congress, Joint Economic Committee (1964, p. 96), and the figure for mainland China was provided by Professor Alexander Eckstein. Where the figures for communist countries were given as G.N.P. at market prices we deflated them by 10 per cent to give estimates of G.D.P. at factor cost. All these estimates are subject to error, on the order of perhaps ± 20 per cent for communist countries and more than that for some underdeveloped states.

We must acknowledge that trade in commodities gives an incomplete measure of economic interdependence, even within the limits of a bilateral relationship. A full analysis would require data on investment, foreign aid, receipts from shipping, tourism, and other "invisibles." Country-to-country matrices of this kind of transaction, however, are simply not available, and, as these items typically account for only about 25 per cent of total foreign exchange receipts, the omission is perhaps not too serious.[6] If we were to expand our interest in transactions to other kinds of interaction, especially direct contact between citizens of different countries, we might also examine data on the movement of persons, such as migrants, tourists, and students. The *political* relevance of such contacts, however, is neither simple nor uniform. Though I have employed such data elsewhere (Russett, 1963, 1965) and have argued that in the Anglo-American case they usually measure influences which promote political integration, the effect is by no means as clear when two widely disparate cultures, like a European and an Oriental one, are involved. Other factors, such as the length of stay and the nature of the contacts, also make a great difference. Two recent surveys of the literature on the effects of travel and exchange of persons give ambiguous and highly qualified answers (Pool, 1965, and Mishler, 1965).

A second reason is simply the unavailability of data on most other kinds of interaction. Only a very limited matrix, including fewer than 20 countries, could be compiled for student exchange, and other kinds of travel data are even more scarce. Data on movement from and especially to many major states, including the Communist countries, is almost entirely absent. While for some purposes one could still omit such countries or assume that missing data really indicated no exchange, the already ambiguous relation of such variables to politics would leave the entire operation too dubious. The sole exception might be for data on country-to-country flows of mail, as this is an indicator of personal contact at virtually all levels of the political system, elite and mass. But even here the problem of missing data is serious, if not prohibitive,[7] and other studies (Russett, 1963, p. 126; Russett, 1965, pp. 36, 43; Puchala, 1966) have shown trade and mail flows to be highly correlated. For the purposes of this study the additional investment required in gathering and processing the mail flow data did not seem worthwhile, but it is a feasible and perhaps enlightening path of research.

As in the previous chapters, from our data on commodity trade we have derived what is, in effect, a matrix of sociometric choices, where each country's "preference" for every other country is expressed by the ratio of

[6] Wooley (1966) has compiled such data among world *areas,* but not yet among individual countries.

[7] Brams' (1965a) INDIFF program incorporates a method of estimating missing data that might be very helpful here.

their mutual trade to its G.D.P. Direct factor analysis remains our basic method for finding clusters of countries, but each matrix demands two solutions, each of which is equally compelling by any theoretical criteria. While the procedure has not previously been applied to trade data by other scholars, the same kind of analysis has been performed on the more common types of sociometric information by Duncan MacRae, Jr. (1960), and by Wright and Evitts (1961). MacRae did a direct factor analysis on a set of non-symmetrical sociometric data derived by asking prison inmates to name their friends, allowing the men to appear in the matrix both as choosers and chosen. For fairly obvious reasons he found a more nearly reciprocal pattern of relationships than those we shall uncover from trading patterns, but the principle is just the same. In drawing our conclusions below we shall identify as interdependent groups only those instances where the basic pattern of countries' factor loadings is similar in both analyses of the asymmetric matrix.[8] (In the first factor analysis the row countries are treated as variables, and in the second, with the matrix transposed, the column countries become the variables. The list of countries is of course the same in both, but because the matrix is asymmetric the off-diagonal cells are reversed.)

As before, we have standardized the input values to produce proximity measures with a range between zero and one (of course the matrix still is not symmetric since i to j is not the same as j to i), and thus give the loadings in the resulting factor matrix a fairly familiar range (again zero to one). But unlike the inputs to our previous analyses, the distribution of T_{ij}/GDP values is highly skewed. The vast majority are quite small, with trade between two states amounting to less than one per cent of the annual income of either. Yet there are some high values, in one case in 1963 up to 108 per cent of G.D.P. for exports and imports combined. If standardized simply from the raw values most of the consequent proximity measures would be less than 0.01.

A solution comes from combining pragmatism with theory: the $T_{ij}/$G.D.P. values were first multiplied by 10,000 to remove the decimal and then logged to the base ten before being submitted to our usual standardiza-

---

[8] Our understanding of "interdependence" here is of a bilateral relationship, since the trade must make a direct impact on both states. Another definition that might be explored in future analyses would accept a triangular relationship in lieu of reciprocal pairs. By this criterion the triangular pattern of trade which sent molasses from the West Indies to colonial Massachusetts, rum from Massachusetts to England, and fish and textiles back from England to the Caribbean, would meet the test. The political effects of such a relationship, however, will be rather different from those of a bilateral one.

Berry (1967) also uses factor analysis on commodity flow data, but by correlating columns (rather than using direct factor analysis) obtains first groups of units with similar trade origins and, for the transposed matrix, units with similar destinations—not *interacting* groups.

tion formula (T_{ij} divided by T max). The result is a distribution which, except for the excessive number of zeros (no trade) at the low end is roughly normal, and it was because of this approximation to normality that I chose the $\log_{10}$ transformation rather than some other. Theory prevails on the grounds that the effect of trade on a political system is *not* linear, but subject in some degree to diminishing returns. Economists have long employed the notion of decreasing marginal utility as a central feature in many analyses. Surely it does seem correct to assume that the political effect of an increase in trade of from 0.1 to 10.1 per cent of a country's G.D.P. will be associated with more profound political consequences than will an increase of from 50 to 60 per cent. Empirically, Havana's shift of political allegiance in the early 1960's was marked by a jump in Cuban-Soviet trade from less than 1 per cent of Cuba's G.D.P. in 1959 to about 29 per cent in 1963. The East European countries' trade with the Soviet Union in 1963 averaged about 12 per cent of their G.D.P.'s. Except for Albania (no trade reported) the range was between about 6 and 20 per cent. Thus a logarithmic transformation which greatly condenses the scale at the upper limit appears consonant with our aims and not contradictory to them.[9]

This logarithmic transformation compromises, without destroying, the size effect mentioned above. It remains true that for an economically very large country and for a very small one the same trade figure will still produce very different proximity measures when divided by the G.D.P. of each. The G.D.P. of the United States, for instance, is roughly 1000 times that of Cambodia. A small dollar value of trade between them might amount to 0.01 per cent of American G.D.P. but to 10 per cent of Cam-

[9] This still does not say whether we have the *most* appropriate transformation, and our results remain to some degree dependent upon the choice of scale, or metric. In principle, the nonmetric techniques discussed earlier (pp. 56–57) could be used. Lingoes (1965b) has produced several versions of the procedure, one of which, designated SSA–II, can be applied to an asymmetric matrix such as this. Unfortunately none of the routines available at the time of writing could handle a matrix nearly as large as 115 by 115, being limited instead to 55 countries (Lingoes) or 60 (Kruskal, 1965a). But even though I could thus not use the method for the full analysis, as a check on the effects of scale, I performed a direct factor analysis on a subset of 55 countries, input the same matrix into Lingoes' routine, and compared the two. The results were somewhat different (overall r=0.84), but all but one of the clusters in one analysis were clearly recognizable in the other. Much earlier in this project I had another trade matrix, which I submitted to two different transformations—$\log_{10}$ and square root—before factoring. Again the clusters were a bit dissimilar but most groupings in one could still be found in the other. They also are quite similar to those obtained by correlating the columns before factoring—an exploratory and not fully appropriate procedure I employed earlier (Russett, 1967). Thus while the choice of scale does matter some, I think the results of the following analyses are important and the metric theoretically more appropriate than retreating to mere rank-orders. Whatever hesitations do apply to the trade groupings on this ground are less relevant to the analyses in the earlier parts of the book, where the metrics are even more "natural" and more clearly buttressed by theoretical considerations.

bodia's. When logged this would give a proximity index of 0.75 for Cambodia, and 0.0 for the United States. But in the case of two countries of somewhat closer size the effects are far less drastic and intuitively satisfactory. The United Kingdom's G.D.P. is approximately ten times that of Switzerland, hence the same trade figure would produce a difference only on the order of between 0.50 for one and 0.75 for the other in the proximity index. They would thus appear as quite interdependent. Even a difference of 100 times in G.D.P. would give some interdependence, with indices of 0.75 and 0.25 for this example.[10]

Table 8.1 shown on pages 134 through 138, presents the nine major clusters of trading nations identified by the analysis. Each cluster has to be identified by *two* factors, one from the column analysis and one from the row analysis. Consistent with MacRae's procedure we have labelled them, respectively, "Choosers" and "Chosen." Since the entries in each cell depend upon mutual trade expressed as a (logged) proportion of the row country's G.D.P., the analysis with the rows as variables picks out groups of nations which depend on, or tend to "choose," similar trading partners—they will share the characteristic of having a higher than average fraction of their economies devoted to trade with the same nations. But when the columns are treated as variables, the analysis picks out those states *into* whose economies they enter heavily, and identifies countries which in common are "chosen" by, or depended on by, the same countries.

Thus with three nations, Chile, Paraguay, and the United States, the total volume of trade between Chile and the United States is the same, by definition, for each country, as is the volume of trade between Chile and Paraguay the same for both. But because of differences in the size of their economies, Chile enters more heavily into (is chosen by) Paraguay than into the United States; however, the United States enters more heavily into Chile's economy than does Paraguay. Paraguay enters some into Chile, but only trivially into the United States. By *inter*dependence we must identify groups of states which both choose and are chosen by each other. Chile and Paraguay are in this sense interdependent, but are not sufficiently chosen by the United States to make all three "interdependent."

In the table we list Chooser and Chosen factors in parallel columns. Only countries which show loadings exceeding the mean factor loading (averaged over each of the two entire matrices) on *both* are listed. The Choosers are given first, since they more nearly resemble in their orderings the now-familiar geopolitical regions we have found in earlier chapters. For this list the ordering is approximately what would be obtained from factoring

[10] Brams (1965b, p. 76) points out that the Savage-Deutsch null model also has the effect of treating the marginal increment of one unit as less important for an already high level of trade than for a low one.

a symmetrical matrix of indices of relative acceptance, except that there was an entry for each country's "trade" with itself (actually its G.D.P.). The list of Chosen countries, of course, is often led by one or more of the major industrial and trading powers of the world, especially the United States, the United Kingdom, and the German Federal Republic. As in previous analyses, the countries at the top of the list are most closely associated with the cluster, and we approach the more marginal members as we move down. A country which is toward the bottom of both lists is obviously rather peripheral to the grouping; so, in the sense of a somewhat weak *inter*dependence, is a state that appears near the very end even of one. The relatively pure cases of interdependence are toward the top of both. Because of the frequency with which many countries appear in more than one group no map presentation was attempted.

This particular direct factor analysis routine, with its specific and for our purposes theoretically essential provision for the size effect, does not produce factor loadings that necessarily vary between zero and unity, or between plus one and minus one. Many of the loadings exceed unity, but except for its unfamiliarity this need not concern the reader. The relative importance (of each factor for a particular country, and of various countries for each factor) is still indicated by the loadings.[11]

NINE CLUSTERS

One grouping is composed primarily of Western Hemisphere nations, especially those bordering the Caribbean Sea.[12] The Choosers are headed by the six states of Central America, followed by Venezuela, Trinidad, and Colombia. Canada, Mexico, and the United States are further down the list, with the former two also taking a mid-position on the Chosen factor. A number of major industrial states take middle-to-low spots among the

[11] In the more familiar forms of factor analysis, if all the variance were extracted the sum of each country's squared factor loadings would equal unity. MacRae (1960) points out that if one wishes to ignore the size effect one can here, also, norm the loadings so that their squares sum to unity.

[12] Because the loadings for each country would not sum to unity, the normal criterion of "eigen values equal to or greater than unity" offers no good basis for the decision about how many factors to rotate. To my knowledge no generally accepted criterion exists. I chose here to rotate the ten factors with sums of squares greater than one per cent. As a check for the 1954 analysis in the next chapter, I rotated both eight and eleven factors, but it did not change the factor structure in any notable way (the first eight factors in both versions showed an average agreement index of 0.99). Only nine pairs of factors are reported in the table because the rotated tenth in both analyses accounted for very little variance, had few high loadings, and showed less than the usual amount of agreement between Chooser and Chosen factors. By the decisions applied to the nine reported groupings it would have had but five members, Greece, Iceland, Turkey, Israel, and Liberia.

TABLE 8.1
Trade Groupings in 1963

Choosers		Chosen	
North and Central America			
El Salvador	2.42	United States	2.30
Panama	2.41	West Germany	1.89
Costa Rica	2.25	Japan	1.79
Nicaragua	2.24	El Salvador	1.55
Guatemala	2.10	Netherlands	1.53
Honduras	2.05	United Kingdom	1.40
Venezuela	2.02	Venezuela	1.38
Trinidad	2.01	Guatemala	1.37
Netherlands	1.67	Belgium-Lux.	1.35
Colombia	1.60	Mexico	1.32
Belgium-Lux.	1.50	Canada	1.26
Sweden	1.49	Italy	1.24
Norway	1.46	France	1.19
Switzerland	1.45	Honduras	1.18
Denmark	1.41	Nicaragua	1.18
West Germany	1.39	Sweden	1.18
Canada	1.30	Switzerland	1.17
Finland	1.28	Costa Rica	1.13
Spain	1.20	Panama	1.05
Mexico	1.19	Colombia	1.03
United States	1.18	Denmark	1.01
United Kingdom	1.13	Austria	0.83
Austria	1.07	Spain	0.78
Japan	0.99	Norway	0.78
Italy	0.92	Finland	0.73
France	0.82	Trinidad	0.51
South America			
Peru	1.33	Argentina	2.21
Uruguay	1.27	Brazil	2.09
Argentina	1.27	Italy	2.05
Paraguay	1.23	Sweden	1.88
Chile	1.18	Switzerland	1.80
Brazil	1.09	Spain	1.76
Algeria	0.78	Chile	1.65
Spain	0.75	Venezuela	1.50
Saudi Arabia	0.67	Paraguay	1.48
Venezuela	0.65	Uruguay	1.18
Switzerland	0.64	Saudi Arabia	0.67
Italy	0.63	Algeria	0.62
Ecuador	0.61	Ecuador	0.52
Sweden	0.59	Peru	0.50

Choosers		Chosen	
		British Caribbean	
British Guiana	1.31	United Kingdom	2.30
Trinidad	1.25	Canada	2.11
Jamaica	1.22	Trinidad	1.38
Ghana	0.92	Norway	1.34
Saudi Arabia	0.77	Jamaica	1.06
New Zealand	0.75	New Zealand	0.95
Canada	0.75	British Guiana	0.85
Norway	0.63	Saudi Arabia	0.74
Nigeria	0.62	Ghana	0.65
United Kingdom	0.60	Nigeria	0.48
		Commonwealth	
Kenya	1.95	United Kingdom	2.73
Iran	1.77	West Germany	2.22
Mauritius	1.74	South Africa	2.05
Uganda	1.68	Japan	1.92
Tanganyika	1.55	Netherlands	1.87
South Africa	1.44	France	1.87
Ceylon	1.43	Belgium-Lux.	1.86
Congo (L)	1.41	Italy	1.85
United Kingdom	1.37	Iran	1.83
Belgium-Lux.	1.25	Australia	1.71
Pakistan	1.18	Canada	1.53
Ireland	1.16	Sweden	1.37
Australia	1.15	Pakistan	1.24
New Zealand	1.12	Switzerland	1.24
Iraq	1.12	Congo (L)	1.15
Sudan	1.09	Denmark	1.14
Malaysia	1.07	Kenya	1.11
Burma	1.06	New Zealand	1.10
Netherlands	1.04	Spain	1.06
India	0.93	Ceylon	1.03
West Germany	0.91	Israel	0.96
Madagascar	0.90	Ireland	0.90
Israel	0.89	Austria	0.81
Canada	0.87	Malaysia	0.76
Switzerland	0.86	Norway	0.74
Finland	0.80	Finland	0.73
Sweden	0.80	Burma	0.73
Italy	0.79	Portugal	0.71
Japan	0.76	Tanganyika	0.70
Portugal	0.73	Sudan	0.66
Greece	0.68	Mauritius	0.65
Austria	0.66	Iraq	0.59
France	0.65	Uganda	0.57
Norway	0.64	Greece	0.50
Spain	0.60	Madagascar	0.47

TABLE 8.1

Trade Groupings in 1963

Choosers		Chosen	
French Community			
Ivory Coast	2.38	France	3.38
Senegal	2.27	West Germany	2.20
Congo (B)	1.91	United Kingdom	2.00
Cameroun	1.84	Netherlands	1.99
Dahomey	1.80	Senegal	1.87
Niger	1.67	Italy	1.79
France	1.65	Ivory Coast	1.73
Upper Volta	1.63	Belgium-Lux.	1.71
Togo	1.62	Morocco	1.61
Morocco	1.60	Algeria	1.48
Mali	1.45	Spain	1.39
Algeria	1.42	Nigeria	1.29
Cambodia	1.39	Venezuela	1.17
Madagascar	1.34	Cameroun	1.07
Nigeria	1.33	Sweden	1.07
Tunisia	1.29	Mali	1.04
Netherlands	1.19	Dahomey	0.98
Iraq	1.15	Niger	0.95
Belgium-Lux.	1.12	Cambodia	0.91
Portugal	1.10	Portugal	0.90
Ghana	1.08	Upper Volta	0.90
Italy	0.92	Denmark	0.84
West Germany	0.89	Tunisia	0.78
Spain	0.89	Switzerland	0.78
Venezuela	0.86	Iraq	0.75
Switzerland	0.84	Ghana	0.71
Norway	0.82	Madagascar	0.66
Denmark	0.77	South Africa	0.61
Sweden	0.76	Togo	0.58
United Kingdom	0.74	Norway	0.57
South Africa	0.69	Congo (B)	0.53
Western Europe			
Netherlands	1.36	France	1.67
United Kingdom	1.23	West Germany	1.67
Belgium-Lux.	1.18	United Kingdom	1.62
Denmark	1.13	Italy	1.44
West Germany	1.00	Netherlands	1.27
Switzerland	0.83	Belgium-Lux.	1.06
Italy	0.76	Switzerland	0.90
France	0.70	Israel	0.65
Austria	0.64	Austria	0.56
Israel	0.63	Denmark	0.54

Choosers		Chosen	
		Eastern Europe	
Romania	2.66	U.S.S.R.	2.54
Czechoslovakia	2.37	Czechoslovakia	1.96
Cuba	2.30	Poland	1.92
Egypt	2.21	Yugoslavia	1.31
Finland	2.13	East Germany	1.25
Hungary	2.10	United Kingdom	1.20
Poland	2.09	India	1.20
Austria	2.07	China	1.16
Yugoslavia	2.04	West Germany	1.00
Bulgaria	1.91	Romania	0.99
East Germany	1.77	Hungary	0.97
Switzerland	1.73	Cuba	0.97
Netherlands	1.72	Italy	0.89
Sweden	1.71	Bulgaria	0.85
Italy	1.66	Japan	0.78
West Germany	1.63	Indonesia	0.77
U.S.S.R.	1.59	France	0.74
United Kingdom	1.55	Egypt	0.64
Burma	1.41	Austria	0.62
India	1.23	Burma	0.58
France	1.23	Netherlands	0.57
Indonesia	1.10	Finland	0.52
Pakistan	0.93	Switzerland	0.51
China	0.81	Sweden	0.48
Japan	0.79	Pakistan	0.47
		Arabs	
Lebanon	1.81	Italy	3.28
Saudi Arabia	1.53	Netherlands	2.74
Syria	1.47	Egypt	2.25
Jordan	1.46	Lebanon	2.00
Kuwait	1.27	Syria	1.83
Iraq	1.23	Iraq	1.74
Sudan	0.99	Saudi Arabia	1.55
Egypt	0.87	Sudan	1.42
Libya	0.84	Jordan	1.23
Italy	0.68	Kuwait	1.22
Cyprus	0.68	Libya	0.91
Netherlands	0.61	Cyprus	0.73
		Asia	
Malaysia	1.99	Japan	2.48
Thailand	1.84	United States	2.36
Taiwan	1.82	West Germany	1.79
South Vietnam	1.72	United Kingdom	1.76
Philippines	1.69	Australia	1.73

TABLE 8.1

Trade Groupings in 1963

Choosers		Chosen	
		Asia (Cont.)	
Japan	1.63	Thailand	1.68
Indonesia	1.49	Indonesia	1.53
Australia	1.45	France	1.51
Burma	1.42	Malaysia	1.47
Laos	1.41	Philippines	1.45
Kuwait	1.41	Italy	1.39
South Korea	1.35	Taiwan	1.33
Saudi Arabia	1.33	Netherlands	1.31
Iran	1.16	South Vietnam	1.13
Ceylon	1.15	Canada	1.08
Iraq	1.14	South Korea	1.04
New Zealand	0.99	India	1.01
West Germany	0.89	Switzerland	1.00
United States	0.88	Belgium-Lux.	0.94
Netherlands	0.87	Sweden	0.86
Pakistan	0.85	Iran	0.80
United Kingdom	0.84	Burma	0.74
Belgium-Lux.	0.80	Denmark	0.74
Switzerland	0.80	Pakistan	0.71
Denmark	0.79	Saudi Arabia	0.69
Canada	0.78	Norway	0.67
Saudi Arabia	0.77	South Africa	0.66
India	0.75	New Zealand	0.62
Italy	0.70	Kuwait	0.61
Norway	0.69	Brazil	0.60
Austria	0.68	Austria	0.55
Sweden	0.67	Iraq	0.54
Mexico	0.64	Mexico	0.54
Yugoslavia	0.64	Yugoslavia	0.50
France	0.62	Laos	0.49
Brazil	0.61	Ceylon	0.48

Not Listed in Any Group

Afghanistan	Haiti
Albania	Iceland
Bolivia	Liberia
Central African Republic	Mauritania
Chad	Nepal
Dominican Republic	Sierra Leone
Ethiopia	Somalia
Gabon	Turkey
Guinea	Yemen

Choosers, and middle-to-high positions among the Chosen—they are important to the American nations, but are not themselves so deeply affected by economic events in Latin America. Most South American countries, however, are notably missing from this group. Only Colombia and Venezuela, at the top of the continent, are included. Other significant exclusions are the Caribbean island states: Haiti, Dominican Republic, and of course Cuba. Cuba's trade is now directed primarily to the communist countries; Haiti and the Dominican Republic are no more than moderately high up the list of Choosers, and well below the mean of Chosen countries. This is a result not merely of their small size—the Dominican Republic is bigger than five of the six Central American states—but more of the sparsity of commerce between the islands and the mainland. They trade mostly with the United States and some industrial nations of Europe. Ties among the five members of the Central American Common Market, however, are especially important. Past—even distant—political ties also may be relevant, as all of these Latin American states except Mexico once belonged either to Gran Colombia or to one of the Central American federations.

Two other clusters can be found in the Western Hemisphere. One is labelled "South America," and is composed exclusively of nations in the lower continent and a few from across the Atlantic. Venezuela is the only Latin American state to appear both in this group and in the previous one, indicating their separateness. Although Venezuela is not a member of the Latin American Free Trade Area, the first six Choosers are, as is Ecuador and absent Colombia and Mexico, whose ties are primarily with Central America. Bolivia, which like Venezuela did not join LAFTA, falls far down the Chosen list and is therefore not put with the group. Saudi Arabia appears with it, largely because it is a major source of Latin American petroleum imports and has now begun also to take many goods from the Western Hemisphere in return. Spain, with its linguistic and cultural ties to the continent, ranks above all other Europeans as a Chooser and over most of them as Chosen also. Italy does almost as well, but Portugal's bonds with Brazil are not sufficient to bring her in.

The third new world grouping is called "British Caribbean" for fairly obvious reasons, though it numbers several other Commonwealth nations as well: Ghana, New Zealand, Nigeria, Canada, and the United Kingdom itself. Saudi Arabia is again present, especially as a major supplier of oil to the Trinidad refineries, as is Norway which traditionally has had strong trading bonds with the Commonwealth and Sterling Area. But no *Latin* American country makes this cluster. Guyana, Jamaica, and to a lesser extent Trinidad (which made North and Central America) are physically Western Hemisphere, but in no very important way economically interdependent with most of the nations there. Here, with a group that spans four continents and excludes many close neighbors, is evidence of the power of a political relationship.

The British Commonwealth is closely identified with another cluster too. The first seven Choosers, and half of all its members, either are presently or were until rather recently (Burma, Ireland, Israel, Sudan, and South Africa) part of the Commonwealth or British Empire (Iraq and Israel as League of Nations mandates.) Some others once had British spheres of influence (Iran) or are geographically located close to several British territories (Congo, Madagascar). All the continental states usually considered part of Western Europe are present also, but except for the Low Countries, with their historic ties and proximity to Britain, they are well down into the lower half of the Chooser list. This cluster includes nations from all six continents, and except for tiny Kuwait and Sierra Leone, which fell below the overall mean on the Chosen list, either this grouping or the previous one incorporates every nation which has since the end of 1922 been a part of the British Commonwealth or Empire. Although the Commonwealth failed to show up as a distinct large grouping in most of the analyses of previous chapters (with the international organization analysis a marginal exception) it clearly emerges as a major influence on economic patterns. Even here, however, it turns up as two groups joined together by a common link with the mother country, rather than just *one* fully interdependent cluster where most of the ex-colonies trade heavily with each other as well as with the former metropolitan state.

An even stronger case for the primacy of politics applies to the French experience. The single cluster labelled "French Community" lists former French territories for all of its first 14 members on the Chooser list. Among the African ex-colonies only four (Chad, Gabon, Central African Republic, and Mauritania) which partly because of their size did not affect the others enough to make the Chosen list, are missing, as is Guinea, which withdrew prematurely from the French Union, bringing on a serious rupture with France and some of the other colonies. Some Western European nations, and a few non-French Africans, come in toward the bottom. The most heavily involved Western European states, note, are from the Common Market, which has a special economic relationship to the French territories. Notable by their absence, however, are two of the three former associated states of Indochina. Cambodia is tightly joined economically to the rest of the French territories, but Laos and South Vietnam are not. Even so, the French achievement is remarkable in two respects. First, major metropolitan-colony economic bonds were forged, and have been retained since independence, in virtually all parts of the empire. Second, and more striking, is the degree to which the pattern is not purely that of *empire* in the sense of colonies tied only to the mother country, as spokes to the hub of a wheel.

These are political units that are linked not only to the imperial power, but, to a very substantial extent, to each other as well. However important the colonial relationship undoubtedly was, there is something of a true economic community here in addition.[13] Partly geography is responsible—four French African countries are landlocked and can reach the outside world *only* in transit across another French African's territory—but that is not all.

A much smaller group, of ten, is readily identifiable as "Western Europe." Unlike the preceding three groups, this one reflects the power of proximity, or possibly of current politics, more than of past political relations. It is composed of the six states of the European Common Market (Belgium and Luxembourg are already in a full customs union and report their trade as of a single unit), and several others that are geographically contiguous to one or more Common Market countries (Denmark, Switzerland, Austria). Israel comes in, marginally, near the bottom of both lists. Note the presence, near the top of both lists, Chooser as well as Chosen, of the United Kingdom. As of 1963, at least, Great Britain retained powerful commercial ties to the European continent, ties that were economically every bit as important as those to the Commonwealth. Britain's presence both here and in the two Commonwealth groupings is graphic evidence of the reality of her self-conceived role as bridge. The method employed in this book is not appropriate for finding very small groups except when they are very isolated from the rest of the world (like Iberia in the 1963 UN Session), but the absence of a distinct Scandinavian cluster, and Denmark's close ties with its southern neighbors, nevertheless bear remarking.

"Eastern Europe" turns up as one more distinct cluster incorporating a substantial number of European nations, including especially, but hardly exclusively, the communist countries. Most of those most closely associated with the group, near the top of both listings, indeed have communist governments. Cuba's political orientation is very evident here; only two other nations, both physically located in East Europe, focus their commerce more sharply toward the other communists. Yugoslavia, despite its political non-alignment, is almost as high up on the Chooser list as the "satellite" states, and is actually higher than Bulgaria and East Germany. The U.S.S.R. is revealed as somewhat more commercially cosmopolitan than its neighbors, though because of its great size it nevertheless leads the Chosen factor. Egypt's close economic relations with the communist countries are well known, but perhaps their strength (number four among the Choosers) is not fully appreciated. Two other non-communist nations, but which are nevertheless geographically proximate to the Soviet area (Finland and Austria) are

[13] Merritt (1966) effectively makes this distinction between the economic empire (hub and spokes) and the more nearly *interdependent* web which he found to characterize colonial America in the eighteenth century.

almost as tightly involved. West Germany, Britain, Sweden, France, and several Asian states—Burma, India, Indonesia, Pakistan, and Japan—also trade rather heavily with the communist countries. The first three Asians are of course politically neutralist, the latter two, especially Japan, are not. China's alienation from what was once called the Sino-Soviet bloc is very evident indeed, for China directs less of its trade toward Eastern Europe than do several non-communist Asians. Notable by its absence is China's ally, Albania. It fails to make the "interdependent" grouping partly because of its small size and a consequent low loading on the Chosen factor. More than its size matters, however. It has become relatively autarchic, conducting only a limited foreign trade. Its loading on the Chooser factor was but 1.99, above Bulgaria but below Yugoslavia, Poland, Hungary, Cuba, Czechoslovakia, Romania, and several non-communists.

Moving on to the rest of the underdeveloped world, two more clusters emerge. One can easily be identified with the Arab countries. Nine of its twelve members are members of the Arab League; only still-isolated Yemen and the three former French African territories of the Maghreb are missing. This could be considered a geographic rather than purely a politically or culturally-based grouping, and on the whole it is, as the involvement of Italy and Cyprus indicate. Israel is not present for obvious reasons, including not just passive Arab hostility, but the economic boycott as well. Turkey also is absent, despite the fact that all of these Arab nations were, in the not too distant past, part of the Ottoman Empire. If the pursuit of economic advantage is always the *primum mobile* of imperialism, the Turks must be recorded as singular failures.

Finally we have a group that includes virtually all of non-communist Asia except for the remote and land-locked states of Afghanistan and Nepal. Southeast Asia is strongly represented at the top of the Chooser list, with states like India, Pakistan, and Iran coming further down. New Zealand, and especially Australia, score fairly high because of trade with their Pacific neighbors. Some, but not a majority, of the Arab nations are included, as are South Vietnam and Laos (but not Cambodia), who were absent from the French Community grouping. Japan is heavily involved with nations once coveted for the Co-Prosperity Sphere, and especially with countries the Japanese occupied during World War II or decades earlier (Taiwan and South Korea).

These nine distinct and substantial groups are the most we have found for any of the clustering criteria examined in this book. Small differences in method and cutting points for determining the existence of a group, plus the complications introduced here by demanding a cluster by both Chosen and Chooser definitions, fuzz the comparison slightly. These differences, however, are not sufficient in themselves to account for the greater number of groups discovered. The world is more fragmented economically than according to any of the other gross criteria employed in the volume. It is divided into quite a number of partially overlapping but yet distinct multinational trading groups.

Geographic influences on trade are powerful, as they have been for all the variety of groupings we have looked at in the last seven chapters, but it appears (subject to more rigorous measurement below) that the role of proximity can be exaggerated. Distance can be surmounted if the incentives are strong, especially for maritime countries. Much of the cost of marine transport is in loading and unloading, so that the actual mileage to be travelled may be a secondary factor. Nearly half the countries examined are joined to one or more clusters not identified primarily with their geographic neighbors. (This is true, however, for only two, Austria and Switzerland, of the dozen land-locked nations.) Both politics and culture have major effects on commercial choice, as is evident in almost all the groupings. Asia, Western Europe, and the two Latin American aggregates can be explained almost as well by proximity as by politics or culture; the separate factors cannot simply be sorted out. But the Eastern Europe, French, and two British clusters all span three to six continents and exude the heritage of colonialism or more modern varieties of empire-building. The Arab grouping is well defined geographically, but more is seen to be at stake with the absence of Turkey and the exclusion of Israel, geographically in its heart. In fact, one can learn almost as much from the exclusions as from the inclusions.

We have not yet provided much evidence on the causal relation between trade and the flag, but we have amply demonstrated their interdependence, a relationship strong enough to shrink the miles in many cases. Nor is trade merely a matter of a simple division of labor between industrial and primary-producing nations. Many of our groups are composed overwhelmingly of *either* underdeveloped (Central America, South America, Arab, Asia) or developed (Western Europe) nations, who nevertheless find a substantial degree of comparative advantage among themselves despite their overall similarities in resources and productive patterns. And several of the colonial-based groups, most especially the French, are composed of a congeries of states, some similar economically, some very dissimilar, who nevertheless form a quite interdependent entity. Specialists trying to account for trade preferences often produce partially correct but limited explanations —a geographer grasping at distance and transport costs, an economist stressing crude comparative advantage, a political leader emphasizing institutional ties and legal favors or restrictions. Each has a part, but only a part, of the whole.

9

THE CONTINUITY OF TRADING PATTERNS

TRADE GROUPINGS IN 1954

THE TITLE OF THIS CHAPTER BETRAYS ITS MAJOR FINDING: trading relationships have not changed very much since the early 1950's. The year 1954 was selected as a basis for comparison with the 1963 results. By that time the reconstruction of Europe, and of the network of international trade so badly disrupted by World War II, had largely succeeded. Per capita income in all the European countries had for several years surpassed the 1938 level, and while substantial reconstruction of housing and public facilities remained incomplete in 1954 for several nations, most industrial plant and equipment had been restored or replaced. The year 1954 also marked the end of rearmament and the Korean War boom for the world's primary producers, and of the most acute balance of payments pressures on the economies of Europe. In short, 1954 was the first relatively "normal" year of economic activity experienced by most of the world in more than a decade and a half. It thus serves as a good baseline for comparing with the 1963 trade patterns, yet is sufficiently earlier, almost a decade, to show the effects of accumulated incremental change. Also, it is far enough back to get into the period of dollar shortages and discrimination against exports from North America, so that we may expect some distortion, and subsequent readjustment as restrictions were eased.

For 1954 we can examine commercial relations among 93 political entities, not too many fewer than the 115 we had for 1963. In the earlier year French Equatorial Africa, French West Africa, and Indochina reported as colonial units rather than as the separate states they were later to become. Also, several underdeveloped nations who either are small and account for little of world trade, or who are rather isolated and for whom foreign commerce has never been terribly important, did not report in 1954 but finally did so by 1963. They include Liberia, Libya, Malta, Nepal, Yemen, Afghanistan, Somalia, and Kuwait. The same procedures applied to the 1963 data

TABLE 9.1
Trade Groupings in 1954

Choosers		Chosen	

North and Central America

Choosers		Chosen	
El Salvador	2.75	United States	3.24
Costa Rica	2.71	West Germany	2.48
Panama	2.60	Canada	2.45
Nicaragua	2.58	United Kingdom	2.30
Honduras	2.52	Mexico	2.26
Venezuela	2.25	Netherlands	2.24
Cuba	2.25	Belgium-Lux.	2.19
Peru	2.24	Venezuela	2.14
Colombia	2.24	Cuba	2.01
Guatemala	2.23	Switzerland	1.99
Ecuador	2.18	Japan	1.99
Dominican Republic	1.97	Colombia	1.97
Mexico	1.93	Sweden	1.93
Uruguay	1.86	France	1.89
Chile	1.80	Italy	1.89
Canada	1.77	El Salvador	1.76
United States	1.73	Peru	1.73
Netherlands	1.70	Denmark	1.60
Belgium-Lux.	1.69	Spain	1.60
Switzerland	1.68	Panama	1.60
Sweden	1.54	Honduras	1.60
West Germany	1.53	Costa Rica	1.57
Brazil	1.49	Norway	1.55
Argentina	1.48	Nicaragua	1.50
Norway	1.45	Chile	1.34
Philippines	1.44	Guatemala	1.26
Denmark	1.41	Ecuador	1.23
Spain	1.36	Austria	1.12
Japan	1.34	Dominican Republic	1.04
United Kingdom	1.27	Uruguay	1.03
Austria	1.12	Argentina	1.00
Italy	1.10	Philippines	0.90
France	1.01	Brazil	0.89

South America

Choosers		Chosen	
Brazil	1.49	Brazil	2.58
Argentina	1.46	Argentina	2.50
Chile	1.33	Chile	1.88
Bolivia	1.28	Uruguay	1.79
Uruguay	1.28	Peru	1.26
Peru	0.97	Philippines	1.24
Philippines	0.97	Bolivia	0.90

TABLE 9.1 (Cont.)
Trade Groupings in 1954

Choosers		Chosen	
Commonwealth			
Trinidad	2.02	United Kingdom	2.49
Gold Coast	1.64	South Africa	2.01
New Zealand	1.21	New Zealand	1.84
Ireland	1.20	Ireland	1.69
Nigeria	1.08	Trinidad	1.63
South Africa	1.05	Portugal	1.47
Jamaica	1.03	Gold Coast	1.47
Portugal	0.99	Nigeria	1.28
United Kingdom	0.95	Jamaica	0.99
French Community			
French Morocco	2.56	France	2.70
Fr. Equat. Africa	2.41	Algeria	2.30
Fr. Cameroons	2.30	French Morocco	2.21
Algeria	2.30	Fr. West Africa	2.09
Fr. West Africa	2.23	Netherlands	1.87
Madagascar	2.14	West Germany	1.84
Indochina	1.95	Fr. Equat. Africa	1.77
France	1.79	Belgium-Lux.	1.70
Tunisia	1.66	Indochina	1.69
Belgian Congo	1.33	Italy	1.69
Netherlands	1.27	Fr. Cameroons	1.63
Nigeria	1.25	Sweden	1.62
Portugal	1.21	Switzerland	1.56
Denmark	1.19	Denmark	1.54
Belgium-Lux.	1.16	Madagascar	1.49
Cuba	1.13	Spain	1.49
Finland	1.12	Norway	1.42
Switzerland	1.12	Brazil	1.21
Norway	1.10	Portugal	1.20
Spain	1.08	Finland	1.18
Sweden	1.08	Egypt	1.15
Venezuela	1.04	Tunisia	1.14
Brazil	1.04	Nigeria	1.14
Egypt	1.00	Cuba	1.12
West Germany	0.96	Belgian Congo	1.07
Italy	0.96	Venezuela	1.07

Choosers		Chosen	
		North Atlantic	
Netherlands	3.17	United States	4.51
Belgium-Lux.	3.05	United Kingdom	4.38
United Kingdom	2.96	West Germany	3.86
West Germany	2.75	France	3.55
Sweden	2.56	Netherlands	3.45
Switzerland	2.54	Japan	3.34
France	2.43	Italy	3.32
Denmark	2.38	Belgium-Lux.	3.18
Italy	2.33	Sweden	2.81
Norway	2.28	Canada	2.73
Japan	2.20	India	2.67
Malaya & Sing.	2.15	Switzerland	2.52
Austria	2.07	Denmark	2.28
United States	1.90	Czechoslovakia	2.14
Canada	1.85	Norway	1.88
Spain	1.63	Spain	1.65
Czechoslovakia	1.58	Australia	1.54
Australia	1.50	Austria	1.53
South Africa	1.48	South Africa	1.24
Egypt	1.46	Malaya & Sing.	1.19
India	1.40	Egypt	0.99
Hungary	1.13	Hungary	0.96
		Eastern Europe	
Finland	2.75	U.S.S.R.	3.45
Hungary	2.71	East Germany	2.91
East Germany	2.65	Czechoslovakia	2.77
Czechoslovakia	2.65	Hungary	2.61
Bulgaria	2.39	Poland	2.50
Iceland	2.38	West Germany	2.38
Poland	2.36	Finland	2.32
Romania	2.36	Romania	2.21
Austria	2.35	United Kingdom	2.13
Turkey	2.15	Austria	2.08
Egypt	2.12	Italy	2.06
U.S.S.R.	2.12	China	1.98
Greece	2.12	Turkey	1.95
Switzerland	2.00	France	1.92
Norway	1.93	Netherlands	1.91
Denmark	1.93	Bulgaria	1.87
Netherlands	1.92	Sweden	1.85
Syria	1.92	Switzerland	1.84
Lebanon	1.90	Belgium-Lux.	1.81
Sweden	1.89	Egypt	1.75
West Germany	1.88	Denmark	1.73
Israel	1.88	Norway	1.64
Belgium-Lux.	1.87	Yugoslavia	1.63
Yugoslavia	1.81	Greece	1.60

TABLE 9.1 (Cont.)
Trade Groupings in 1954

Choosers		Chosen	
		Eastern Europe (Cont.)	
China	1.75	Brazil	1.60
Fr. Morocco	1.70	Israel	1.25
Uruguay	1.69	Argentina	1.24
Italy	1.68	Australia	1.17
United Kingdom	1.57	Indonesia	1.12
Brazil	1.56	India	1.03
Argentina	1.53	Iceland	0.99
Malaya & Sing.	1.53	Malaya & Sing.	0.96
France	1.47	Uruguay	0.94
Iran	1.42	Fr. Morocco	0.87
Australia	1.39	Iran	0.85
Indonesia	1.37	Syria	0.84
India	0.93	Lebanon	0.84
		Middle East	
Lebanon	2.06	Saudi Arabia	2.49
Saudi Arabia	1.96	Italy	2.47
Cyprus	1.81	Egypt	2.24
Syria	1.77	Iraq	2.11
Iraq	1.62	Syria	2.00
Sudan	1.50	Lebanon	1.97
Tanganyika	1.32	Sudan	1.94
Belgian Congo	1.30	Greece	1.79
Uganda	1.28	Turkey	1.70
Greece	1.23	Yugoslavia	1.62
Egypt	1.16	Belgian Congo	1.54
Turkey	1.15	Cyprus	1.47
Kenya	1.13	Kenya	1.47
Ethiopia	1.12	Tanganyika	1.45
Yugoslavia	1.08	Uganda	1.43
Italy	0.97	Ethiopia	1.27
		Asia	
Malaya & Sing.	3.08	Malaya & Sing.	2.45
Ceylon	2.73	Japan	2.16
Burma	2.55	Australia	2.02
Mauritius	2.48	Indonesia	2.01
Iraq	2.34	India	1.94
Thailand	2.28	China	1.84
Australia	2.27	United Kingdom	1.80
Saudi Arabia	2.23	Ceylon	1.78
Indonesia	2.11	Thailand	1.74

Choosers		Chosen	
		Asia (Cont.)	
Japan	2.08	United States	1.72
India	2.06	Burma	1.66
United Kingdom	1.91	West Germany	1.47
Taiwan	1.87	Pakistan	1.45
Pakistan	1.85	Netherlands	1.33
South Africa	1.81	France	1.27
New Zealand	1.80	Canada	1.25
Egypt	1.80	Belgium-Lux.	1.25
Netherlands	1.74	South Africa	1.23
Belgium-Lux.	1.72	Taiwan	1.20
Philippines	1.63	Indochina	1.15
Iran	1.59	Italy	1.13
West Germany	1.53	Philippines	1.08
Indochina	1.51	Iran	1.07
Switzerland	1.50	New Zealand	1.07
Italy	1.48	Switzerland	1.06
Canada	1.40	Sweden	1.03
Sweden	1.37	Egypt	1.00
France	1.28	Mauritius	0.93
China	1.24	Iraq	0.93
South Korea	1.22	Saudi Arabia	0.91
United States	1.09	South Korea	0.85

Not Listed in Any Group

Albania	British Guiana
Haiti	Paraguay

were used on the 1954 material. Eight factors accounted for more than 1 per cent of the variance each and were rotated, and all are substantively meaningful. We have again used the overall mean loading as the cutoff point below which we will not consider a country to be associated with a particular group, but, largely because fewer factors were rotated, the mean loading here is higher than in the preceding chapter.

The first, once again identified as "North and Central America," closely resembles the group to which we assigned the same name for 1963. Here too the Chooser factor is headed by the Central American states, though for this pre-Central American Common Market year Guatemala is tenth instead of fifth. Cuba, before Castro, is heavily involved with the continental nations bordering the Caribbean as, more surprisingly, are the Dominican Republic and Peru and even Ecuador from South America. In fact, most of the South American states—Chile, Uruguay, Brazil, and Argentina—are here, even though they are fairly far down the list and were no longer even present in the 1963 cluster. Of all the republics, only Haiti, Bolivia, and Paraguay were absent. This is a longer grouping than we found in 1963, primarily because it includes more Latins. The more restricted 1963 clustering comprised no South Americans below Colombia and Venezuela, indicating that the hemisphere became economically more divided over the nine years following 1954.

The "South America" cluster, not large in 1963, was even smaller in 1954. Bolivia is included in this table, as it was not for the more recent year, but Ecuador and Venezuela are missing. So too are all the extra-American nations such as Spain, Switzerland, and Saudi Arabia. The Philippines, however, are present, as they were near the bottom of the North and Central America lists. This was still a period of acute dollar shortages for many European and Asian countries, and they used quotas and currency restrictions to limit their imports from the so-called Dollar Area: those nations which linked their currencies to the United States monetary unit. The Philippines, recently independent, maintained a favorable balance of payments with the United States during this period and retained most of their commercial bonds. As a consequence they both were able to pay for imports from the dollar-linked nations of the Western Hemisphere, and because of their monetary strength had but limited export access to markets in Asia and Europe. Hence we find them grouping with the South Americans.

No distinctive British Caribbean group emerges for 1954, but there is a cluster unambiguously identified with a number of Commonwealth countries. It actually includes most of the British Caribbean countries with the primary exception of British Guiana, which fell just too low on the Chosen factor. Also present are South Africa, Ireland, and British-connected Portugal, which by 1963 were part of the separate Commonwealth cluster.

The French Union comes through with great clarity, as in the previous chapter. Eight French-associated polities were included in this analysis; these eight lead the Chooser factor, and four even lead the Chosen factor as well. Below them, once again, are some non-French colonies in West Africa (Belgian Congo and Nigeria) and a fair representation of West Europeans. In both years it is an extremely tight and interdependent grouping, with non-French units coming into the Chooser list only after the French ones have been accounted for. Political independence brought some minor market diversification, however. In 1963 the second, third, and fourth positions on the Chosen factor were taken up by West European nations, but under the colonial regimes of 1954 Algeria, Morocco, and French West Africa were more preferred. (West Africa, as a bigger unit than its several fragments in 1963, might well be higher, but this explanation does not hold for the other two.)

We find no West European grouping in 1954, but instead a broader aggregation that has to be given a "North Atlantic" label. Except for Sweden's inclusion and Israel's absence, the same states that appeared in the later, more limited group lead this one. But below them are the United States, Canada, and several non-European nations, most of them British colonies or ex-colonies. Japan, Egypt, Czechoslovakia, and at the very bottom, Hungary are also present. Thus despite the dollar gap and trade discrimination, the United States and Canada were more closely linked economically to Western Europe in 1954 than in the 1960's. The growth of the Common Market has meant, as many observers predicted, a kind of increased European parochialism, and with the smaller but tighter continental grouping, an increasing economic as well as military and political trend toward the "dumbbell" expression of NATO. This is the tendency that the Trade Expansion Act of 1962, with its special provision for complete tariff abolition on goods for which the United States and the Common Market accounted for 80 per cent or more of world trade, was meant to reverse. With the exclusion of Britain from the EEC that provision has become ineffective, and the tendency for the Atlantic Ocean increasingly to split the NATO market has gone uncorrected.

Finland, a non-communist state, leads the "Eastern Europe" Chooser factor in 1954, but is then followed by the Soviet satellites. Some contemporary observers of the period had already consigned Finland to the Soviet bloc, as some of their fellows were to do later for Iraq, Ghana, and Indonesia. Possibly the tight economic integration of Finland with the communist countries in part explains that bit of misperception, though much of the Finns' trade was involuntary—war reparations—rather than the consequence of a free choice of markets and suppliers. Iceland is high also; this was the year of fishing-grounds conflict between Iceland and Great Britain, and when the Soviet Union rescued the Icelanders' economy by relieving them of their one substantial export, fish, which was temporarily blocked from its normal market in the United Kingdom. On the other hand, Yugoslav relations with Eastern Europe were still extremely strained in 1954, and this is reflected in Belgrade's *much* lower position in the cluster than in 1963.

Although we know that the foreign trade of the communist countries expanded mightily (by 150 per cent overall, and 240 per cent with non-communists) with the opening of many doors in the decade following Stalin's death, the Eastern Europe cluster was actually larger in 1954 than in 1963. The reason for this seeming paradox is really quite simple. Partly because of the American strategic embargo, and partly because of Soviet preferences for self-sufficiency, many countries in the non-communist world conducted little or no trade at all with the Soviet bloc. Hence virtually all those that had *any* substantial commercial relations with communist nations appear here. Note, nevertheless, the high positions of both Egypt and Syria. These were among the first nations in the 1950's to exhibit a fairly marked and sharp eastward shift in their political orientations, and were among the first to seek large shipments of Russian arms.

As in the previous chapter, two more groupings complete the mapping, and account for most of the underdeveloped states. The first is called "Middle East" rather than Arabs as in 1963, for although the independent Arab nations lead it, and none who reported are absent, it is a broader cluster. Cyprus is third in the Chooser list, and several other non-Arab Mediterranean countries—Greece, Turkey, Yugoslavia, and Italy—are also incorporated. In addition we find the units of East Africa, especially the British colonies of Kenya, Uganda, and Tanganyika, who conducted a fair amount of commercial intercourse with each other and with the Middle East. These states of the East African customs union moved together into the Commonwealth grouping of 1963, indicating a very modest shift in their trade orientation over the decade while remaining together.

Finally is again an Asian grouping, corresponding in general to the cluster of the same name in 1963. Here too, though to a more limited extent, the most closely associated countries are in Southeast Asia. Also present are most Arabs, Mauritius and South Africa, the Commonwealth dominions of Australia, and a number of West European nations. The United States is present in the 1954 table, but much further down both lists than in 1963; its subsequent increased political involvement in Southeast Asia is reflected in the trading patterns. France and the United Kingdom, both of which were below the United States position in 1963, are above it here in the 1954 listing.

THE STABILITY OF TRADE RELATIONS

Thus we have eight clusters of trading states which, except for the fractionation of the Commonwealth, very closely match the 1963 groupings. The closeness of the fit is evident in Table 9.2, which gives all indices of agreement over 0.50 between the two years, first for Choosers and then for Chosen.

In both sets the North and Central America and the French Community groupings are essentially identical, except of course for the new states added by independence and fission to the French cluster in 1963. The Asia group is also quite constant, with some rather minor changes noted above. South America is stable, though in 1963 it picks off and adds at the margin several European polities that were previously identified with the North Atlantic aggregate. Eastern Europe and the Arabs (or Middle East) appear static enough in the Chooser comparisons, but from the Chosen half of the table it is apparent that a certain merging has occurred, as the

TABLE 9.2
Indices of Agreement Between Trade Groups

Choosers		
1954		1963
North & Central America ——— 0.98 ——————→		North & Central America
South America ——————— 0.82		South America
North Atlantic ——————— 0.53		South America
Middle East ——————— 0.80 ——→		Arabs
Asia ——————————— 0.89 ——————→		Asia
Eastern Europe ——————— 0.97 ——————→		Eastern Europe
North Atlantic ——————— 0.91 ——————→		Western Europe
French Community ————— 0.97 ——————→		French Community
Asia ——————————— 0.76 ——————→		Commonwealth
Commonwealth ————————— 0.90 ——————→		British Caribbean

Overall product-moment correlation between studies is 0.97.

Chosen		
1954		1963
North & Central America ——— 0.98 ——————→		North & Central America
South America ——————— 0.86 ——————→		South America
Middle East ——————— 0.78		Arabs
Eastern Europe ——————— 0.55		Arabs
Asia ——————————— 0.90 ——————→		Asia
Eastern Europe ——————— 0.63		Eastern Europe
Middle East ——————— 0.72		Eastern Europe
North Atlantic ——————— 0.53 ———————		Western Europe
French Community ————— 0.96 ———————		French Community
Commonwealth ————————— 0.69		Commonwealth
Asia ——————————— 0.51		Commonwealth
Commonwealth ————————— 0.69		British Caribbean
North Atlantic ——————— 0.50		British Caribbean

Overall product-moment correlation between studies is 0.95.

communist nations have expanded their commercial as well as political activities in the Middle East and have established well-traveled routes to Cairo and other Arab capitals. (Though not evident in Table 8.1 because they were not high on the Chooser list, the communist East European states loaded heavily on the Arab Chosen listing as well as on East Europe.) Soviet commercial vessels have passed through the Bosporus with greater effect than the Czarist navy ever could do. The two Commonwealth groupings show up here as resulting from both a fissioning of the Commonwealth cluster in 1954 and a fusion of both parts with a somewhat wider aggregate of non-British territories. For the Choosers most of the 1954 Commonwealth influence is exerted on the British Caribbean, with the 1963 Commonwealth derived in large part from the British portions of Asia. (The index between the two Commonwealth factors in each year is a modest 0.44, and so does not appear in the table as a major continuity.) For the Chosen the Commonwealth influence is clearer, with Asia contributing to the 1963 Commonwealth and a few North Atlantic states affecting the Caribbean cluster. Overall, the correlation between the two years is an extraordinary 0.95 for one and 0.97 for the other, figures that exceed the levels achieved either for the continuity of United Nations voting (0.91) or for international organization membership (0.93). More than 90 per cent of the variance in 1963 trade patterns could have been predicted, for units which existed and reported their trade a decade earlier, from the 1954 network. Economic man is impressively a creature of habit.

INTERNATIONAL TRADE AND POLITICAL CHANGE

Before leaving this topic, however, we should also look at the d^2 to pick out the deviant cases, the countries that could not have been well predicted from earlier commerce alone. Some of this has been done impressionistically in previous paragraphs, but a brief rigorous check still will prove instructive. For the two comparisons the mean difference, or d^2, is 0.76. All the countries exceeding that average in *both* analyses are listed in Table 9.3 on p. 155.

As we found for United Nations voting, Cuba easily tops both lists of trade changes with a sharp drop in her Western Hemisphere connections, and her new-found association with Eastern Europe and China. This is hardly a surprise. What is astonishing is to find Paraguay near the very top of both lists. No political shift even approaching the magnitude of Cuba's has occurred for Paraguay, and the trade changes demand explanation. Two adjustments are responsible. First, Paraguay has over the decade become appreciably more closely linked to the South American states on or near its borders. It was tightly situated in the South American grouping for 1963, but not so for 1954. Second, and much less expected, however, considering Paraguay's small size, there is a sizeable amount of commercial intercourse between it and the communist states of Eastern Europe. General Stroessner's country carries on a rather un-South American proportion of its trade with Yugoslavia, East Germany, Czechoslovakia, Hungary, and Romania. The volume is not enough to give Paraguay a position at all high on the Eastern Europe Chosen factor, and even on the Choosers its loading is only 1.00, or not much above the mean. But for Paraguay to be carrying on any substantial trade at all with the Communists is quite a shift, and along with its greater involvement in South America produces a high index of change.

TABLE 9.3

**Countries With Major Shifts in Trading Patterns on
Both Chooser and Chosen Factors, 1954–63**

Choosers		Chosen	
Cuba	3.81	Cuba	4.64
Paraguay	2.91	Iran	3.37
Iran	2.53	Paraguay	2.25
Ceylon	1.71	Japan	1.93
Cyprus	1.39	Iraq	1.73
Iraq	1.33	India	1.70
Iceland	1.24	Yugoslavia	1.58
India	1.21	Israel	1.42
Ghana (Gold Coast)	0.94	Morocco	1.16
Morocco	0.93	Ceylon	1.14
East Germany	0.90	Dominican Republic	1.09
Israel	0.88	Algeria	1.08
Japan	0.88	Iceland	1.03
Yugoslavia	0.86	Ghana (Gold Coast)	1.02
Trinidad	0.85	East Germany	0.92
Algeria	0.84	Cyprus	0.84
Dominican Republic	0.79	Trinidad	0.82

Overall mean = 0.76

Movement into or out of the East European group accounts for a high proportion of all the changes. Further down on the list India, Ceylon, and Iraq all owe their d^2 indices primarily to their new trade relations, acquired since the death of Stalin and since the 1958 revolution in the case of Iraq, with Eastern Europe. Iraq also, and less predictably, shows a certain increase in trade with the French area. Yugoslavia has been somewhat shut out of the Middle East, as this has evolved into a more strictly Arab grouping, but it has renewed its earlier trading ties with Eastern Europe, ties that were disrupted by Tito's break with the Cominform in 1948. Israel and Iceland, on the other hand, are less dependent on trade with the communist nations than they were in 1954. Iceland's commerce with the communists has always been discernible but small; the great fish trade of 1954 was something of an aberration. So was the brief consequent flirtation of some Icelanders with a neutralist foreign policy. Following the fish deal and strained relations with Britain, the local Communist Party won many seats in parliament and there was talk of expelling NATO from its airbase at Keflavik. This soon died down. East Germany has also become less dependent on trade with the COMECON countries. It still remains near the top of the list, but has in the past several years broadened its worldwide contacts to at least a pale shadow of the Federal Republic's far-flung commerce.

Iran owes its high d^2 to a general diffusion of its contacts, but especially to increased trade with many countries of the British Commonwealth. Possibly this is largely a recovery of Iran's normal trade with the United Kingdom and several other Commonwealth countries after the disruption of their relations by Premier Mossadegh's nationalization of British oil holdings. (Recall that Iran also, in its United Nations alignments, has moved closer to the West.) Both Trinidad and Ghana (Gold Coast) owe their positions in this table to the splitting of the 1954 Commonwealth into two components, one being associated especially with the Caribbean.

Strong evidence of the political decline of empires is strikingly absent from these analyses. Most former colonies continue to trade almost as much with former colonial rulers, and fellow colonies, as they did before independence. The only major exceptions are for two French territories, Morocco and Algeria. They have used their new sovereignty to widen their commercial relations substantially; while they still are high on the French Community, their loadings, and rankings, are down notably. The Moroccan case is nevertheless contaminated slightly by the fact that the present state incorporates not just French Morocco, but the smaller territories of Spanish Morocco and Tangier as well. Part of its apparent change may be due merely to the absorption of real estate which had never been so closely tied to France. Of the remaining shifts, Japan shows less trade with the North Atlantic area but strengthened contacts with the Commonwealth countries and with the Arabs, in large part doubtless a resumption of Japan's pre-war commercial arrangements. Cyprus, like Yugoslavia, has a proportionately diminished trade with the Arabs, and the Dominican Republic, with a reduction in economic exchange with the Central American states, may be a victim of the Central American Common Market's success. Political unrest in Santo Domingo during 1963 disrupted a good bit of its total trade in any case.

As in previous analyses, the total number of substantial changes is quite small, and in a majority of cases can be at least tentatively explained in political terms. Two instances (Algeria and Morocco) are clearly related to the achievement of independence by former colonies; two (Iraq and Cuba) underwent revolutionary domestic changes of regime during the period and another (Iran) seems to have settled into a different pattern following an earlier change of regime. Two more seem related to cold war orientations: Iceland's brief flirtation with the Soviets, and Yugoslavia's limited but more lasting rapprochement with Eastern Europe. Japan recovered its full sovereignty in 1952 and this is probably reflected in its later broadening of trade relations; possibly Cyprus' achievement of independence in 1960 may also have had some commercial consequences.

Thus political change occurred in at least nine of the 17 cases of major change, though the causal and temporal relation of that change to trading patterns is in some instances quite unclear, and politics is by no means always involved. It seems fairly certain that the independence of the French North African territories, loosening some of the shackles imposed by colonial economic policy, preceded and made possible the commercial changes. The cold war-related shifts are not of so uniform a pattern. An earlier examination (Russett, 1962) showed a distinct rise in trade with the Soviet bloc *before* substantial political changes in Iceland and Yugoslavia, but the same study showed *no* prior increase in Iraqui trade with the communists, and nothing of the sort preceded Castro's accession to power in Cuba. No easy or uniform answer to the chicken-egg question emerges from the analysis so far. We shall return to it in a subsequent chapter, but without expecting to find that the causal relationship always runs the same way.

10

CONTIGUOUS REGIONS

A PROXIMATE SOLUTION

IN DISCUSSIONS OF REGIONAL DELINEATION, CONTIGUITY is usually considered to be a necessary if not sufficient condition for the identification of a region. In writings on international integration it is thought to be a helpful though not sufficient condition for political integration. Over all the areas of the world currently amalgamated under common governments there are only two nations divided by the intruding land mass of another country: Pakistan and the United States. In the latter case the non-contiguous section, Alaska, is of marginal political and economic importance, but the Pakistani case comprises a far more significant instance. East and West Pakistan, with roughly equal populations, are separated by almost 1000 miles of Indian territory. The two segments differ substantially in several economic and cultural respects, and their continued union in the state of Pakistan is somewhat tenuous. A few other nations have various portions of their land masses set off from each other by water, but in only three cases, Indonesia, Malaysia, and the United States (mainland—Hawaii) are the distances from one island to any other important one as great as 100 miles. The first two instances again provide examples of states where national integration is less than firmly established, and a key barrier to its fulfillment is indeed the divisive distance.

Distance can be overcome by money and technology. In a rich society like the United States, high speed air travel can much reduce the economic distance among its component units and make possible the full integration of Hawaii and Alaska into the union. As transportation becomes even faster and relatively still cheaper, we may see other examples of political union among widely separated areas. Yet the barrier of distance remains severe and instances of high political integration in the absence of contiguity are rare.[1]

[1] It is widely acknowledged that communications tend to be greatest for units that are in physical proximity to each other. See, for example, Berelson and Steiner (1964, p. 349) and March and Simon (1958, pp. 128–29). The economic literature emphasizes time—cost distance as distinguished from physical distance. See also Hawley (1950), pp. 236–38.

Naturally proximity alone does not guarantee integration, as innumerable examples demonstrate.

To round out this study we shall finally look for groups of countries which form into clusters by reason of their nearness to each other. As a measure of geographical distance we shall use simply the straight-line mileage between the capitals of any two countries. The air distance between capitals was obtained where possible from the great-circle distances given by the International Air Transport Association's listing. The IATA's distances are actually for the mileage between the principal airports serving the capitals, and while this introduces slight inaccuracies of perhaps 10 or 20 miles, the error is trivial for the world, where distances average about 6000 miles. The majority of measurements, however, were not given by IATA and had to be taken by tape measure from a large globe. Some inaccuracy is likely here too, but with the large 18-inch diameter globe employed the mean error should not exceed 1 per cent, or 60 miles.

Two aspects of this operationalization deserve discussion. The capital was chosen as the *political* center of the country, appropriate to a study of the conditions of political integration. An alternative would have been the geographic center of the country, but not infrequently such a point bears little resemblance to an area of commercial or political importance. For example, the geographic centers of Brazil, Canada, and Libya are, each in a different way, virtual wildernesses. In practice, the political capital is usually rather near the geographic center of a country. Where it is not, it is nevertheless almost always an area of high population density, the country's major center of economic activity, and, by definition, the focus of political attention. Treating it as the heart of the nation seldom will lead us far astray.[2] In most cases where one might be disposed to argue with the decision at most a very few hundred miles are at issue, again to be put against an average country-to-country distance of roughly 6000 miles. The most serious exceptions are the United States and Russia. But for the Soviet Union it still seems not inappropriate to place its "center" fairly near Europe. Using Washington rather than Chicago or St. Louis as the center of the United States is less defensible, despite the Eastern seaboard's residual claims to primacy. But it seemed best to stick to a consistent rule, given our focus on politics, and even so it makes little actual difference in the analysis. The distance between either Washington or Chicago and other capitals in the Western Hemisphere is trivial, and the expanse of ocean separating North America from the other continents reduces the proportionate effect even of latitudinal measure. It will, however, bring the United States somewhat closer to Europe in the following results. Where there was a choice between

[2] See the interesting graphic presentation by Cole (1964, p. 310) on the relative distances of various capitals from Moscow and Peking.

two cities each of which was described in some sense as the capital (e.g., Rio de Janeiro and Brasilia, Sucre and La Paz in Bolivia, Vientiane and Luang Prabang in Laos) we did in fact pick the one nearer the physical center.

The other part of this decision that might be questioned was the use of great-circle distances rather than some measure of economic distance, say the shortest rail and/or sea route. If we were in fact concerned with economic distance, how to ship heavy or bulky goods most cheaply, or just to compare distance with our trade data alone, this would have been the appropriate choice. It would even have been the only defensible choice just a couple of decades ago. But with the advent of jet air travel and direct or near-direct connections among most of the world's major capitals, a choice based on the economics of surface travel no longer was necessary. For a measure of the span that men must travel in person, or the gap to be covered by weapons of mass destruction, the straight line is a better approximation.

The methodology was thereafter of the sort that is by now familiar to the reader. A matrix of the distance from each state's capital to that of every other country was constructed: a square, symmetrical matrix. All the values were then standardized by dividing each by the largest distance in the matrix (New Zealand to Spain, almost 12,400 miles) and subtracting the dividend from one. This simultaneously converted them to a range of zero to one and changed the distances into proximities, with the shortest distance in the entire table (Congo-Leopoldville to Congo-Brazzaville, less than 25 miles), becoming 0.998. (The formula is again $1 = \dfrac{Dij}{D\ Max.}$) Unities were inserted in the diagonal, making the proximity from each country to itself equal to 1.0.

Since most readers will from school geography already have some idea of the physical dispersion of countries around the globe they may find the results of this analysis rather less than astounding. It will be useful, nevertheless, to have the data in the form of a factor matrix for systematic comparison with the other criteria. By matching these factors against those from homogeneity, international organization membership, and so forth, we will be able to assess the contribution of geography to each. Furthermore, applying factor analysis here, to a set of data most of us know well, gives us an opportunity to validate the method in a different way. Here, if at any point, we bring to it well-informed images of how countries *ought* to cluster together.

Six factors had eigen values greater than one, but only four of them, when rotated, had more than one loading as high as 0.50. Those four are sufficient to classify each of the 118 countries that has been used in any of the previous analyses. It may be well to point out, in light of the obvious three-dimensional model that the globe provides, that the factors or dimensions of this exercise are *not* equivalent to the dimensions of terrestrial space. For the Euclidean three-dimensional model to apply we would have to measure the straight-line distances, through the earth, between capitals—the equivalent of digging a hole to China. Just because neither goods nor people normally travel that way, we instead have measured the great circle distances around the surface of the sphere. Since these are not Euclidean distances we cannot expect to get out the three Euclidean dimensions. Here, as in the preceding four chapters, we are using factor analysis as a means of reducing the data of a large matrix in a way that allows us more readily to understand the interdependencies among the points. We are not using it to find in any absolute sense *the* minimum or maximum number of dimensions necessary to describe the globe. We say simply that the configuration of political units in the world happens to be such that four factors are able to depict them in an informative way. If we had considered each of the 50 states of the U.S.A. as separate political entities we would doubtless have had a fifth major factor centered in North America—the clustering of the points, not the geometry of the globe, determines the number of factors.

FOUR CLUSTERS

Each of these factors can readily be matched with a familiar geographic label: "Europe," "Western Hemisphere," "Asia," and "Africa." The first one picks out all the nations which are physically part of the European continent, plus the offshore islands of Cyprus, Malta, Britain, and Ireland. The original data were as-the-crow-flies distances; for the crow there is no Iron Curtain. We find no distinction between Eastern Europe and Western Europe. The core is right in the heart of the continent—Czechoslovakia, East Germany, Denmark, and Luxembourg head the list. Ireland and the Soviet Union, on either flank, are still primarily and equally a part of the group. The U.S.S.R. does load moderately also on the Asia factor, but with Moscow as the capital it mainly faces west. If we ignore water and mountain barriers to *land* travel, Europe emerges, from Galway to the Urals, as a compact and coherent physical unit. Even Iceland, though off to the periphery and with some proximity to the Western Hemisphere, is a part. So too is Turkey in this analysis, even though its capital, Ankara, is actually in Asia Minor. The Turks' usual insistence that they live in a European country has geographic merit. All the states of Southern Europe and the Mediterranean also are unquestionably here despite a fairly low position on the list and a slight affinity for the Africa factor. More unexpected is the discovery that Iran, Israel, and all the Arab states except southernmost Yemen have their highest loadings on this factor too. For North Africa, the

TABLE 10.1
Geographic Regions

	Factor 1 30%	Factor 2 22%	Factor 3 17%	Factor 4 20%
Europe				
Denmark	0.85	0.31	0.27	0.25
East Germany	0.85	0.31	0.28	0.26
Czechoslovakia	0.85	0.29	0.26	0.29
Luxembourg	0.85	0.32	0.23	0.31
West Germany	0.84	0.33	0.24	0.29
Belgium	0.84	0.34	0.23	0.29
Switzerland	0.84	0.31	0.22	0.33
Austria	0.84	0.27	0.27	0.32
Hungary	0.84	0.26	0.29	0.32
France	0.83	0.34	0.22	0.31
Netherlands	0.83	0.34	0.24	0.29
Sweden	0.83	0.31	0.33	0.22
Yugoslavia	0.83	0.25	0.28	0.36
Poland	0.83	0.27	0.32	0.27
United Kingdom	0.82	0.36	0.23	0.29
Norway	0.82	0.34	0.30	0.21
Finland	0.82	0.29	0.36	0.20
Romania	0.82	0.23	0.31	0.34
Italy	0.81	0.28	0.23	0.39
Bulgaria	0.81	0.24	0.30	0.36
Albania	0.81	0.25	0.27	0.39
Ireland	0.79	0.39	0.21	0.28
U.S.S.R.	0.79	0.24	0.40	0.24
Greece	0.78	0.22	0.29	0.43
Tunisia	0.77	0.29	0.21	0.46
Malta	0.77	0.27	0.23	0.47
Spain	0.76	0.38	0.16	0.42
Turkey	0.76	0.19	0.35	0.39
Iceland	0.73	0.46	0.26	0.18
Algeria	0.73	0.34	0.19	0.47
Portugal	0.73	0.41	0.15	0.42
Cyprus	0.73	0.18	0.35	0.44
Libya	0.73	0.27	0.22	0.51
Syria	0.71	0.17	0.37	0.44
Lebanon	0.71	0.17	0.37	0.45
Israel	0.70	0.16	0.36	0.48
*Egypt	0.70	0.17	0.34	0.50
Jordan	0.70	0.16	0.37	0.47
Morocco	0.70	0.39	0.13	0.49
Iraq	0.69	0.13	0.44	0.43
*Iran	0.66	0.12	0.49	0.39
*Kuwait	0.63	0.11	0.47	0.47
*Saudi Arabia	0.58	0.11	0.46	0.52

	Factor 1 30%	Factor 2 22%	Factor 3 17%	Factor 4 20%
	Western Hemisphere			
El Salvador	0.22	_0.94_	0.11	0.07
Honduras	0.22	_0.94_	0.10	0.09
Panama	0.22	_0.94_	0.05	0.15
Guatemala	0.22	_0.93_	0.12	0.06
Nicaragua	0.22	_0.93_	0.08	0.11
Costa Rica	0.21	_0.93_	0.07	0.13
Ecuador	0.18	_0.92_	0.01	0.19
Colombia	0.22	_0.91_	0.01	0.22
Jamaica	0.28	_0.91_	0.07	0.15
Cuba	0.29	_0.90_	0.11	0.11
Haiti	0.30	_0.90_	0.06	0.19
Mexico	0.23	_0.89_	0.18	0.00
Dominican Republic	0.31	_0.89_	0.05	0.21
Venezuela	0.28	_0.88_	0.01	0.26
Peru	0.13	_0.88_	0.02	0.25
Puerto Rico	0.33	_0.87_	0.04	0.24
Trinidad	0.31	_0.85_	0.00	0.30
Guyana	0.30	_0.83_	0.02	0.34
United States	_0.42_	_0.80_	0.16	0.10
Bolivia	0.14	_0.80_	0.05	0.36
Canada	_0.48_	_0.76_	0.20	0.07
Chile	0.04	_0.75_	0.02	0.37
Paraguay	0.13	_0.74_	0.02	_0.41_
Brazil	0.20	_0.72_	0.02	_0.47_
Argentina	0.09	_0.70_	0.00	_0.43_
Uruguay	0.09	_0.69_	0.00	_0.46_
	Asia			
Philippines	0.25	0.05	_0.91_	0.10
Taiwan	0.30	0.09	_0.90_	0.07
South Vietnam	0.27	0.04	_0.90_	0.24
Cambodia	0.29	0.04	_0.89_	0.24
Laos	0.33	0.01	_0.88_	0.23
Indonesia	0.20	0.08	_0.87_	0.27
Malaysia	0.27	0.07	_0.87_	0.28
Thailand	0.32	0.38	_0.86_	0.25
South Korea	0.35	0.19	_0.86_	0.00
Burma	0.35	0.02	_0.84_	0.28
Japan	0.32	0.24	_0.83_	0.07
China	_0.40_	0.15	_0.83_	0.07
Australia	0.18	0.29	_0.78_	0.10
Nepal	_0.45_	0.03	_0.76_	0.30
Mongolia	_0.48_	0.16	_0.76_	0.10
Ceylon	0.36	0.05	_0.74_	_0.42_

TABLE 10.1

Geographic Regions

	Factor 1 30%	Factor 2 22%	Factor 3 17%	Factor 4 20%
Asia (Cont.)				
India	_0.49_	0.04	_0.71_	0.33
New Zealand	0.34	_0.47_	_0.70_	0.09
*Pakistan	_0.54_	0.07	_0.66_	0.33
*Afghanistan	_0.57_	0.08	_0.63_	0.33
Africa				
Cameroun	_0.43_	0.28	0.21	_0.80_
Congo (L)	0.37	0.26	0.25	_0.80_
Gabon	_0.40_	0.30	0.20	_0.80_
Congo (B)	0.38	0.26	0.25	_0.79_
Nigeria	_0.44_	0.34	0.16	_0.78_
Dahomey	_0.45_	0.34	0.15	_0.78_
Togo	_0.45_	0.35	0.15	_0.78_
Ghana	_0.44_	0.36	0.14	_0.77_
Central African Republic	_0.44_	0.23	0.26	_0.77_
South Africa	0.22	0.20	0.35	_0.74_
Ivory Coast	_0.43_	_0.40_	0.13	_0.74_
Uganda	_0.41_	0.15	0.37	_0.73_
Upper Volta	_0.50_	0.37	0.14	_0.73_
Chad	_0.51_	0.25	0.24	_0.73_
Niger	_0.51_	0.34	0.15	_0.73_
Liberia	_0.43_	_0.45_	0.09	_0.73_
Kenya	0.39	0.13	_0.40_	_0.72_
Tanganyika	0.34	0.12	_0.41_	_0.72_
Sierra Leone	_0.44_	_0.46_	0.08	_0.71_
Mali	_0.47_	_0.43_	0.11	_0.71_
Madagascar	0.25	0.09	_0.47_	_0.69_
Guinea	_0.45_	_0.47_	0.08	_0.69_
*Ethiopia	_0.48_	0.12	_0.40_	_0.66_
*Somalia	_0.42_	0.08	_0.47_	_0.65_
*Senegal	_0.49_	_0.49_	0.07	_0.64_
*Sudan	_0.55_	0.15	0.35	_0.64_
*Mauritius	0.24	0.04	_0.54_	_0.62_
*Mauritania	_0.52_	_0.48_	0.08	_0.62_
*Yemen	_0.52_	0.09	_0.45_	_0.60_

* Two or more loadings above 0.40, with the highest r^2 less than twice the second highest.

Sahara intrudes with greater distances from Black Africa than the Mediterranean does from the nations on the other side of the basin.

The Western Hemisphere is even more clear-cut and identifiable. Countries with the highest loadings are in Central America, spreading out in a circle to Mexico, the Caribbean, Colombia, and Ecuador, and finally dropping off about equally toward Hudson's Bay in one direction and the Straits of Magellan in the other. The United States and Canada have, with their eastern capitals, some affinity for Europe but are still quite solidly with this cluster. And four of the southernmost countries load slightly on the factor identified with the other big continent under the Southern Cross, but are yet very clearly part of the Americas. Whatever faults it may have from a cultural or political viewpoint, the Pan-American vision accurately depicts the relations of physical proximity and separation in the hemisphere. The image of a Western Hemisphere is of course itself an Americanocentric notion that would not readily occur to a Eurasian, but with the great oceanic distances separating its countries from the rest of the world it still does make some sense.

Third, and slightly less neat, is the Asia cluster. Its core is to be found in Southeast Asia, in the area of the Philippines, Taiwan, and the states of former French Indo-China. On the side of inclusions, Australia and New Zealand may be mild surprises (though New Zealand is sufficiently east to load somewhat on the Western Hemisphere factor too). Notable by their absence are almost all the states of the Middle East. Israel, Iran, and the Arab countries have their highest loadings either with "Europe" or with "Africa," and for most it is a matter of having their highest loadings with "Europe" and their second with "Africa." Only for Iraq, Iran, and the Arabian peninsula are subsidiary loadings on Asia very important. Afghanistan, Pakistan, and some other countries of the Asian heartland also have secondary loadings with "Europe," but are primarily on factor three.

Finally there is Africa, which with slightly more accuracy we might limit to sub-Saharan Africa since the nations along the Mediterranean littoral have only secondary loadings on this fourth factor. Its heart is in equatorial Africa, the area of Cameroun, the two Congo Republics (Brazzaville and Leopoldville), and Gabon. The Sudan and Mauritania, partially Arab and Saharan states, also are found with it. Mauritius and the Malagasy Republic, both islands in the Indian Ocean, show their location by having subsidiary loadings on Asia. And quite a few of the nations of West Africa bear some modest relation to the Europe or "Western Hemisphere" factors. These secondary loadings, however, are typically 0.50 or less as compared with at least 0.70 on Africa. There are about a dozen Middle Eastern and North African countries with moderately high loadings on both the first factor, identified with Europe, and either the third (Asia) or the fourth (Africa). Since the picture is not at all clear, and some countries actually load on all three of these factors, I have not separated them into a distinct cluster. But except for Mauritius (which does not load at all on

Factor 1) all the asterisked states at the bottom of the first, third, and fourth groupings are so characterized.

We have now completed our examination of how countries can be grouped by different criteria. It is time to work toward a synthesis, both for theory and for some conclusions about the prospects for political integration in each of the major regions. In the following chapter we shall look first at the general question of how closely the delineations by the various criteria do coincide, and then examine how they change over time.

11

REGIONS OF THE WORLD

REGIONS AND SUBSYSTEMS

"PEACE BY PIECES" IS A WELL KNOWN FUNCTIONALIST aphorism. It could as well be the slogan of an enthusiast for regional integration, whether that advocate sees regionalism as a step in the creation of "building blocks" for worldwide institutions, or as a plateau for the development of a multibloc international system. Whatever the purpose, the emphasis on piece work is widespread. Given such an outlook, just what potential pieces can be identified from the various aggregates examined here; what clusters of countries, or regions, exhibit the characteristics required for integration or seem to have a significant potential to become integrated blocs?

We shall in this chapter be strict constructionists, asking what aggregates show essentially the same *boundaries* as identified by different criteria. That is, in the general systems sense, what groupings can properly be termed subsystems of the international system; what clusters include the same nations, and only those nations, whether aggregated according to sociocultural similarity, common political orientations, institutional memberships, transactions, or proximity? Are there indeed *any* such aggregates where the boundaries consistently coincide from one characteristic to the next? Such an area would, by definition, be one that not only was relatively homogeneous and showed high interaction, but clear distinctiveness from the rest of the world and low rates of transaction with its neighbors.

The traditional nation-state best typifies such a unit, with a clearly defined political boundary that marks the boundary of a monetary system and a set of customs and currency controls which provide a barrier to foreign trade, a cultural and often a linguistic dividing line, and perhaps a distinct change in popular political values as well. These boundaries may be extremely divisive and impermeable, such as those between Israel and Jordan or Egypt, or divide less distinctive and more interacting units such as those of the new Western Europe. But whether the boundary is an iron curtain or merely a white picket fence, it is likely to coincide for all these characteristics. Where it does not, such as the enclave of German-speaking people in the Italian Alps, or those parts of Canada that are tied especially tightly to the United States economy, stresses arise and there may be demands either that the boundaries be brought into coincidence (the German-speaking areas be returned to the Austrian political and economic unit) or, under other circumstances, sometimes for the removal of the boundary altogether and the political unification of the entire area. While there will nevertheless always be examples of fuzzy or incongruent boundaries between nation-states, those boundaries are virtually certain to be sharper and more consistent than those delineating international subsystems or regions. A second question relevant to finding areas of integration concerns the *absolute level* of capabilities—homogeneity, economic interdependence, etc. —that is achieved within the area defined by a given boundary. We shall postpone examination of that question to the next chapter.

There is *no* region or aggregate of national units that can in the very strict sense of boundary congruence be identified as a subsystem of the international system. As suggested in chapter one, such a subsystem must be identified empirically by the agreement of several different criteria. Trade interdependence could establish one set of limits, but these would have to match closely with others.[1] Inclusion in any of our regions always marks a rather arbitrary point on a continuum, not something that can always be identified as the simple presence or absence of a characteristic.[2] This is a common enough problem in social research where for our intellectual convenience we often convert problems of "more-or-less" to ones of "yes-or-no," and we can bear in mind that our cut-offs, though presented as lines, must be remembered also as shaded zones. Even allowing for this arbitrariness, however, there is in our findings no area where the inclusions and exclusions are the same over all criteria.

COMMUNIST EASTERN EUROPE

Searching one's knowledge of world politics for an example of a group of states marked by high intra-group homogeneity, clear qualitative differ-

[1] See, for example, Talcott Parsons' (1961, pp. 324–25) identification of a system as marked by a high level of interactions and also some degree of complementarity of expectations. Etzioni (1965, p. 6) uses the term merely to refer to interdependent units, emphasizing that a *system* need not be *integrated*. I, of course, agree with the latter, since common membership in a system is necessary for integration but not sufficient.

[2] In the most rigorous general systems usage, however, one would expect to find boundaries marked by step-level changes in the quantity of information transmitted (Miller, 1965, p. 385). Perhaps this would, however, be true of national systems, emphasizing once again how loose or "open" are our regional approximations to subsystems.

ences from nearby states outside the group, and especially distinct trans-action boundaries, brings quickly to mind the "Soviet Bloc," or, less anach-ronistically, the Soviet Union and its allies of Eastern Europe. But political events of the past several years, buttressed by the evidence of this volume, show how far even that area is from deserving, in the rigorous sense, a label like "Sino-Soviet Bloc" or "Communist International System."[3] We shall study this and several other aggregates which have at least some of the characteristics of a subsystem with the aid of a graphic presentation illustrated in Figure 11.1.

Each of the factor analyses of previous chapters (for homogeneity, similar political behavior, institutional ties, trade transactions, and prox-imity) was compared with the others for approximately the same point in time (trade in 1954, U.N. behavior in 1952, and international organizations in 1951 are compared with each other, as are trade and U.N. voting in 1963, and international organizations in 1962). Each of these is also com-pared with the cultural homogeneity and proximity analyses, which were done for only one point in time.[4] For each of these sets of analyses we have a total of ten paired comparisons. By finding a factor which is more or less closely identified with an area that we hypothesize may have some of the characteristics of a subsystem, and following it through one comparison after another for the factor or factors which it most closely resembles in other analyses, we can discover the degree to which the boundaries do indeed coincide over different criteria. A group which fell *between* factors (e.g., Latin America in the late 1963 UN) will not match well with a group which was closely identified with a *single* factor in another analysis—as is appropriate because of the former's indistinct boundaries.

The graph shows, for Communist Eastern Europe, the two sets of com-parisons, on the left for the early 1950's and on the right for the early 1960's, divided by the center line. Each paired comparison is marked off at the margin, and the names of the two factors being matched are given just below the labels identifying the empirical domains being compared. The center line indicates the value of 1.00 for the index of agreement between two factors, and this tapers off on either side toward an index of 0.50. The points marking the actual agreement scores are connected by the jagged lines running down the figure. Thus if there were an Eastern Europe factor that coincided exactly with another factor in each of the other

[3] If "system" is defined differently, of course, the term may still apply (e.g., Modelski, 1961).

[4] Unless one is prepared to engage in rather finer geological measurements than could be carried out on a table-model globe, proximity is unchanging anyway. Cultural homogeneity is of course not static, but problems of the accuracy and availability of ecological data are still too serious to permit confident assessment of any but the most gross changes over a period as short as a decade, and it was not attempted.

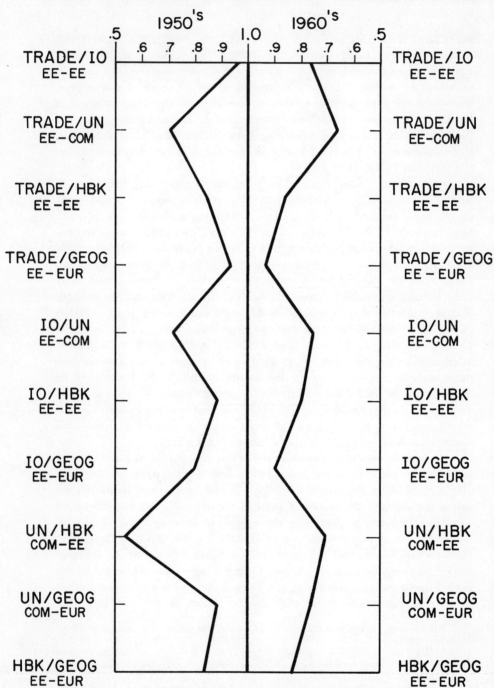

FIGURE 11.1: Communist Eastern Europe

analyses for that time period, its continuity would be marked by the center line at 1.00. The amount of actual deviation from such an ideal is measured, over all ten comparisons, by the area between the jagged line and the center.[5]

There is a core group of states, made up of the U.S.S.R., Poland, Czechoslovakia, Romania, Bulgaria, and Hungary, that are always found together. In no case, however, do the boundaries encompass only these nations. For the early 1960's Albania is usually present also, but for the United Nations voting cluster, and for international organization member-ships (IO) as well, it is distinctly marginal, and entirely absent for trade. Its recent independent pattern of behavior, in fact, has served to bring Albania's overall pattern into greater consistency, since it was even in the 1950's very poorly tied into the East European group by the interactional and structural bonds of trade and organizational membership. Had those links been stronger in the early years either the desire or the ability to pursue such an independent policy later might have been prevented.

Not only is China the mainstay of Albanian defiance of Moscow, in structural and behavioral terms its relationship to Eastern Europe is much like Albania's, only more. Institutionally it is aloof from the European com-munist organizations, and has always been so. For a while it carried on a fair volume of trade with the Soviet Union and, to a lesser extent, with other communist states, but its size has always permitted a high degree of economic self-sufficiency. As a very poor and Asian nation, its sociocultural profile from the *Handbook* (Hbk) shows much more clearly some of the tendencies exhibited by Albania. Distance, and Mao's historical accession to power without Soviet military support, provide further bases of indepen-dence. It was not during the period analyzed a member of the United Nations, but its other behavior in international politics indicates that it would hardly have been more conforming with the bloc than was Albania in 1963. China's ties to the other communist countries have never been as strong as those of the East European states, hence its recent behavioral independence is not surprising.

According to the measures employed in chapter two, Yugoslavia is not notably different in culture or social organization from the other communist

[5] All indices of agreement of 0.50 or higher between factors are listed as an appendix to this chapter. The graphs are limited to illustrating those matches that seem to trace a single cluster. For trade, only the Chooser analyses were used in the comparisons, since addition of the Chosen factors would have complicated the presen-tation and discussion without adding substantial information. (The Chooser and Chosen analyses correlated an average of 0.90 with each other for 1954 and 1963. As indicated earlier, the Chooser factor gives a better indication of preference, though not of impact.) Because of difficulties in data gathering the years measured for each criterion are not always the same, especially for the early 1950's. The high agreement between each of these and the corresponding analysis for as much as a decade later, however, strongly indicate that little noise is introduced by this necessity.

states; it is geographically proximate and carries on a high level of commercial transactions with them. But the Yugoslav government has chosen neither to tie itself intimately to its neighbors by a large number of institutional bonds, nor to behave too much like them in international politics. Actually the close economic association is a fairly recent phenomenon, for during the years while Yugoslav political independence was being established Belgrade either cut off, or had terminated by the bloc, the bulk of its normal trade with the East. Only with the improvement in political relations over the past decade has the trade level returned to something approaching the original volume, at the same time without diminishing notably the commerce that had been established with the West during the interim. Finland, Austria, Egypt, and a number of other states of Central Europe and the Mediterranean carry on substantial trade with the communists but are not otherwise closely associated with them.

In most respects East Germany does not differ greatly from the other communist states. It is not a member of the United Nations, but if it were it surely would vote no more independently than Poland or Czechoslovakia. But in institutional ties at the level of formal governmental organizations it is, like China and much more than Albania, very isolated indeed. Much of this is in the communist system compensated by a functional equivalent, the formally non-governmental but politically most relevant ties among communist parties. The presence of 20 Red Army divisions also provides a unique "bond." Nevertheless the lack of broad intergovernmental organizations linking East Germany with other communist states might some day make a difference to a government that wanted to find an extra degree of freedom.

Cuba is of course geographically very distant from the other communist nations, and is but loosely connected with them in some other ways too. The socio-cultural data from the *Handbook* were largely for the late 1950's and so did not take account of the changes introduced by Fidel Castro. Had they done so, Cuba's factor loadings in that analysis probably would not have been very different from, say, such a semideveloped East European state as Romania. By a combination of choice and the United States-directed embargo, Cuba's trade has become heavily directed toward Eastern Europe, and in international politics Havana acts like a good communist capital. However, it is not yet a member of many of the purely communist organizations, and given the irrelevance to it of many of the purely East European institutions is not likely to develop many. This, plus distance, plus the partly forced and artificial character of its current foreign trade pattern, plus the social and cultural subtleties that would not fully show up on the gross *Handbook* dimensions in any event, provide much of the potential for a future independent course by Cuba. Yet the longer current bonds are maintained, the stronger they are likely to become. With spill-over into the

cultural and organizational realms, the accretion of ties over the years probably makes a completely independent course less likely the longer it is delayed.

Even for the communist "subsystem," therefore, the term *subsystem* is
inexact and the boundaries are indistinct. For some purposes Yugoslavia,
Cuba, China, East Germany, and Albania are in, for others one or more of
them are not. It is not, in any precise sense, a bloc. Nor is this entirely a phenomenon of the post-Stalin thaw and the surfacing polycentrist tendencies.
Examination of the graph shows that the fit among the factors was only
slightly tighter in the 1950's than since. Yugoslavia's political independence
was very evident even then, as were the weak institutional ties of China,
Albania, and East Germany to the rest of the bloc. The admission of a
number of reliable East European states to the United Nations has perhaps
disguised, on the measure of voting, some increases in behavioral independence and compensated for the maverick activities of Albania. The entry of
mainland China, which would hardly be more docile, would make these
disparities more evident.

Still, much of the evidence of polycentrism in the 1960's can be seen as
the natural and even expectable result of the failure to create more bonds,
across a number of dimensions, in the previous decade. What remained latent
during the period of Soviet military occupation of Eastern Europe, and was
suppressed by strategic factors and the atmosphere of military tension in the
1950's, has since become manifest. Under Romania's leadership efforts to
weaken the controls exerted by institutions have spread from the economic
sphere (COMECON) to the military (Warsaw Pact). Unless force, in
substantial quantities, is employed to reunify the bloc, the prospects for a
return of the wayward are poor.[6] There has been some trend among the
communist states for the patterns of cultural relationship, transaction, behavior, and institutional structure to be brought into agreement, and this
is to be expected since each of these promotes the other. But the opposite
side of the coin is that the absence of several contributes to the atrophy of
those that are present. The prospects for retaining the long-term allegiance
of Cuba and East Germany are suspect, and will require, by the other communist states, assiduous cultivation over a wide range of activities.

LATIN AMERICA, WESTERN COMMUNITY, AND ASIA

Latin America is another region of common parlance, and one where,
in the 1950's at least, the congruence of differently defined boundaries was
quite high, in most instances exhibiting an index of agreement above 0.90.

---

[6] Note the very interesting proposition of Etzioni (1965, p. 73) that the relationship between coercion and successful unification is curvilinear; i.e., some force can
help, but much creates strains that will result in eventual dissolution.

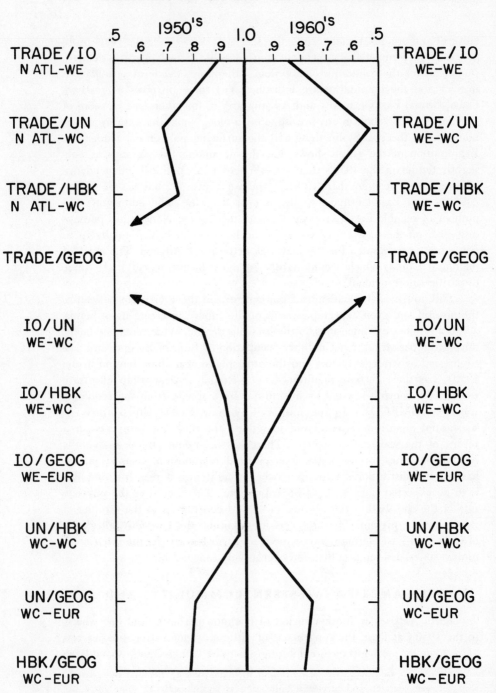

FIGURE 11.2: Latin America

Institutional structure, behavior, transactions, cultural homogeneity, and geographic proximity all gave much the same patterns. As Figure 11.2 shows, the major discrepancy was for trade, where the hemisphere was split into two components, a North and Central American aggregate, and one for South America. The North and Central American group provides the closer fit, but a second jagged line, farther from the 1.0 mark, is included to identify South America's fit as well.

Recall the pattern of clustering in previous chapters and it will be apparent that not all of Latin America is equally involved in this potential subsystem, but rather that the core group is to be found in Central America and other continental states bordering on the Caribbean, with the nations in the lower half of South America, and of course the United States and Canada, very much more marginal. The group of socio-culturally homogeneous states, as defined by the *Handbook* variables, excluded Haiti, the British colonies, Argentina, and, on the whole, Uruguay, Chile, Puerto Rico, and Cuba. The latter were appreciably more developed economically, and hence characterized by a more urban or industrial culture than the less-developed majority. The highest loadings on the Western Hemisphere factor from the analysis of geographical proximities were also for Central American states, with the North American nations and Chile-Uruguay-Argentina about equally far down the list.

Some of these divisive tendencies were reaffirmed in the analyses for the 1960's, to the point that most of the agreement scores are lower for the right-hand half of the graph. Cuba and the Dominican Republic were no longer identified with the Central American trading group, Cuba of course becoming heavily involved with Eastern Europe instead. Cuba, the Dominican Republic, and Uruguay also had by then slipped quite far down the list of states who belonged to large numbers of Latin-American oriented international organizations. Haiti had always been very marginal. And Cuba's behavior in the United Nations was emphatically not that of a Latin American nation, but of a communist (East European) state. Haiti, Bolivia, and Uruguay had, by 1963, reinforced earlier tendencies to vote often with the Afro-Asian neutralists, and the Latin Americans in general did not show a high degree of cohesion. By noting their fairly high loadings on two different factors we were able, in chapter four, to identify a general Latin American group, but the dispersion was substantial with some members absent and some, like Argentina, quite closely identified with the Western Community. By some, but hardly all, criteria, the Iberian mother-countries were more like Latin America as a whole than were some of the states physically located in the hemisphere.

In sum, Latin America in the 1950's possessed many of the attributes of an international subsystem, especially if one looked not at the 20 republics in toto, but most closely at the group of nations in Central America and the area once known as Gran Colombia. But by the beginning of the 1960's some of this had disappeared. North America, which had always been so distinct culturally, was not less so, and in United Nations voting behavior, trade, and international organization membership, there had been a distinct falling off of several states from the Caribbean and the southern half of South America. Of all the world's geographic regions, Latin America as a whole exhibited the sharpest decline in intra-regional trade as a proportion of its total income over the decade (see next chapter). The Latin American Free Trade Area experienced very little success in correcting the situation, though trade among the *Central* American states, with their common market, did rise substantially; hence the finding of chapter nine of a more distinct split into *two* Latin trading groups. There is, perhaps, a rising degree of coherence in mainland Central America on several counts, but the area is not yet sufficiently distinct from its neighbors by most criteria to constitute a subsystem by itself. Extrapolating the trends of the past decade, prospects for the next few years seem to be possibly for rising unity in Central America, but not elsewhere, either in the sense of an all-encompassing Latin American system or of a competing center in the southern continent. In the entire Western Hemisphere the composition of various clusterings (by homogeneity, trade, etc.) differs too greatly, and varies from smallish subgroups to encompassing the entire two continents, to constitute the boundaries of a tight subsystem.

Many of these same general comments apply to the *Western Community* which, like the previous major aggregates, includes a core group of countries who are included by any criteria, but for which the other exclusions and inclusions vary widely. For trade, international organizations, and geography a group readily identifiable as Western Europe constitutes this core. (The agreement between the trade and geography factors, however, was so poor as to be less than 0.50, as is indicated by the arrows pointing beyond the 0.50 line on the graph.) At its heart are the countries of the Common Market, plus Austria, Switzerland, Denmark and surprisingly, the United Kingdom. These are to be found in each of the Western Community or Western Europe clusters. By the criteria examined here, this group of countries does possess the minimal requirements for political integration. Whether the present degree of integration will grow, or whether the needs for political unification can be met, is a question we cannot answer from this general overview. But this cluster of ten nations is the largest aggregate to be found over all five criteria in the entire analysis. The strength of Britain's ties with the continent is especially notable, and may hold a major portent for the future.

Except for the fairly tight trading group of the 1960's, the other clusters

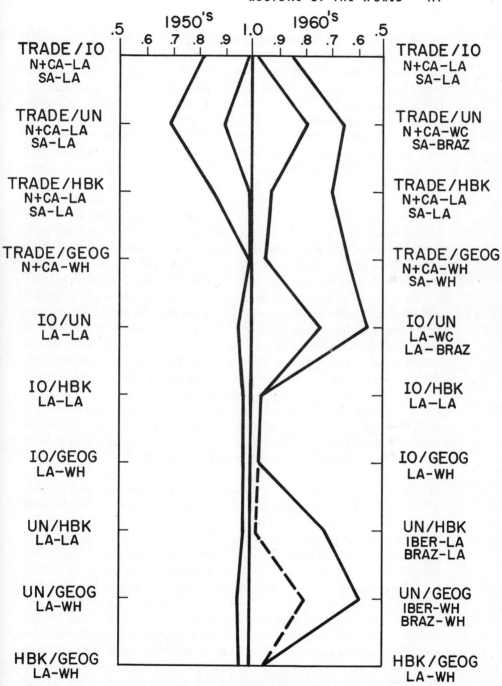

FIGURE 11.3:   Western Community

include most or all of the remaining non-communist states of Europe. Spain and Portugal are absent from the socio-cultural and United Nations clusters, and marginal geographically and institutionally as well. Turkey's cultural differences are profound, and it is also linked but weakly by commercial bonds to Europe. Its continued association with the European nations in international organizations, and the maintenance of its very pro-Western orientation in international politics and the United Nations, is open to doubt since these orientations draw only limited reinforcement. Cyprus was found to be fairly Western in culture, but not joined with many European states by trade, institutions, or political behavior.

The strongly European characteristics of this grouping are shown by the in-and-out nature of some non-European states' relations to it. The United States and Canada share a common Western culture with their European allies, and generally agree with them on most of the issues of international politics which are posed in the United Nations General Assembly. Their physical distance, however, is reflected in, and reinforced by, only a limited degree of association in international organizations and a limited commercial dependence upon them. The same remarks apply, with greater force, for Australia and especially for New Zealand, whose current institutional and transactional bonds with the rest of the Western Community are indeed tenuous. Israel, and more surprisingly Japan, however, belong with the European countries on every criterion except proximity (and Israel is not really so distant). For international organization membership they rank low in the Western Community list, and strictly speaking Israel's United Nations voting pattern looks more like that of a Latin American country than of a European. But despite its location Israel was one of the small group of countries identified as Western Europe on the 1963 trade analysis, and while Japan was outside that group it nevertheless fell only just below the cut-off mark employed. If the world of the next several decades is to see a very general kind of agreement and common interest among the Western industrialized countries, with interests that come increasingly into conflict with the non-Western underdeveloped nations of Asia and Africa, Israel and Japan, now "have" states, are much more likely to be aligned with their rich developed fellows than with their geographic neighbors.

Yet these results suggest that the prospects for widespread co-operation and presentation of a common front should not be exaggerated. In the ideal-type sense defined for this book there is no Western or North Atlantic subsystem, and though there is a core area of Western Europe, its edges are too inconsistent to constitute boundaries in any strict sense. Nor has there been any identifiable trend toward sharpening these boundaries. The differences among the clusters identified by the various criteria were, on the average, every bit as great in the 1960's as in the 1950's.

We shall look at a number of other regional subgroups in the following pages, but only one, *Asia*, has sufficient continuity from one criterion to another in both periods to warrant serious consideration as a possible international subsystem. The level of agreement here actually is no better than for the Western Community, and appreciably lower than for either Eastern Europe or Latin America. The closest fit is obtained for the broadest groupings—the Afro-Asians from the United Nations, and the Afro-Asians as defined by a broad sort of cultural homogeneity. These are not *just* Asian groupings, but ones that include a substantial number of Arab North African states as well. A more limited Asian group showed up in each of the trade, international organization, and, naturally, the geographic analyses. They agree rather well with each other, but usually not at all well with the all-encompassing clusters from the UN and *Handbook* studies.

In any case these are very large aggregates which hide considerable diversity, and once more there are substantial variations in the inclusions and exclusions. Japan is pretty regularly absent; it is Asian in hardly more than the strict geographic sense, plus substantial commercial involvement with its Southeast Asian neighbors and, especially, former colonies. The Afro-Asian cluster of states who vote together regularly in the General Assembly is certainly broad enough in geographical terms, but it omits a large number of countries that vote with the West at least on Cold War issues. Such states include some Arab and Southeast Asian states, and the very pro-U.S. voting records of Japan, Taiwan, and the Philippines. South Korea and South Vietnam would surely, had they been UN members, also not have behaved as cold war neutralists. The Philippines was absent from the Asian socio-cultural group, primarily because of the strong differentiating role that religion took on in that inductive analysis. The international organization cluster for Asia included most non-communist Asian nations except for politically untouchable Taiwan and Afghanistan and Nepal, whose geographic isolation has permitted them to remain as aloof from international trade and world politics as almost any modern political unit. China is absent from all of these Asian clusters except for geography and modest commercial ties; the same would doubtless have been true for North Vietnam and North Korea had we possessed enough data to include them formally in the analyses.

Aside from the boundary problem, there is not even any major Asian cluster that simply can meet the demand of inclusion in the same group over all five criteria. Seven states cluster together on at least four: socio-cultural similarity, trade, international organization membership, and proximity. They differ greatly, however, in their orientations in international politics. On many issues, especially cold war ones, Malaysia, Pakistan, and Thailand have voted with the developed Western nations, to the point

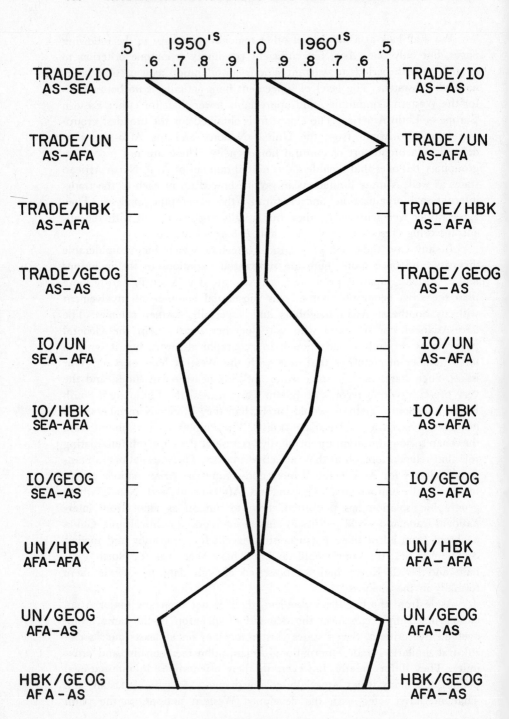

FIGURE 11.4:   Asia

where in 1963 their United Nations voting patterns were about the same as most Latin Americans. India, Indonesia, Burma, and Ceylon, however, were leaders of the Afro-Asian neutralist group. Possibly governmental changes in some of these states (as in Indonesia) or the rise of China to complicate the simple cold war divisions of the original United States-Soviet conflict (as it has affected the original alignments of both Pakistan and India) will mitigate the division between these two sub-groups. The effect so far, however, has been moderate, and the split continued to be manifested on issues like seating Communist China in 1966. And the bonds would still be highly tenuous; for instance by our indices India and Pakistan do not differ notably, but it is perfectly obvious that their antagonisms are more profound than their current, relatively minor, and perhaps temporary variations in cold war outlook.

REGIONS AND INAPPROPRIATE COMPARISON

Thus there is no sharply identifiable Asian or Southeast Asian system either, even less than could be found for other areas. There is a real danger, in the facile use of regional labels we all employ when discussing international relations or comparative politics, of comparing the incomparable. In so many respects Japan is *not* an Asian country, nor Haiti a Latin American one, nor Turkey either a European or an Asian state, that to expect them to behave like their geographic neighbors, or to have political and social systems like them, is often extremely misleading. Similar strictures apply, with only a little less force, to treating Argentina or Uruguay as typical Latin Americans, Spain and Portugal as Western Europeans (Latin America begins at the Pyrenees), or even the Philippines as an Asian state.

These distinctions naturally are well-known to an area specialist on Latin America or Southeast Asia, and he may not find many new insights here for considering the particular intellectual problems of his specialty. The firm evidence of these differences may nevertheless surprise him, since comparative data to document and sharpen his more intuitive perceptions are not always readily available. Also, it is sometimes possible to become so engrossed with one's particular tree as to forget to ask systematically how it is similar to, and differs from, the adjoining flora. And for the analyst with more general interests and lacking a regional specialization, or for the regional specialist when he wants to go beyond the geographic area of his expertise, these findings may be more instructive. To assume uncritically that the kind of general program for economic development and political stability that worked well in Chile would have equal success in, say, Honduras, would be extremely unsound. Similarly, to treat Spain as potentially like France, only poorer, might be very unwise. Note that this argument is not that no use can be made of cross-national comparisons, or that the experiences of one state cannot suggest the prospects for another, or that every case is unique and must be considered as a *tabula rasa*. The whole methodological approach of this volume is just the contrary. It is always an empirical question as to when and under what circumstances one can generalize from one nation's experience to another's. But some cautions and general guidelines are required to suggest where such comparisons may be most fruitful and where there is a special risk that they will be misleading. I would suggest that they can most successfully be attempted between countries within the same group as defined by *all* criteria of this volume. Whatever the incomparabilities and risks in analysis, the most valid results should arise with countries that cluster together by all or at least most of the criteria.

For there is indeed, for each major aggregate, a core, a limited number of states found in each of the clusters. Nor is the disagreement from one criterion to the next so violent that we cannot expect, in a general sense, to find the same states associated from one analysis to the next. The Philippines and Pakistan are absent from one or two, but they are more likely to be found with an indentifiable Asian grouping than not. The *majority* of states grouped with Asia on trade will be there for international organizations, and vice versa. Thus in a general sense the regional labels we use when discussing international relations or comparative politics do hold. There is in the strict meaning of the term no all-purpose region, but for many purposes Asia or Latin America correctly connotes the same cluster of states by most criteria. One primary danger is of being too confident that this general observation will hold in the particular case. The other is in employing the *geographic* labels carelessly. Our moral is that for purposes of generalization one should not refer to Asia unless one specifically means to refer to countries with a certain *physical* proximity to each other and distance from the rest of the world. For some types of strategic analysis, perhaps, such a usage is proper. But the political systems of Asia form a much less valid subject for generalization. It would be far safer, and productive of more accurate propositions, to discuss "the political systems of the non-communist underdeveloped states of Asia." While inelegant, the precision obtained by excluding such very deviant cases as Japan and mainland China should bring its own rewards.

SMALLER REGIONAL GROUPINGS

There are several other aggregates of nations that do not have overall boundaries even as sharply delineated as those of the above four groups, and thus cannot be considered promising candidates for the label of subsystem or "all-purpose" region. They are clusters of states that agree very substantially over two or three criteria, but fall within a much larger group-ing, with poor internal differentiation, for the others.

One of the most important such groups is the Arab or *Middle East* cluster. By indices employed in chapter two it did not stand out as separate from the other Afro-Asian states, but the addition of other variables to that analysis might well have brought out the distinctive character of this rela-tively compact and identifiable geographic area. It emerged clearly from the analysis of international organization membership as a predominantly Arab group except for the absence of Yemen and the marginal inclusion of Iran and Israel. Much the same group, but without Iran and Israel, was found in the trading patterns, save for the absence of the former French North African territories—Morocco, Tunisia, and Algeria—which carried on the bulk of their commerce within the franc area. Both of these were more clearly Arab groups (rather than general Middle East) in the 1960's than in the 1950's, indicating *some* progress toward Arab unity. All the members of the trading cluster shared the further historic bond of inclusion, in the relatively recent past, within the Ottoman Empire, though Turkey itself was consistently outside any current Arab aggregate.

In international politics, however, there was another division that did not coincide with these. Most of the Arab countries voted with the Afro-Asian states on the great majority of issues in 1963, and they were helped to do so by the virtual absence of Palestine-related issues from the 18th Session agenda, the one policy dimension on which the Arabs unite and can be readily distinguished from other Afro-Asians. But a minority of the Arabs, three of the remaining monarchies plus Mauritania and democratic Lebanon, hived off to form an identifiable Conservative Arab grouping. While this separate group was larger than it had been in previous sessions, its roots nevertheless go back at least to 1957, shortly after Libya and Jordan were admitted. Saudi Arabia balances somewhere between the two groups.

Arab unity is still a myth and perhaps an aspiration, not yet a reality. If one is looking for clusters that emerge by all of the criteria we set, it requires at least three to account for most of the Arab states. One can perhaps be called the radical or revolutionary Arabs of the geographic heart-land: Egypt, Syria, Iraq, and Sudan. A second is Algeria, Morocco, and Tunisia of the Maghreb, and the other comprises the geographically dis-persed states of Jordan, Libya, Lebanon, and Kuwait. This last is especially tenuous, since important political and economic characteristics of Lebanon make it marginal, and, as of 1963 at least, Kuwait had not yet obtained membership in too many of the international organizations of the area. Saudi Arabia, and much more so Yemen, cannot readily be placed with either, and Yemen's situation is unlikely to change before its problems of political regime are settled. The governments of the radical states have at various times made moves, serious or half-hearted, toward political unification, but, except for the brief union of Syria and Egypt, nothing has come of it. Their experiences of the past few years do not encourage much confidence in their prospects for the immediate future. Yet except possibly for the Maghreb states, their potential is greater than it is anywhere else in the Middle East. That alone is sufficient commentary on the likelihood that a strong and wide-ranging Arab nation will emerge during the lifetimes of the area's present rulers.

Possibly better prospects lie in black *Africa,* especially among most of the former French colonies there. Excluding the Arabs, all the ex-French African territories except the radical states of Guinea and Mali vote together (with others) in the cluster we labelled Brazzaville Africans. These same nations (again with Guinea absent) belonged to the Former French Africa cluster we identified in the international organization analysis. And except for some of the smallest and/or landlocked states, they again appear together (with France, North Africa, and former Indo-China) as a distinctive trading group. While we had insufficient data to incorporate them in the socio-cultural analysis of chapter two, it is certain that, in a very gross sense, they would have hung together. Altogether they form a group with sufficiently distinct boundaries in 1963 that we should illustrate the congruence with another graph, Figure 11.5. No comparisons are given for the 1950's because too few French African territories were included in the analyses for the matchings to be instructive.

Remember the presence of the former *Belgian* Congo in each of these groups. Congo (Leopoldville) was not a part of the former colonial empire, yet it trades substantially with the French Africans, votes with them in the General Assembly, and belongs to most of the same international organizations. While it is sometimes a marginal member of these clusters (especially for international organizations) its presence here at all is instructive, indicating that this French African group is an association chosen by the leaders of independent nations, not a hang-over from the past. It seems even more a case of voluntary choice when one recalls the Congo's geographic position. The country is substantially to the south of most of the French territories. It borders on two, but is not at the center of French Africa, thus providing the opportunity for an association without compelling it. Perhaps this aggregation, particularly the Congo's inclusion, is made possible only by the presence of French-speaking elites in power everywhere, and will not outlast the eventual politicization of the speakers of different African languages and dialects. But for the moment these governments do seem drawn together for at least limited purposes in a way that is not wholly accounted for by their colonial past.

Although it included the Belgian Congo, and did not incorporate

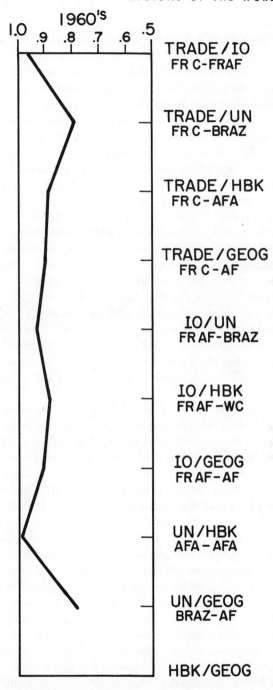

FIGURE 11.5:   Former French Africa

France or the former French territories of Asia or North Africa, the lineage between the preceding group and the French Union was quite apparent. No such clear lineage exists for the British Commonwealth, which is split into many, sometimes overlapping, subgroups. The states predominantly settled by Europeans (Canada, Australia, New Zealand, and the United Kingdom itself, but not South Africa) vote together regularly in the United Nations, carry on substantial mutual trade, and certainly have very similar socio-cultural profiles. These links are not, however, bolstered by a substantial number of common international organization memberships, with New Zealand's bonds to the others being especially weak in this regard. And of course these four nations are dispersed across the face of the earth. The Western Hemisphere states of Trinidad, former British Guiana, and Jamaica share similar broad socio-cultural profiles, trade some with each other (though British Guiana's ties were weak), and vote much the same way in the General Assembly (again omitting British Guiana, which was not then a member). Yet even this small group is not joined by many institutional bonds, and the failure of the West Indian Federation is still a recent memory. Among the ex-British colonies of Asia there is also no very notable unity except among quite small groups. As we showed during the broader Asian discussion above, Malaysia, Pakistan, India, Ceylon, and Burma share some common links, but their behavior on issues of international politics splits them into a pair and a triplet, and even then the bonds are not overly numerous or strong.

Already we have found that French Africa is distinct from the former British and Italian colonies and from the long-time independents (Liberia and Ethiopia). Nor is the division so simple as, for the major clusters, merely French and British. We did identify a cluster of Former British African states in the international organization analysis, and on the whole these states (except Sierra Leone) voted together pretty regularly in the United Nations. But East and West African states split up in their trading patterns, with Uganda, Tanganyika, and Kenya going with the larger Commonwealth group, and Ghana and Nigeria more heavily involved with the cluster that included the former British colonies in the Caribbean. So again, any attempt to discover a Commonwealth aggregate would succeed in finding no more than two or three countries per group, with over the entire world at least five such small clusters. This confirms the impression we gained while looking at one attribute at a time: the Commonwealth, as a worldwide association bringing together many nations of diverse characteristics, is an extremely amorphous and fractionated group. The divisions and differences within it are so great, and the bridges so few and narrow, that it is hard to see how it has the potential for any significant upgrading or reunification. Quite the opposite—its divisions have become deeper and more numerous over the past decade, and as the reality of the Commonwealth has become more amorphous, many Britons' ardor for it has wandered toward Europe.

Much of the world therefore remains fragmented, and this is especially true of the separate nations which were part of the former colonial empires. Only in West Africa among the French colonies has the legacy of colonialism included the bequest of many widespread and congruent ties among the once dependent territories. Elsewhere in Africa, Asia, and the Middle East one finds at most three or four nations that cluster together on all the criteria we have assembled. In the world at large, the divisions throughout the underdeveloped areas make the emergence of a big semi-continental have-not power, with great influence in international politics, a negligible prospect.

The situation is somewhat different in Latin America, where perhaps as many as nine states in Central and northern South America are consistently found together, and three more (Chile, Argentina, and, more tenuously in the UN, Uruguay) in the southern part of the Hemisphere. The size of the Central American group is impressive, and it will bear watching.

A half dozen countries in Eastern Europe always cluster together, with several others often with them, and no rival clustering in sight. The origin of this aggregation is obvious—Red Army occupation at the end of World War II, with the subsequent imposition of communist governments in each state. Yet Soviet armed forces have now been withdrawn from most of these nations (they remain stationed in Poland and Hungary, and very substantial in East Germany) and many of the rigid controls of the Stalin era have been relaxed or removed. The consequence has indeed been greater but still limited national independence on the part of virtually all these states, with Albania and Romania the most dramatic current examples. But force was not the only cement for these nations, or if it was it has now been replaced by other bonds of institutions, similarity, interaction, and common interests vis-a-vis the international system. Though it will never return to the monolith which we saw in public during the Stalin years, the unity of Eastern Europe is based on real ties and has a strength that must not be ignored. Under the impact of new strategic conditions the bloc has moved from a coercive attempt at semi-amalgamation to a more pluralistic effort. The new structure is likely to produce higher mutual responsiveness than could the old one.

Western Europe's original unity was the product not of military occupation and externally imposed force, but of common needs for co-operation in reconstruction and protection against a common threat. That unity was already sufficient for the threat indeed to be perceived as a *common* one rather than providing a potential external ally whose help might be used by one European state against another. That in itself is most significant. The unity has been fostered by many consciously and semi-consciously con-

TABLE 11.1

All Indices of Agreement Exceeding .50 Among Factors at Approximately the Same Point in Time, 1950's and 1960's

1960's			Trade								UN					
	N. & C. America	S. America	West. Eur.	East. Eur.	British Carib.	British Com.	French Com.	Arabs	Asia	West. Com.	Iberia	Braz. Afr.	Communists	Afro-Asia	Cons. Arabs
Geography Africa					.55	.78	.90					.79		.56	
Asia				.94					.97					.53	
Europe										.75	.50		.76	.64	
West. Hem.	.95	.64			.75					.79	.59		.55		
Handbook Afro-Asia						.62	.88	.57	.96					.99	.67
East. Eur.				.87								.71			
Latin Am.	.93	.70								.98	.72				
West. Com.			.74			.77				.96			.55		
Asia									.97	.50			.76		
Arabs								.75					.81		
IO French Afr.							.96					.93			
British Afr.						.78	.85						.83		
East. Eur.				.77								.76			
Latin Am.	.98	.85								.74		.57			
West. Eur.			.84	.51						.71					
Cons. Arab							.84								
UN Afro-Asia			.50	.80					.52						
Communists			.67												
Braz. Afr.		.66				.79									
Iberia															
West. Com.	.79		.53						.64						

UN	West. Com.	Latin Am.	Communists	Afro-Asia
West. Com.		.92	.68	.83 .51
Latin Am.		.69		.73
Communists			.70	
Afro-Asia		.59		.84 .96

TABLE 11.1

Correlation matrix comparing regional classification schemes.

Column groups (read across): **Trade (1950's)** · **UN** · **IO** · **Handbook**
Row groups (read down): **IO** · **Handbook** · **Geography**

	Trade — N. & C. America	S. America	N. Atlantic	East. Eur.	British Com.	French Com.	Mid. East	Asia	UN — West. Com.	Latin Am.	Communists	Afro-Asia	IO — West. Eur.	Latin Am.	East. Eur.	White Com.	Mid. East	Arabia	S. E. Asia	Handbook — West. Com.	Latin Am.	East. Eur.	Afro-Asia
IO West. Eur.			.88						.83				.99							.85			
Latin Am.	.98	.81								.95				.97							.97		
East. Eur.				.95											.90							.80	
White Com.					.74	.50			.50		.92					.89							
Mid. East							.62																
Arabia																							
S. E. Asia							.62	.58				.88							.80				.80
Handbook West. Com.									.80				.96			.78							
Latin Am.										.97				.97						.96			
East. Eur.			.84		.63						.53				.97							.83	
Afro-Asia			.74		.67	.90	.66				.88	.62				.80	.86	.87	.76	.78			.60
Geography West. Hem.	.99								.99	.95			.92	.97		.96				.78	.96		.69
Europe		.85		.93								.98	.96		.97	.80				.60			
Asia							.65	.94				.98				.88	.50	.98	.75	.83			
Africa																	.56	.67	.94			.56	

structed bonds over the past two decades, with the result that there is now a total of about ten nations who consistently are clustered together. No doubt this unity has its limits and cannot uncritically be projected into a probability of political unification—past difficulties between France and her partners surely are not simply passing squabbles. No doubt too the degree of integration is higher for the Six of the Common Market than it is between them and the states on their fringes—Denmark, Switzerland, Austria, and the United Kingdom—which go to make up the ten countries mentioned. But even allowing for both these weaknesses, Western Europe makes up the largest aggregate of states which group together in the entire world. No other area can claim so many states joined by even the network which cements the most separate of the ten.

Nor is there likely to be any such group within the next few decades. In every instance in the preceding chapters where we had information on the agreement of clusterings over time, we dwelt at length on their stability and continuity (indices of agreement exceeding 0.90 for all the ten-year comparisons).[7] The cases where trade, organizational memberships, or even voting behavior changed radically were few indeed. This vividly illustrates what we should already know, that the growth of such ties is a slow process of accretion, not something that can be expected to occur over the course of only a few years. Political integration must be built up bit by bit, as the achievement of one bond creates the possibility of constructing another. If Western Europe still has far to go, other areas of the world have a yet longer road before them. It will be many years before even Western Europe's limited present achievement is surpassed elsewhere.

Neither does there seem to be much prospect for the re-integration of the two areas where the most notable fault-lines have appeared in recent years. The differences between the Soviet Union and Eastern Europe on the one hand, and mainland China on the other, are numerous and profound. They are very likely to continue to pursue divergent policies, with at best a limited military alliance or tacit agreement for defense *in extremis.* Similarly if less drastically, the divisions in the Atlantic Alliance have become somewhat more pronounced, and are reflected not merely in the political behavior of France or a few other European countries, but in some of the background conditions as well.

[7] Incidentally, this finding of very high continuity argues strongly for the basic accuracy and reliability of the data used in the analyses. Whatever difficulties in measurement, reporting, and recording doubtlessly exist, these indices of agreement, for data gathered independently, greatly circumscribe the problems of data error which must worry us.

12

CONFLICT AND INTEGRATION

LEVELS OF REGIONAL ACCOMPLISHMENT

SO FAR WE HAVE CONCENTRATED ON DISCOVERING AREAS of the world where countries shared such attributes as economic interdependence, similar social and cultural characteristics, or similar political orientations. We have assumed that these had something to do with the political behavior of countries toward each other, since so much of the conventional wisdom of international relations asserts that they do make a difference. Yet although we defined political integration as a favorable ratio of loads to capabilities which results in responsiveness, we have produced no *measures* of integration that might be matched against the attributes which are supposed to affect it.

At the beginning of the book we set as our goal the mapping of the geographic distribution of these attributes and, where possible, the discovery of how they influenced and reinforced each other. A worldwide empirical study of how they affect responsiveness is beyond the scope of the book, and must be built up from more intensive and detailed study of single regions or even single pairs of countries. Responsiveness is a difficult phenomenon to measure reliably at the level of international politics, and I devoted an entire previous volume (Russett, 1963) to trying to do so for just the United States and Britain and relate the results to a study of their apparent causes. Even there it was far easier to measure the variables which are supposed to influence responsiveness than to get more than a rather gross measure of the dependent variable itself. Accordingly I have not attempted to do so for the macro-analysis of this volume.

Nevertheless we need not resign ourselves entirely to marking time until further research can fill the void; we can at least examine the relation between our clusterings and the frequency of violent conflict. Avoiding war is part of a minimal requirement of responsiveness, and we identified the condition of successful political integration with the ability to work out conflict, with a minimum of violence and without one party always making the important concessions. On the other hand, it must be clear that violent conflict is not simply the opposite of integration, nor its avoidance sufficient evidence that two states are highly integrated. As suggested in the previous statement, conflict may be suppressed by the operation of a relationship where one party dominates the other. Or conflict may be avoided merely because the actions of the nations in question are not relevant or salient to each other (they have nothing to fight about), or by an elaborate process of deterrence, without implying that the parties in question manifest any great ability to respond constructively to each other's needs or to work out solutions to joint problems.

Nor even can we facilely assume that conflict will be eliminated in areas that cluster together by one or more criteria, since capabilities within the group may not be high *absolutely,* but only by comparison with those between group members and outside states.[1] The mere fact that internal bonds exceed inter-group bonds, even to such a degree of consistency that a clearly-defined subsystem emerges, does not necessarily mean that the internal links are numerous enough to suffice for high integration. An attempt to promote integration that proceeded not by fostering *intra*-group bonds, but merely by cutting *inter*-group ties, could not succeed. Several important empirical questions are thus involved in asking to what extent our clusterings are associated with the avoidance of violence.

For some of the bonds discussed in the book it is not easy to devise satisfactory measures of their density within groups, but for two of them relatively simple indices are readily at hand. A count of the number of international organizations which include the members of the group is one, on the assumption that capabilities tend to be directly associated with the number of co-memberships. To measure economic interdependence a slightly more complex indicator is required; it is directly analogous to that used in chapters eight and nine, the ratio of intra-regional trade in 1963 to the Gross Domestic Product of the nations in the region. Table 12.1 presents this information for six major areas.[2] The subsequent discussion evaluates the achievements only in terms of the capabilities considered in this volume. It does not substitute for a definitive statement about each area, such as might be made from detailed regional analyses of the patterns of these and other relevant variables, but does point up striking and notable conditions.

---

[1] Nor would I deny that conflict within a group, even in violent forms, can sometimes contribute to its later integration, as by building common norms or settling outstanding disputes (e.g., Coser, 1956). We are concerned here, however, with the *concurrent* relation between conflict and integration.

[2] Trade data from United Nations, 1966a, pp. 398–405; G.D.P. data from United Nations, 1966b, pp. 499–503. Some data are estimated; regions are defined by 1966a. Co-membership data are approximate and refer only to those countries most closely associated with the grouping in chapter six.

TABLE 12.1

Economic and Institutional Bonds Among Nations Within Regional Groups

	Intra-Regional Trade as a Per Cent of G.D.P.	
	1954	*1963*
Western Europe	15	20
Middle East	9	9
Eastern Europe	6	7
Non-communist Asia	9	7
Africa	4	3
Latin America	4	2
	Common International Organization Memberships	
	1951	*1962*
Western Europe	40	75
Latin America	25	42
Middle East	12	35
Non-communist Asia	10	30
Eastern Europe	14	28
Africa*	—	15-25

* Not enough states independent in 1951; the first 1962 figures apply to the former French Africans and the second to former British East Africa.

Most impressive is the performance of *Western Europe* (including the British Isles) which, even in the early 1950's and without the slightest doubt by 1963, stands far above any other group on both criteria. European trade and institutions have an enormous impact on the international politics of the area. On the less easily measured dimensions too Western Europe performs well. One can talk about a common Western culture that, despite its differences from state to state, clearly is unmatched for homogeneity in any other major region. Democratic attitudes have slowly become more entrenched in most of the states that had totalitarian governments before World War II. Despite the dangers to it, the prospects for democracy now look far better in West Germany and Italy than they did 20 years ago, and even Spain is slowly liberalizing.

Rather surprisingly, the second best record on trade, and the third on international institution-building, is recorded for the *Middle East*. Combined with what would appear to be a relatively high degree of cultural homogeneity, this may to some extent soften the rather negative conclusions on the prospects for Arab unity expressed in the previous chapter. Nevertheless the political divisions between radicals and monarchies in the area are, as we noted, still deep and far-reaching, preventing common action even

on matters of such salience and surface agreement as the common enemy
Israel. Furthermore, the pattern of economic interdependence is not uniform,
with the Maghreb states rather cut off from the others. Some of this, however, and especially the political division, may ease if the political life-span
of the Middle Eastern kings proves to be short. (*Uneasy lies the head* . . .)

Latin America has built up substantial capabilities and ranks second
by one criterion (international organizations), but looks very bad by the
other (intra-group trade). Trade within the region, never substantial, has
in recent years swelled only slightly in total dollar value and has fallen far
behind the growth in total income. Impressionistically one would' probably
say that cultural homogeneity is moderate. Due to severe differences in
income between say, Argentina and Central America, and the importance
in many areas of Indian or mestizo cultures despite a Spanish overlay in the
cities, cultural uniformity is perhaps less than in Europe, but surely greater
than in other parts of the *tiers monde*. In international politics the Latin
American countries split more than do the Europeans, but not nearly to the
extent that regularly occurs in Asia.

Within *Eastern Europe* on the other hand the number of international
organizations remains low even despite a doubling over the decade, but
intra-regional trade is fairly high, namely about 7 per cent of G.D.P. (and
more than twice as high if the autarchic Soviet Union is not counted). This
is rather surprising in light of the virtual self-sufficiency imposed on the
Soviet bloc during the Stalin era, and the substantial reaching out to the
non-communist world that resulted from easing restrictions in the late 1950's.
One might have expected that the new trade with capitalist nations would
come at the expense of commerce within Eastern Europe, but in fact both
have grown greatly. Only here and in Western Europe has intra-regional
trade grown faster than income. A substantial degree of homogeneity of
political and social attitudes probably has also developed in Eastern Europe,
where by now the majority of the populace accepts a major element of state
ownership and economic control (though not necessarily with the current
political controls). The relationship between the Soviet Union and these
countries is now based more on consensus and common interests than it was
two decades ago, when naked force and suppression were much more evident.

The record of non-communist *Asia* is in both aspects of the table only
average or below, despite a rather rapid growth in Asian institutions. In the
previous chapter we noted the political divisions among the nations in that
part of the globe; the degree of social and cultural homogeneity is also, by
any criterion, slight indeed. Within Western Europe by contrast the same
alphabet and related languages are employed, religious differences among
Protestants, Catholics, and even agnostics educated in the Judeo-Christian
tradition are less deep, and political cultures are, except for Iberia, not so

terribly different across the non-communist part of the continent. By this standard the Asians have far to go. Perhaps one of the major subgroups has close enough bonds to form the nucleus for notable achievement in the foreseeable future—the degree of cooperation between Thailand and Malaysia, for example, is already substantial—but it seems extremely unlikely that it will take the form of supranational institutions or extend across a very wide area.

The emergence of a stable Asian or Southeast Asian grouping, capable of containing Communist China without substantial assistance from the United States, also appears unlikely. Any such grouping, to be successful, would have to include most of Southeast Asia and either India or Japan, and by far would be most effective if both the latter were involved. Some small indications of greater Japanese involvement in Southeast Asia ar becoming evident, as in the recent decision to form an Asia and Pacific Council (ASPAC) but these are at a level probably below the bare minimum needed to sustain a coalition for long, and there are very few Indian-Japanese bonds. Some things, perhaps on the order of cooperation for economic development, can be accomplished from such a base, but it is hardly a propitious foundation for long withstanding the strains that a military alliance against a strong neighboring power would inevitably impose.

Finally, with the least imposing record overall, is ex-colonial *Africa*. In addition to these low levels of accomplishment, it is easy enough to list other real and powerful divisive forces in Africa—differences of language, tribe, political values, income levels, westernization, and religion, to name only some of the most salient. These differences were certainly great enough to prevent the maintenance of colonial-imposed unity after independence, as in the case of such efforts as the Mali Federation (Foltz, 1965). Yet in the previous chapter we did find a notable degree of congruence among the various regional criteria, especially in the former French African areas. While we cannot eliminate the possibility that the similar clusterings found are merely the result of past political unification in the colonial empire, rather than a portent for the future or even just a now obsolete phenomenon that cannot be long maintained at the present level, there are several straws in the wind suggesting that something in addition to a carryover from the past is at work.

One involves the distinctive character of the trade pattern arising from colonial rule. The amount of intra-regional trade overall is higher than in Latin America. And more than is typical in an empire, there was a fair amount of trade among the French colonies, just as between the colonies and the metropolitan country. This provides a base of mutual interaction that can have important consequences in future politics. Another involves consideration of the Mali Federation's failure. Mali is, with Guinea, the only sub-Saharan former French territory that did not vote with the Brazza-ville group, and furthermore it was near the very bottom of the list of states with organizational ties that we identified as Former French Africans. In other words, the failure of the Mali Federation (of Mali and Senegal) is not a failure of one of the abstractly most promising efforts at West African unity, but rather of one that contained, from the beginning, some special handicaps that may not have counterparts in other less ambitious attempts to promote integration.

With this basic information about the levels of integrative capabilities in various clusters in hand, let us turn to examine data on the frequency of violence in different areas. We shall first look at the relation of inter-national conflict to countries' presence or absence in particular *kinds* of groups (trade, international organization, etc.) and then develop a more complete explanation by relating conflict to the *level* of capabilities achieved.

SALIENCE AND WAR

Of the countries which have been involved in conflict since the end of World War II, 41 pairs have engaged in one or more wars, battles, or skirmishes that left at least an estimated 100 men dead on both sides com-bined. We can look at these pairs to discover whether the two countries clustered together by one of the criteria posed in earlier chapters. The pairs include both wars among independent states and a large number of colonial wars. Table 12.1 lists the pairs which have fought, with their characteristics. The listing includes only wars between troops or para-military forces of states which have concerned us in this book; Portugal-Angola, for instance, is not listed since we have not been able to get enough data on Angola to discuss it elsewhere. Actions carried out under the aegis of international forces of the United Nations or OAS are excluded except for the United States, which initiated the interventions in Korea and the Dominican Re-public. The 100 death cut-off mark is arbitrary and often the evidence concerning casualty lists is incomplete or ambiguous. Yet the threshold is high enough to exclude trivial incidents like border shootings, overflights by military aircraft, and "accidents," and also high enough to give us confidence that all such events were at least reported in the world's news media. For much lower casualty totals, especially between remote or politi-cally unimportant states, the clashes are not always recorded.

The total figures at the end of the table show first the percentage of warring pairs that shared membership in the same cluster by each criterion. Below that is the percentage of *all* pairs that shared membership in the same cluster in the 1960's, for comparative purposes. The latter is an "expected" value, equivalent to the percentage of all warring pairs that

TABLE 12.2

Pairs of Countries Involved in Conflict Resulting in Over 100 Battle-Related Fatalities, 1946–65, With Data on Cluster Memberships

Countries and Year(s) of Conflict	Both Were Members of Same Cluster For:				
	IO	Geog	Trade	SC	UN
†U.K.-Malaya Guerillas, 1946–56	X		X		
†Netherlands-Indonesia, 1946–49	X		X		
†France-Vietnam Guerillas, 1946–54			X	*	0
†India-Pakistan, 1947–49; 1950–54; 1965	X	X	X	X	
Israel-Egypt, 1947–49; 1956		X			
Israel-Jordan, 1947–49; 1953		X			
Israel-Lebanon, 1947–49		X			
Israel-Iraq, 1947–49		X			
Israel-Syria, 1947–49; 1962–63	X	X			
France-Madagascar, 1947–48			X	*	
†South Korea-China, 1950–53		X		*	
†U.S.-China, 1950–53					*
France-Tunisia, 1952, 1961		X	X		
†U.K.-Kenya Mau-Mau, 1952–55			X	*	*
France-Morocco, 1952–56		X	X		
†France-Algeria, 1954–62		X	X		
China-Taiwan, 1954–56; 1958		X			*
U.K.-Cyprus, 1955–59		X			
France-Cameroun, 1956–58			X	*	
France-Egypt, 1956		X	X		
U.K.-Egypt, 1956		X	X		
U.K.-Yemen, 1956–60				*	
†U.S.S.R.-Hungary, 1956	X	X	X	X	X
Spain-Morocco, 1958		X	X		
U.S.-Lebanon Rebels, 1958					
Dominican Rep.-Cuba, 1959	X	X		X	X
Belgium-Congo, 1960–63			X	*	
Ethiopia-Somalia, 1960–61; 1963–64		X		X*	X
†U.S.-Vietnam Guerillas, 1961–65			X	*	0
Egypt-Syria Rebels, 1961–62	X	X	X	X	X
U.S.-Cuba, 1961	X	X			
†India-China, 1962		X			
Saudi Arabia-Yemen, 1962–65				X*	
Egypt-Saudi Arabia, 1962–65	X	X	X	X*	
Egypt-Yemen, 1962–65				X*	X
Algeria-Morocco, 1963–64	X	X	X	X	X
. Malaysia-Indonesia, 1963–65	X	X	X	X	
U.K.-Indonesia, 1964–65	X		X		
Turkey-Cyprus, 1964		X			
U.S.-Laos Guerillas, 1965			X	*	
U.S.-Dominican Rep. Rebels, 1965	X	X			0

		Countries and Year(s) of Conflict			
	IO	Geog	Trade	SC	UN
Percentage of all *warring* pairs that shared membership in the same cluster	32%	63%	53%	24%	16%
Percentage of *all* pairs that shared membership in the same cluster in 1960's	14%	26%	25%	21%	16%

CODE:

X = Countries belonged to the same groupings.

Blank = Countries belonged to different groupings, or to none.

* = One country not included in the analysis of the relevant previous chapter, but its presence or absence in the same grouping as the other country was estimated.

0 = One country not included in the relevant analysis of a previous chapter; data insufficient for estimation.

† = Combined battle deaths for pair probably exceeded 5,000. *This* total does not include cases where deaths were primarily between internal belligerents even though a foreign power was involved (e.g., Congo).

Source: Report prepared by Office of National Security Studies, Bendix Systems Division, Ann Arbor, Michigan, 1966.

Membership in clusters was assessed according to the analysis for the year closest to that of the conflict. If one country was included in the more recent, but not the earlier, analysis, the more recent one was used regardless of conflict date. If there were two separate conflicts several years apart, necessitating examination of clusters for both the 1950's and the 1960's (e.g., Israel-Syria) membership in the same cluster·for either year resulted in the entry of an X. In the case of conflicts involving more than two countries, all opposing pairs were listed even if a particular pair might not have suffered 100 war deaths.

would belong to the same grouping if the groupings were totally irrelevant to the probabilities that two states would fight each other. This second row of percentages is not a perfect baseline, since some of the clusterings above are assessed for the 1950's rather than the 1960's, but it provides an approximate figure for comparison.

Overall, *none* of the five characteristics—clustering by common institutional membership, proximity, economic interdependence, socio-cultural similarity, or similarity of UN voting behavior—in itself makes war between two countries *less* likely. This unexpected finding emerges unmistakably at the bottom of the table. At best, cultural similarity and voting behavior make essentially no difference in the probability of conflict; countries that cluster together by these last two criteria are neither less nor much more likely than other states to fight each other. But countries belonging to the same groupings by organizational membership, proximity, or trade are more than *twice* as likely to fight than are nations which belong to different groups, or to none. Clearly the conventional wisdom which asserts that political institutions always bring an end to war, or that "Good trade insures good will," (Leech, 1959, p. 142, quoting the author of the McKinley Tariff!) is very mistaken. None of these relations is sufficient to prevent war.

In fact, the point can be made very much more strongly—common grouping by all of these five conditions *together* is not sufficient to prevent war. Three of the 41 pairs of countries in the above table of warring states actually belonged to the same cluster by all the criteria (U.S.S.R.-Hungary, Egypt-Syria, and Algeria-Morocco). And not only did membership in the same cluster even for all five characteristics fail to prevent war, states that shared such memberships were very much more likely to fight. No more than 3 per cent of all the pairs of states examined in this book belong to the same groupings by all five criteria, even when some estimations are made for cases where the data are incomplete. But 3 of 41 is approximately 7 per cent: such nations are *more than twice as likely to fight*. All five of these conditions may be necessary to prevent war between states that are salient to each other, but not even all five together are sufficient to do so.

This finding demands a reformulation of some assumptions about international integration and conflict. While few writers would, if pressed, maintain that these are the only conditions relevant to the problem, and none has actually produced an exhaustive checklist of conditions, these nevertheless come up repeatedly in the great majority of existing theoretical and empirical studies. Since grouping according to these conditions is not an adequate explanation we need to go back to our theoretical generators and testing-grounds.

Previous efforts are of course not wholly devoid of virtue, and to a substantial extent the findings could have been anticipated or can be explained in retrospect. At the very least, while the above associations are valuable for showing that the characteristics do not prevent war they surely do not establish that they *cause* war. The fact that they are associated with violent conflict may merely be spurious, the result of some third influence. Nor are we so helpless as to be left only with these gross findings; a closer look at the results shows some further interesting patterns. For example, countries that fight are *never* associated *only* in clusters defined by socio-cultural characteristics, or by voting behavior, or by both together.[3] This is a much stronger statement than simply that obtained from the gross totals. Countries which share similar socio-cultural patterns, or share similar orientations in world politics, do not fight each other unless they are brought

---

[3] Actually the pairs Egypt-Saudi Arabia and Saudi Arabia-Yemen make a formal exception to this statement, since by marginal differences in the factor loadings Saudi Arabia fell into a different geographical cluster than did the other two. But obviously Saudi Arabia is close to them, and the clusterings should not be applied over-rigidly in this instance.

together by proximity or by economic interdependence. Thus we can rule out the possibility that similarity, by itself, is a cause of war. Not a very profound statement, perhaps, but we can build more on it. For the same is also true of international organization memberships. Despite the fact that in the gross totals countries in the same institutional clusters were more than twice as likely to fight (and several other conflicts were colonial wars, with a territory trying to break an institutional bond with the imperial power), this attribute too is never found alone, nor only in company with socio-cultural and/or behavioral similarities. Again, proximity or interdependence must be added to make a deadly quarrel; the interactions arising from contacts in intergovernmental organizations are not enough. (This does not indicate what the effect of *supranational* institutions would be.)

The same cannot be said for the groupings by geographical proximity or by trade patterns. Each of these is often found as the sole example of common clustering, or often the two are found together without others. Over half the warring pairs of nations shared memberships only in clusters defined by trade and/or geography. These conditions, then, remain as candidates for the role of *cause* in any theory of the origins of international violence. The reasons are not hard to imagine for trade; we mentioned earlier some of the ways that economic exchange might bring burdens to a political relationship if one of the parties felt it was making a bad bargain or being exploited. This is especially likely to happen in a colonial relationship, as evidenced by the fact that of the seven instances in the above table where the conflicting states clustered together only by trade, five are wars between colony and metropolitan power.

Although the statistical relationship between geographical clustering and conflict is much the same as between trade clusterings and conflict, it seems less appropriate to consider proximity a cause of war. Except in some sense for border disputes, countries do not fight each other *because* they are physically close; they merely happen to have the *opportunity* to fight because they are close. Proximity becomes the catalyst. Until this century the barriers of distance were so great that the vast majority of wars took place between near or adjacent states; widely separate states simply could not make their power sufficiently effective on each other's territory for sustained conflict to be feasible.[4] The principal exceptions were for wars between the great industrial colonial powers and their weak colonies-to-be, where the disparity of power was so great that even at half-way around the globe enough remained to permit conquest. With the acquisition of modern

[4] One of the finest theoretical statements of this problem remains that of Boulding (1962) and his treatment of the loss-of-strength gradient. Richardson (1960, p. 177) and Wright (1942, p. 1477) also consider the positive relation between propinquity and war.

equipment for rapid transportation and communication in the twentieth century, great powers have found themselves able to fight even each other over great distances, but the smaller nations have yet to reach this happy state of affairs. Save for the colonial wars and the United States-China conflict in Korea, all the battles in Table 12.1 were fought between states which were near each other. Proximity is not a cause of war, but it makes nations salient to each other, providing them with issues over which they can fight if other capabilities are low and with the opportunity to make their power felt on each other's territory.[5]

A re-examination of theories of international conflict and of international integration must begin with the understanding that war is not eliminated within the groupings delineated by the variables examined in this volume; those clusterings do not guarantee a high level of responsiveness, but merely show some possibilities for it. Some variables, such as similarity of social and cultural attributes, or of political orientation, may make the peaceful resolution of conflict more likely or at least do not prejudice the case. In terms of our formulation about loads and capabilities, they bring more of the latter. Most of the theoretical considerations of the problem agree with this statement. On theoretical grounds one can think of reasons why institutions might create serious loads, and we discussed some of these earlier in the book. But the empirical evidence of this chapter indicates that international organizations bring at least as many capabilities. Clustering by common membership *alone* does not delineate an area where the probability of war is greater than average. At the same time common memberships seem not to bring many *extra* capabilities for dealing with loads other than the ones immediately concerned—overall they do not *lower* the probabilities of violence between participating states.

Other variables may, under the wrong circumstances, actually be associated with an increase in the likelihood of violence. Trade may not itself bring major loads under all conditions, but it is frequently somehow *associated* with them. The countries that are heavily interdependent economically often have a number of common problems which can give rise to conflict; trade brings a salience that may, while creating capabilities, also make loads. Geographical proximity is also associated with loads such as border disputes (one cannot accurately say that it *causes* those difficulties) and often makes wars possible by bringing nations within range of each other's effective power. *Two general classes of war can be distinguished*. One is that between dissimilar states, who fight because certain loads arise on their relationships even if they are not physically near each other or economically interdependent. The other is between states who share organizational memberships or similar socio-cultural attributes or political orienta-

---

[5] Note Quincy Wright's (1955, p. 566) proposition from his field theory: if psychic distances diminish less rapidly than strategic distances, war will occur.

tions. These nations fight *only* if their relationship is complicated by loads associated with proximity or relative interdependence.[6]

CLUSTERINGS AND THE LEVEL OF CAPABILITIES

Another and even more important point returns to the concern about the *level* of capabilities available to deal with the loads put upon them. Generally the evidence indicates that conflict *is* related to the growth of capabilities for integration, but *not* in any linear or other simple way. When capabilities—and hence the mutual salience of two countries—are very low, violent conflict is likely to be absent. When capabilities and salience are moderate and narrowly focused, conflict may be quite common. But when capabilities are numerous and varied, the relationship is seldom marked by violence. If the pattern of adjustment and responsiveness proves to be a reciprocal one, we can also say that integration is high. Any *one* carrier of capability brings its peculiar burdens as well as capabilities. (This is perhaps especially true of trade and proximity, but not only of them.) These burdens are likely to be specific to particular interests in the political system, and need to be counteracted by rewarding relationships associated with capabilities attached to other points in the system. To insure a broad coverage so that capabilities will affect substantially the entire political system requires various *types* of ties, not just a few intense ones.

Study of the region-by-region pattern of violent conflict helps clarify matters. Not one of the 41 conflicts occurred either in Western Europe or its immediate fringes. The closest were the two involving Cyprus, and by most criteria Cyprus is outside the group identified with Western Europe. On a number of counts we suggested that Western Europe comprises the most tightly knit group of nations-states on earth. Thanks in large part to the achievements of recent years, Western Europe has emerged not only as a separate area which can in a number of respects be distinguished from other areas, but one where internal bonds, of the sort that promote political integration, have been built up with some success.

The Communist countries have done almost as well at eliminating international conflict among their number; only the U.S.S.R.-Hungary clash of 1956 appears. Partly this may be due to the hopeless disparity in military power between an East European country and the Soviet Union (though that did not dissuade the Hungarians), and part too is surely traceable to the efficient use of military and police power to suppress nascent violence. Yet some real capabilities for mitigating conflict must be present as well.[7]

---

[6] It must be noted that many clashes between dissimilar countries are colonial or counter-insurgency wars between a Western state and unofficial groups within the smaller nation. This set may have to be analyzed separately.

[7] Once more, I do not necessarily equate a rise in capabilities with the political control that the superpowers exert over their allies. The exceptions are much too

The Latin American nations also have exhibited little international war since 1945, only one of any size. Since there are more than twice as many Latin American as East European states, this is an even more creditable performance. Latin America exhibited an unimpressive degree of intra-regional trade, but numerous institutional bonds; the Eastern European countries have not formed a large number of local international organizations, but do carry on a higher than average volume of trade among themselves. Furthermore both groups, and especially the East Europeans, are relatively homogeneous politically and culturally. Apparently this homogeneity counts for a good deal, as indeed was indicated by the findings of the previous section.

In areas lacking these bonds the frequency of violent international conflict is substantially greater. Asia and Africa ranked quite low on most or all of the measures of integrative capability. Conflicts between African states have not been common, but since most of the countries have been independent only since 1960 that is not yet very impressive. Wars between pairs of Asian nations, however, have been quite frequent (5), as have conflicts between Arab countries (5). Apparently the volume of trade and the number of international organizations in the latter area are insufficient to compensate for the differences of political outlook. Finally, wars fought across regions have been very common (27).

Our clusters alone, therefore, do not tell us where integration has been or will be achieved; they merely tell us that for countries within a grouping the capabilities are higher than between a typical country within the group and one outside of it. After a cluster has been identified we must look at the level of capabilities reached before we can begin to know whether sufficient integration exists to reduce the probability of war. Expressed in terms of a probabilistic theory, we can now say that the probability of violent conflict in Western Europe is extremely low, that war is moderately unlikely in Eastern Europe and Latin America, and much more likely within and between other areas of the world.

AN END TO REGIONAL WARS?

On reflection, some extraordinary achievements can be discerned in the first of the above areas. Thirty years ago the countries of Western Europe were involved in numerous wars or threats of war, not just those of France, Germany, and Britain, but Italy and Spain as well. But there has been *no* international violence within the area in more than two decades now, and for some time there has even been *no* serious *expectation* of war or prepara-

---

obvious. It is nonetheless probable that integration, in the mutual responsiveness sense used here, has been inversely related to the imposition of centralized control; e.g., that Eastern Europe is more politically integrated now than under Stalin.

tion for it. A mere ten years ago one could not say with confidence that France and Germany, or perhaps France and Spain, would never fight. We can more readily say so now, and none of these states even takes military precautions against the possibility.[8] Something of utmost importance has occurred in the attitudes and expectations of the peoples of Western Europe, an occurrence that has not been sufficiently widely appreciated or studied with sufficient care.

With more reservations, similar conclusions apply to Latin America and to Eastern Europe. The Western Hemisphere experienced some terribly bitter conflicts in the period between the World Wars, including the bloody Chaco War and a most severe struggle between Haiti and the Dominican Republic. In the late 1940's there was no war, but serious fears were aroused of Argentine expansionism under Peron. But since then there has been but one brief conflict in Central America and, in effect, the virtual cessation of preparations for wars among Latin American countries—the threat from (or to) communist Cuba excepted. Eastern Europe in the 1930's was marked by repeated instances of territorial aggrandizement by Poland against the Baltic states, Hungary against Czechoslovakia and Rumania, Bulgaria against Romania, and others, with innumerable more threats of war and preparations for it. Again there have been no recent wars in the area, and a great abatement of fears of war within Eastern Europe, despite the ingrained hostilities among many of its peoples. This is the least convincing case, since much of this pacific behavior may be due only to the Soviet Union's peacekeeping "presence," and the possibilities of war between Russia and one or more of the smaller states cannot be discounted. But even here something impressive has happened.

An easy explanation is simply that these countries, in Western Europe, Eastern Europe, and Latin America, have stopped fighting among themselves because of the danger of war *between regions,* especially as aspects of the cold war. This explanation is least plausible for Latin America, which is far enough removed from the center of East-West conflict to be free of most of the unifying pressures allegedly produced by an external threat. For the two halves of Europe it works better, and the common danger undoubtedly was largely responsible for the original efforts to bury hatchets. But with the expectations of peaceful change now established, the correlation between external threat and lack of internal violence vanishes. The common danger hypothesis in simple form would have us expect that as the threat passes the risk of intra-regional war would return. Yet recent years have seen precisely the opposite. Just as the danger of a Soviet attack on the West has receded, we can more surely say that the probabilities of a Franco-

[8] The Franco-German case is still not clear. Though I see little evidence for the opinion, a few observers hold that the French desire for an independent nuclear force derives as much from a fear of (a possibly reunified) Germany as of Russia.

German war have faded toward the vanishing point. The last decade has witnessed a reduction of the danger of violent conflict both within and between the halves of the European continent. Some intra-regional disagreements and major conflicts of interest remain, and indeed have been exacerbated by changes in the international system, but within Europe we are more confident than ever that such divisions will not lead to a state of belligerency.

These developments have some important implications for wider international order. The elimination of intra-European wars would mean that never again will the United States be called upon to settle a conflict on that continent, as in effect happened in the two World Wars. Furthermore, the absence of war among the states of Western Europe and Latin America would eliminate opportunities for extra-regional powers to fish in troubled waters; absence of violent conflict reduces both the need and the temptation for external intervention. And as the Soviet Union and China are denied these chances among Western nations, peace in Eastern Europe would remove any similar temptation for the United States. While some Americans may regret the loss, considering its risks it probably would be an opportunity well foregone. In other parts of the world, however, and including most of Asia and Africa, the prospects are for more conflict and new wars among the member states. The invitation, and sometimes the necessity, for outside intervention is almost sure to remain for a long time to come.

Before leaving this topic one further observation must be made about our findings. Very *major* wars involving over 5000 fatalities between states that cluster together by all five of the specified criteria are rare. In fact, of 11 such international conflicts since World War II, only one, the Hungarian revolt against a communist government and the Soviet Union, involved countries that shared membership in all types of groupings. And that, of course, was the case of a state which had been brought into a grouping essentially by military force and whose people were trying to extricate themselves, to reduce their association with the other power. The other two conflicts between countries joined together in all clusters were, for Algeria-Morocco, hardly more than a brief border clash, and, in the case of Egypt-Syria, a secession that was not vigorously resisted. The superior partner chose, for the sake of future relations, not to bring all its power to bear. In situations where military coercion is not a primary centripetal force, therefore, belonging to the same "all-purpose" region may well provide the capabilities for containing violence if not for avoiding it. In this way, where our clusterings coincide they create responsiveness in the sense of capabilities at least for limiting conflict even when the within-group bonds are not numerous enough to prevent it. Should groups of countries become more closely linked by the bonds we have been examining, wars within those clusters may become less severe as well as less frequent.

13

SOME PROBLEMS OF PRIORITY AND CAUSATION

CAUSAL PATTERNS AND EXCEPTIONS

ONE HOPE WITH WHICH I BEGAN THIS UNDERTAKING HAS been somewhat disappointed: only a little consistent evidence on the question of causation has been uncovered. I had hoped to be able to make some general statements about whether international organization memberships tended to follow or precede heavy trading relationships, whether a shift in trade patterns came before or after a change in political orientation. Such statements about temporal sequence would not lead inexorably to causal conclusions, but coupled with careful theory they could point the way. The relationships in fact found, however, are more complex and less regular than this, and the evidence is sparse and often contradictory.

A straightforward way of approaching the question is to compare our clusters *both* across different criteria and over time. For example, we can match international organization clusters with UN voting groups, not for about the same point in time as in the previous chapter, but making two matches, first for organization clusters in the 1950's with UN voting in the 1960's, and then UN voting in the early 1950's with organizations in the 1960's. The closer fit would tell us which led which. In this case the overall correlation coefficient between the UN analysis for 1952 and the international organization analysis for the 1960's was 0.88, whereas the reverse arrangement (organizations for 1951, UN for the 1960's) was but 0.81. From this it seemed clear that behavior was leading institutions rather than the opposite; countries first came to have similar positions on the major issues of international politics, and *then* joined international organizations in common. The same technique showed that behavior also led commercial ties; the UN analysis for 1952 was closer to the trade study for 1963 (0.84) than the 1954 trade analysis was to UN voting in the 1960's (0.78). But trade is not always in the follower's position; it leads institutional ties. The 1950's trade analysis was slightly closer (0.91) to organizations in 1962 than organizations in 1952 were to trade in the 1960's (0.89). We thus had three simple empirical propositions about sequential relationships during the postwar years: institutions follow behavioral patterns, trade also follows behavior, and institutions follow trade. Putting these together into a neat two-step sequence produces the following: Similar orientations in world politics lead to the growth of trade between countries, and the trade, along with the similar political outlooks, leads on to the growth of international organizations which bind the nations together in a formal manner.

Plenty of anecdotal evidence can be produced to support the conclusion. We could spin out a tale of how the countries of continental Western Europe discovered after World War II that they had a number of important common interests as regards the cold war, reconstruction, relations with the United States, and economic relations with the underdeveloped world. The common outlook and consequent ease of communication among their citizenry led to increased commercial intercourse, as buyers preferred goods from other European countries to those from abroad, and European sellers learned how to meet the needs of European buyers. And the economic transactions led to the need for certain controls and regulations to achieve greater mutual advantage from the exchange, to create channels for increasing the trade as it was seen to be mutually beneficial, and from there, via "spill-over" effects, to the creation of other institutions to handle related problems as they arose.

Sticking more closely to the data of this volume, we note that some of the most dramatic shifts of the postwar period follow essentially this sequential pattern. Cuba's economic channels were routed to Eastern Europe by 1963 and it behaved like a thoroughly communist country in that Session of the General Assembly. But its pattern of institutional ties had not changed so drastically. Many of its bonds with the Western Hemisphere had been severed, but it had not yet joined many communist area organizations.[1] Likewise, when Yugoslavia left the communist bloc in the late 1940's this was quickly evident in its trade and UN behavior, but it still clustered, albeit marginally, with the Eastern Europe international organization group in 1951.[2] In the 1960's it had partially returned to the Eastern international trade fold, but *not,* as the above sequence suggests, in its UN voting habits. Still another example fitting the model is Japan, whose trade and UN

[1] *Partly* this may be because at the time data were collected we had to settle for international organization information for 1962, a year earlier than the others. Also, communist party ties across nations are very important, and they do not show up here.

[2] Our trade data are of course for 1954, three years after the international organization material. A look at the raw information for previous years shows conclusively, however, that Yugoslavia's economic isolation from Eastern Europe was firmly established by 1951. In fact, 1954 was the *last* year before Belgrade's eastern trade began to recover.

behavior identified it with the North Atlantic countries before it had joined many of the Western international organizations.

But there are serious difficulties with this accumulation of examples. We have illustrations that behavioral changes presage institutional and trade shifts, but not about which of the latter has precedence. Even while discussing them we have had to make qualifications and hedges. Especially during the discussion of the EEC area we did not prove cause, but merely spun out some comments about sequence with some half-hidden causal inferences slipped in. The theory is not adequate, as it fails to tell us *how* they got from the common outlook to the heavy trade, for instance. These are not insuperable problems. If rigorous theoretical hypotheses about such causal relationships are not exactly common in the literature of international integration, neither are they totally absent from that body of writing nor from social science more generally. And while we can never *prove* causation, and there are special problems in trying to infer causation under the messy conditions of observing international politics, in principle some highly plausible assertions can still be made in combination with the *elimination* of certain other causal possibilities.[3]

By far the most serious qualification regards the ease with which one can come up with counter-examples. Our sequential statements may hold more often than they fail to, but not very much more often Albania in the 1950's was not tightly bound to Eastern Europe, either by trade or institutional links. These gaps presaged its behavioral independence, not the other way around as above. And if we take Albania's UN behavior as a surrogate for China's, the Peking government also fits this pattern. For these cases it would nonetheless be wrong to say that they contradict the sequential pattern first established, since the trade and institutional ties were *never* strong; it is not a matter of their *shifting* and leading to a subsequent change

[3] The path-breaking labor on mathematical techniques for inferring causal relationships in non-experimental research was done by Herbert Simon (1957), pp. 37–49, and refined, developed, and hedged about with the appropriate cautions by the important work of Hubert Blalock (1962, 1964). As Blalock carefully warns, these methods are still very much in the developmental stage, but could under the right conditions be extremely useful with the kind of correlational results given in this book. Unfortunately my data fit insufficiently with the assumptions one has to make to avoid a high risk of erroneous conclusions. The most serious problem stems from the requirement that the independent variables one is using as possible causes in the model not be too highly intercorrelated. But as must be fully apparent impressionistically, and as we shall document below, the correlations among all the variables (clusterings by trade, geography, etc.) here are very high, usually above .80. When the correlations are this high it becomes extremely difficult, due to inevitable "sampling" error (how much would the correlation change by adding ten more countries?) and measurement error, to choose reliably between alternative causal models. Cf. Blalock (1964), p. 89, noting that the correlations in his example of "too high" are lower than ours.

in behavior. Yet if we look for examples of true leads, the search is not a difficult one. The Philippines clustered with Southeast Asia on international organizations; it became less marginal in later years by the trade criterion, and has slowly shifted from a Western Community position in the United Nations to one that involves greater association with the Afro-Asians on colonial and other rich-poor issues.

There are also examples of this kind of movement including entire groups. Still staying with the data of the book, even the EEC example looks questionable. There was a discernible shift toward a faster tightening of the Western European grouping at the expense of a broader Western Community one in both the international organization and trade analyses, but this has not yet even been *followed* by a shift in UN voting. (According to the above it should have been preceded by the behavioral change.) Just the same is true of the better differentiation of an Arab group that has showed up in trade and institutions, but still not in General Assembly behavior. Israel has begun increasingly to run with the Western Europeans in commerce and institutions, but is not more closely allied with them in the UN. And as far as we can tell from our data, the movement toward greater integration in Central America has come virtually simultaneously on all three fronts. Going a bit beyond this immediate set of data, as we did briefly at the close of chapter nine, produces still more counter-examples.

The situation is not much better when we try to infer a general causal relation between socio-cultural similarity and other characteristics. The *Handbook* analysis could be performed for only one time, but that is roughly in the middle (late 1950's) of the entire span under scrutiny so there is a possibility of finding some temporal regularities. Quite often similar *Handbook* profiles predict to (lead) changes in the others. Japan's growing institutional ties with the West, which showed up in 1962 but not in 1951, could have been predicted this way. Again accepting Albania as China's UN substitute, and extrapolating from more general Chinese actions, its behavior too could have been "predicted" by its socio-cultural differences (as well as by its other forms of separateness from the "Sino-Soviet Bloc"). Generally similar but slightly mixed results also come up for Uruguay, where its socio-cultural differences from most of Latin America predict to greater marginality from that area both in institutional ties and in the UN, but *not* trade, and for Israel, where its affinities for Western Europe have led strengthened ties in the trade and institutional spheres, though not in the General Assembly. But just the opposite sequence of events turns up for Yugoslavia (in the *Handbook* analysis it still looked like a Soviet Bloc country, though it did not by the other criteria as far back as the early 1950's), the Philippines (whose socio-cultural similarity to Latin

America trailed behind its otherwise growing involvement with Asia), and Argentina, whose social and cultural resemblance to Europe did not show up on any of the other indices for the 1960's.

In all realism, one cannot expect these procedures to give clearcut and uniform results. We have information on each of the various characteristics for at most two or three points in time. While those periods are sufficiently far apart to leave us very much in the dark about just what occurs in the meantime, they still are so close that in the slow-moving process that characterizes international change we have few very sharp and obvious variations to work with. This is part of the price we pay for our success in finding very high agreement among the clusterings defined by quite different criteria. Analyses spread over several decades doubtless would have produced more variation and more room for examination. Just because there are some regularities for the 1950's and 1960's does not mean that the same temporal or causal relationships applied in earlier eras like the age of empire. Nye (1965b) has concluded from his study of East Africa that the European experience of spill-over from economic transactions to political unification does not occur in conditions of underdevelopment. And surely our analysis is gross, the measures are crude, and they are restricted to certain classes of phenomena and unavoidably miss other aspects and subtleties (though until now this has usually seemed to be a manageable handicap). Further research may be able to refine the investigation appreciably.

CIRCULARITY AND RECIPROCATION

I think the appropriate response is to face squarely the implication that we have indeed found some general regularities to which there are many and important exceptions. While the sequence outlined in the first part of the previous section is the correct one more often than not, there is substantial theoretical reason to believe that the processes can and do frequently work the other way too.

For a colony settled largely by inhabitants of the metropolitan country, as happened in the new world and in Australia, a culture and a political system much like that in the motherland may be maintained for some time even without much current communication. But over the years the characteristics of colonial society will change in response to the peculiarities of the original settlers as they differed from a cross-section of the state from which they came, and in response to local demands and whatever interactions with other societies do spring up. A colonial power is not a punchpress that can stamp out innumerable identical copies either of itself or of some model. A substantial degree of similarity between colony and mother country can nevertheless be maintained if there is a high level of interaction and communication between them.[4] And except by the accident of convergent evolution, similarity between two societies which do not have a common origin can be achieved only by heavy communication and interaction.

On the other hand, similar origins certainly promote communication and interaction (Miller, 1965, p. 402; March and Simon, 1958, pp. 428–29). Overall, a common culture eases communication. Despite Shaw's witticism about the common language and the dangers of taking ease of communication for granted, surely information is transferred more readily between individuals who share similar experiences, outlooks, and cultural patterns than between those who do not. Therefore the causal pattern can and does work either way. Homans (1950, p. 120) states clearly the results of his observations of small groups:

> The more frequently persons interact with one another, the more alike in some respects both their activities and their sentiments tend to become. Moreover, the more a person's activities and sentiments resemble those of others, the more likely it is that interaction between him and others will increase. The process as usual works both ways.

Elsewhere (p. 362) describing the disintegration of Hilltown as a community, he states that the process applies to a descending cycle as well as to an ascending one; a decline in the frequency of interaction leads to a decline in the extent to which norms are common, and vice versa. The same kind of pattern follows for interaction and friendliness, with an important qualification about the symmetry of the relationship: "The more frequently persons interact with one another, when no one of them originates interaction with much greater frequency than the others, the greater is their liking for one another and their feeling of ease in one another's presence" (p. 243). Homans in fact builds his whole theory on a model of reciprocal causation, quoting as his frontispiece Claude Bernard's early description of a homeostatic system:

> The ancient emblem that represents life by the circle formed by a snake biting its tail gives a sufficiently just picture of the state of affairs. In effect, the organization of life in complex organisms does form a closed circle, but one that has a head and a tail, in the sense that all the phenomena of life are not equally important although all take part in the completion of the *circulus* of life. . . . There is in this an organic or social solidarity that keeps up a kind of perpetual motion, until a disturbance or cessation of the action of a necessary vital element shall have broken the equilibrium or brought about a trouble or stoppage in the play of the bodily machine.

[4] Hawley (1950, p. 190) states this well. "In the degree to which the isolation of a unit of territory is complete the occupants acquire a set of responses peculiar to themselves."

Without accepting all of Bernard's (or Homans') analogy between society and the physical organism, it is clear enough that similar possibilities for reciprocal causation exist among the characteristics of international systems identified in this volume. All the phenomena are indeed not equally important, in that some are more often involved in initiating events than others, as we found above. But probably each social element has the capacity to initiate the process under some circumstances, and certainly each plays a crucial role in maintaining it.[5] Naturally it is not a *simultaneous* process of reciprocal causation, although it is sometimes presented that way and it may be difficult or impossible empirically to identify which precedes which. It is in actuality a successive process in which one phenomenon (e.g., interaction) occurs and *then* produces another (e.g., similarity of belief). Finally, I would prefer an explicit concept of an interdependent *system* to that of snake or circle—each phenomenon may directly affect several others, rather than always working in a chain reaction.

We do not have enough information for different points in time to verify this theory directly in the data of this book, but reflection on some of the more obvious changes in interaction and behavior patterns of nations in recent years supports it. For example, one can see it happening between Cuba and the communist countries in the early 1960's. The Havana government's behavior in international politics caused or reinforced hostility in Washington, which in turn cut off much of Cuba's normal trade with the United States, forcing the Cubans to become economically dependent on the communist states, which in turn reinforced belief patterns and behavior favorable to the Soviet Union. Less anecdotally, we have strong—though admittedly not conclusive—evidence of a reciprocal pattern from our own data on the degree to which our various analyses matched others. Below is a table representing a condensation of the information exhibited in Table 11.1; instead of showing the indices of agreement among all clusters it gives the overall correlation between each of our analyses which was conducted for approximately the same point in time. The upper right triangle shows the correlations among studies done for the early 1960's, and the lower left half of the table shows the interrelationships among those done for the early 1950's. The diagonal is left empty since we have presented that information in the earlier chapter.

While the correlations are not as high as we found for comparing the same characteristics over time (they were uniformly over 0.90), the simi-

[5] Similar points of view are exemplified by Hawley's ecological approach, "the world of life as a system of dynamic interdependencies" (1950, p. 3), and Kurt Lewin's (1951) field theory of interdependence. Brian Berry (1967) shares this conception as applied to problems of regional differentiation, and is currently collecting and analyzing data on India which may provide a rigorous test with a mathematical model.

larities are nevertheless quite striking. The average correlation in the entire table is 0.79, meaning that typically almost two-thirds of the variance in the factor pattern of one analysis could be predicted by knowing the factor pattern of the analysis for another criterion performed for about the same time. Note particularly that the lowest correlation for a given analysis is almost always between it and the pattern of geographic proximity. Geographical distance is of course invariant; it alone cannot be changed by social processes. Geography is a physical phenomenon rather than a social one, and while it can act as a cause of social relationships it cannot in turn be caused by them, and so is outside the hypothesized process of reciprocal causation and reinforcement. The fact that it is empirically so imperfectly related to the social phenomena argues powerfully for the existence of a reciprocal and corrective association among the latter.

TABLE 13.1
Overall Correlations Among Factor Analyses

		UN	IO	Hbk	Geog	1960s
		0.84	0.89	0.78	0.83	T
UN	0.86		0.86	0.75	0.44	UN
IO	0.90	0.89		0.82	0.82	IO
Hbk	0.84	0.83	0.83		0.66	Hbk
Geog	0.87	0.64	0.79	0.66		
1950s	T	UN	IO	Hbk		

The low correlation makes another important substantive point that we should note explicitly: geographical distance is a deceptive predictor to clusterings by other criteria. When one looks at the groupings on an impressionistic basis the role of propinquity stands out and seems very important, but its apparent predictive power is rather illusory. It seems powerful only because it is so familiar. We can see the relationship between the groupings and geography because we are so familiar with it. Each of us carries in his head a more or less well-informed image of the geographical relationships among nations; we know it much better, for instance, than we know the detailed patterns of international trade or of international organization memberships. But it is only our ignorance that makes it seem so closely related to the social phenomena. A systematic comparison shows that it is appreciably less closely related to each of the others than they are to themselves; in the 1960's the average correlation between the geographic analysis and the others was more than 0.10 lower than the overall average among the rest of the 1960's analyses. Physical space explains less of international relations than does social space.

EXOGENOUS CHANGE AND EXTERNAL PRESSURES

Often a change will occur in one of the relationships, caused by some event that is essentially exogenous to the interrelationships we have been examining. Cuba's government is overthrown and replaced by one that develops and/or exposes strongly favorable sentiments toward the communist states. The Eastern European states are occupied by the Russian army after World War II and their governments are replaced. Japan regains its sovereignty and is able to pick up many of its former relationships in Asia. Or as in the case of Albania, some behavioral patterns are imposed primarily by force without producing major shifts in all the other patterns, leaving the change incomplete. In each instance an incongruence between the clusterings by one criteria and those of others is created. Forces are then set in motion which will correct the original disturbance, bring the other relationships into line with it, or work out some balance that involves a readjustment both of the one that shifted first and the others as well. There are many discussions of phenomena of this sort in the literature of social science, although systematic studies of the amount of change in one necessary to produce a shift in the other are rare. Very few allow the observer to say whether in fact the original disturbance will be corrected, others will be brought into line, or all will change, and what studies there are apply to such different systems and phenomena from what we have been examining as not to be very informative.

We might at least note the theoretical position of Robert Merton (1957) who discusses at length strains and tensions within systems and the discrepancies among various component elements of social and cultural structure. He sums up his argument (p. 121) with the insight that socially deviant behavior is just as much a product of social structure as is conformist behavior. Possibly of slightly more insight-generating value is Festinger's (1957) theory of cognitive dissonance and some of the empirical work which has followed it (Cf. Brehm and Cohen, 1962). Both Festinger and Osgood and Tannenbaum (1955) have observed that the outcome of an imbalance in attitudes depends upon which evaluation was initially the more firmly rooted, though both of two conflicting attitudes are likely to slip at least a little. Of more direct use perhaps is Festinger's consideration of incongruities between an individual's private attitudes and mere public behavior. He concludes that the most effective way to change both is to offer *just enough* reward or punishment to elicit the overt compliance. An "excessive" reward or threat of punishment may produce the behavioral change but leaves dissonance between it and beliefs. Perhaps this kind of analysis could profitably be applied to explaining Albania's recent change in behavior. Albania may well have been threatened with *too much* punishment, especially out of proportion with the rewards it was receiving. Also, other Eastern European states have received appreciably more rewards, in the form of commercial and institutional ties with other members of the group. The Albanians' trade and organizational bonds with the group have been quite weak, making the entire relationship especially dependent upon the threat of punishment for withdrawal rather than on the rewards of continued membership.

Finally, Festinger and some of the other researchers who have accepted his theory discuss some of the personality characteristics of people who can tolerate substantial degrees of dissonance as compared with those who cannot. While the personality traits are not really relevant to our concern, the question of what kinds of nations can stay for long periods in a position where some of their ties to an area are incongruent with other bonds deserves much attention. Even the simple idea that there may be some variable, other than the bonds themselves, which affects tolerance for incongruity is extremely important. This problem of incongruity is very similar to the idea of "cross-pressures" which we shall develop in more detail in the next chapter. A nation that is linked to one group by some bonds, and to another by different kinds of ties, can be described as cross-pressured, and cross-pressures have long been identified in sociological and political science writings as crucial for the mitigation of conflict. If there is differential influence making some nations readier than others to accept cross-pressures we must investigate it.

Another matter which demands attention is the role of systemic pressures in promoting the integration of groups or subsystems. There has been somewhat more discussion of this problem, again at many different levels of analysis. We can refer again to Homans (1950, pp. 449–50), who notes that a decline in interaction in the external system engaged in by the group leads to a decline in interaction in the internal system, hence to a decline in agreement on norms and, through the descending cycle, to the disintegration of the group. Thus common action vis-a-vis the outside world is a crucial variable. Simon (1957, p. 111) has expressed much of Homans' analysis in mathematical terms, a procedure that has allowed him to deduce some new propositions. For example, he states that the level of activity imposed by the external system that is required to bring the group into existence is greater than the minimum value needed to prevent the group from dissolving once it has been formed. A group can retain its cohesion under less pressure than it took to form it in the first place. Sherif *et al.*'s study (1961) of the behavior of boys at a summer camp showed persuasively the effect of an effort to overcome difficulties imposed from outside as a means of further-ing the integration of the entire group. Common experience of rewarding events was not enough; joint enterprise was necessary.[6]

Many sociologists have worked on aspects of this problem. It is probably unfair to cite only a few, but the comment of Coser (1956, p. 146), "Com-mon values and norms develop in the course of struggling together," is fairly typical. Quincy Wright (1942, vol. 2, p. 1038) concluded part of his massive empirical and theoretical study with the words, "Human communities larger than the primary group have usually been organized by conquest, enlarged by more conquest, and integrated internally through the fear of foreign invasion." And Aron and Lerner (1957) decided that one of the most important reasons for the failure of the French parliament to pass EDC was the apparent diminution in the external threat posed by the Soviet Union and thus a reduction in the need for a tight European coalition. If not supported by underlying bonds an alliance is a fragile thing. Examples such as the American-British-Russian alliance during World War II could be multiplied far beyond their usefulness in the absence of rigorous comparative study. Liska (1962) has a number of valuable observations on the matter.

It would seem that an external threat often serves as a discriminating variable. Where integration is already high, to the point that an external threat is seen by the members of the group as a mutual danger and not a potential ally for one side in internal quarrels, it becomes a force that pro-motes further integration. A common culture frequently promotes mutual identification, a sense of oneness vs. external pressures. If the area is poorly integrated at the time the threat appears, the possibilities of securing such an external ally, or disagreements over priorities and the degree of necessity to cope with the threat, are likely to produce further disintegration. Deutsch *et al.* (1957) concluded essentially this from their comparative study of historical cases, and Simmel (1955, p. 57) states, in a form that is really not terribly helpful: "A state of conflict, however, pulls the members so tightly together and subjects them to such uniform impulse that they either must get completely along with, or completely repel, one another." An im-portant review of the theoretical and empirical literature on this point was undertaken by Robert Hamblin (1958). He also produced limited but persuasive experimental evidence that even with the other necessary condi-tions a crisis or external threat increases a group's integration only if a *co-operative* solution to the crisis can be *perceived*; otherwise the group moves toward disintegration.

On the whole, however, there is little in the available literature that is more than a collection of interesting insights. Very little adequate data

---

[6] Vincent Rock (1964) has tried to apply these findings to produce some sug-gestions for improving United States-Soviet relations.

above the level of small groups can be found. Nor, frankly, has this study contributed much either. There is no clear relation between the apparent relaxation in international pressures, as they have borne both on Eastern Europe and on the Western Alliance, and changes in the interactive, behavioral, or structural data measured here. The relaxation may have something to do with Albania's new independence from the Soviet Union, but certainly Yugoslavia's break in 1948 bore no relation to reduced international tensions. (Possibly it is a case of tensions as the discriminating variable, however, since Tito made his split at the time tensions were increasing.) In point of fact we simply have no systematic information with which to attack the problem. Maybe if our data were carried beyond 1962–1963 into the most recent years, when polycentrism became less mistakable, we would be able to see more than we can here. Much more research is required.

In general, these discussions point up the fact that for a detailed theory of how subsystems are transformed we have many insights but little evidence. Actually, there is good reason to believe that we have identified most of the essential variables from which a rigorous theory of subsystem formation and transformation would be constructed. The high correlations among our variables, both across variables and over time, suggest that we have the makings of a model with substantial power as a probabilistic theory. We even have a number of verbal statements about how the variables are related to one another, and can formulate rigorous hypotheses. These verbal statements could quite well be translated, with a loss of some nuances but with a gain in precision, into mathematical language, much as Simon (1957) has done for the Homans and Festinger models. A set of simultaneous equations is likely to be more useful than simpler cause-and-effect models. But what is much more important now is empirical observation of the processes; the fault is less a lack of mathematical rigor in the theory (though we could certainly use it) than an absence of data. A study in depth of a particular subsystem or approximation thereof, or better a comparative study of two or more subsystems, would allow us to make much more precise statements about the amount of change in one variable that is produced by a given change in another, under what conditions. This requires a detailed examination of data over a rather long period of time. Probably a couple of decades (e.g., essentially the post-war period), with observations taken annually, would be the minimum for making general statements to which we could attach reasonable confidence.

14

REGIONS AND THE FUTURE OF THE GLOBAL SYSTEM

CONGRUENCE AND THE HIERARCHY OF NATURE

SCIENCE GROWS BY A RECIPROCAL AND CUMULATIVE process of hypothesis-formulation and hypothesis-testing. Since this study is not just an exercise in description we have spent the last two chapters testing some hypotheses about conflict and causation, and we must now spell out some more of the hypotheses which motivated the project. A basic one—so basic as not to be very exciting—is actually a null hypothesis: that no significant clusters of countries would be found by any of our various criteria.[1] Clearly we reject the null hypothesis. A more interesting statement, however, was implicit but quite conscious as a result of reading the available literature on regions and regional delineation: that the degree of congruence among the clusters produced inductively by the various criteria would be relatively low; that is, the socio-cultural groupings would not closely resemble the political ones, nor the trade groupings, etc. Although we did not at the outset specify precisely what we meant by relatively low congruence (it might, for instance, have been defined as a particular maximum index of agreement for the relationship between a factor in one study and that in another), and it is never high enough to produce, by a rigorous definition, any international subsystems, the observed congruence is nevertheless in some respects greater than I expected. If we accept as a criterion the statement, "A natural grouping is one which allows the discovery of many more, and more important, resemblances than those originally recognized," (Kaplan, 1964, p. 50) several of our groupings have not performed badly.

The literature on regions and boundaries, which stresses non-congruence, the difficulties of finding agreement among multiple tests, and the hopeless-

[1] "Significant" is here used in the non-technical sense of "meaningful" or "interesting." A rigorous interpretation of statistical significance for this study would require assumptions about random samples and the distribution of values in a universe that cannot be met.

ness of any quest for a universally-accepted definition of a region, is certainly not at all explicit about what is meant by "enough" congruence. No quantitative threshold for accepting two different criteria as giving the "same" results is ever specified. But from reading this material one nevertheless is left with a very strong impression that most writers would not have anticipated quite the degree of congruence uncovered by this study. Howard Odum might have been an exception to this statement, but it was precisely Odum's laborious and brilliant failure to achieve a satisfactory all-purpose delineation of American regions that created or reinforced this attitude in his audience.

If this statement about expectations is accurate not just for the writer but for many other members of the social science guild as well, it is worth asking how the misconception is to be explained. Best, perhaps, by recalling the difference in the level of analysis. Most previous empirical studies have started at the national level, looking beneath it for subgroupings of states, provinces, or districts. Here, of course, we have been searching the international system for subgroups of nation-states. The differences among the component subgroupings of the international system are far greater than those among the states of a nation. Nations are dispersed far more widely in the physical sense, and are bound by no supranational or intergovernmental institutions remotely approaching those of a federal government in strength. So much is obvious, as is the fact that nation-states, whatever their internal diversities, are far more homogeneous politically and culturally than is the world at large. A national government's typical controls over education and communication assure similar socialization processes for all young citizens. In France virtually all schoolchildren of a given age are studying the same lesson on any given day. Only in some federal states like Canada is this authority delegated to large regional sub-units. If we imagine a pair of curves for the distribution of political attitudes in a nation and in the entire international system, that for the world has both a wider range and a less-pronounced central tendency—the curve is flatter.

Much the same is true for economic attributes. The richest 1 per cent of the population of the United States is surely among, and near the top of, the richest 1 per cent of the world's population. But even the poorest 1 per cent of Americans has a higher income than the *average* Indian. The difference in per capita income between Connecticut and Mississippi, the wealthiest and poorest American states respectively, is approximately two to one. Even making quite generous allowances for differences in the domestic purchasing power of national currencies, however, per capita income in the United States exceeds by more than 20 times that of many underdeveloped states in Asia and Africa (Russett *et al.,* 1964, pp. 155–57). Indeed, one of the functions of the nation-state is to develop at least a minimal homogeneity among its citizens. Gunnar Myrdal (1956) has emphasized the role of national governments in equalizing wealth among their citizens while maintaining the differences between them and foreigners. Partly this is a consequence of tariff and other barriers to the movement of goods and factors of production; partly it may result from conscious redistribution among the areas within the country. Federal expenditures for welfare, health, and education are usually designed to return more to poor American states than is extracted from them in taxes. Finally, the relative level of transaction among the states or provinces of a nation is usually much higher than among nations. In all but the smallest countries, a far greater proportion of the goods consumed originate elsewhere in the nation than come from beyond its borders.

Because of the phenomenon of feedback and reciprocal causation discussed previously this is hardly surprising. One process influences another, and we must expect a certain congruence among our various conditions which we have described both as influences on political integration and as criteria for regionalization. The question remains: how *much* congruence and mutual influence?

If a nation-state is relatively homogeneous economically, culturally, and politically, characterized by many institutional bonds at the system (national) level, and marked by a high incidence of transactions among the component subgroupings, *the variance to be explained by regional differences is relatively small*. Thus the effect of the interaction of various influences will be less pronounced. If you build a fire on the hearth of a previously cold and dark house, for a while the contrast between that area and the rest of the dwelling will be marked, and people will be drawn to it for warmth and light as well as for the pleasure of watching the flames. But if the rest of the house is restored to the proper conditions of habitation, piling a couple of logs onto an existing fire will add little to the contrast between the heat and light of the fireplace and the remainder of the house. And while it may continue to attract some of the inhabitants, others will move on to satisfy different needs and desires. In promoting congruence the contrast effect is crucial; the nearer one approaches to homogeneity the less will whatever remains of the variation in one condition (e.g., transactions) be explicable by variation in another (institutions). Some part, and often a very substantial proportion, of trading patterns will always be explicable in terms of economic factors, such as transportation costs, resource patterns, and the complementarity of different producing areas. Some portion of an area's cultural heterogeneity will be traceable to historical accident, such as where migrants from various origins settled. The greater the overall homogeneity or evenness of transaction patterns, the more influential, *relatively*, these other factors are likely to be.

But in a heterogeneous world of great differences, the islands of similarity that do exist take on special importance. The differences among all national units remain sufficiently large that clusters of relative similarity or transaction can be identified rather easily, and the effect of one condition is notably to create or reinforce that of another, resulting in relative congruence among the clusters produced by different criteria. The cluster or "region" thus more nearly resembles a subsystem in the hierarchy between the worldwide system and nation-state subsystems. Complex social systems are organized hierarchically. Every higher level of organization is characterized by drawing together a number of sub-units, which themselves are clusters of sub-units.[2] Society is built up of aggregates: from the individual to the family, the neighborhood, the city, and the political units of province and nation. Some of these clusters, like the family, are fairly tightly bound; others, like the neighborhood in modern suburbia, may be highly homogeneous but characterized by weak interaction and virtually absent political bonds. For many analytical purposes we can move directly from the family or individual to the city government.

International groupings or regions clearly form one of the building blocks in this hierarchy. But how important a step? Over the past several centuries a clear trend is visible, a trend toward the integration of lower levels of the hierarchy into higher ones. Small political units such as city-states have become absorbed into nations, and existing nations have become more thoroughly integrated as the degree of homogeneity and interaction among their component units has risen. The unification of the nation-state which began in Europe and is now progressing in Africa and Asia is a well-studied phenomenon. It is not, of course, a linear trend. Only recently have organizations comparable in scope to the Roman Empire been reached again, and within the past couple of decades we have seen the political disintegration of national empires that had previously been bound together by little other than the political tie (bound to the metropolitan country, of course, but usually with few links among the colonies). Even if there should be a secular trend toward tighter organization at the higher levels of complexity underlying the various cycles, we would have no basis for projecting uncritically this trend to the stage of a world state. Some writers have done so, but systematic efforts to separate hopes and fears from analysis, or to provide anything like a timetable, are virtually non-existent.

ROADS TO THE FUTURE

J. David Singer (1966) has suggested that social scientists pursue the following goals in analysis:

[2] For an excellent discussion of this point see Simon (1962).

We observe structural, cultural, and physical properties of a system in order to describe it in *being;* we observe the rates and direction of change of such properties to describe or predict what it is *becoming;* and we observe their propensities to interact with one another and to respond to external inputs in order to predict, and partially explain, the system's modes of *behaving.*

After having looked at aspects of the being and behaving of the international system, it is time to turn to questions about what it is becoming. Logically, four possibilities exist: 1) There is a continuing progression toward the integration of still larger units, and this progression will pass through a period of several large-scale regional units along with the further integration of a single worldwide system; 2) There is a progression toward the integration of still larger units, but for the foreseeable future it will involve only the integration of regional subsystems and not the entire international system;[3] 3) There is a progression toward the integration of still larger units, but it will proceed directly to the entire global system without leading to the further differentiation of regional subsystems en route; 4) No further integration at either level will occur for some time.

The evidence is sparse and sometimes contradictory, but I think that as general statements the last two possibilities are the least likely. In terms very broadly of the kind of evidence adduced in previous chapters of this book, perhaps the strongest support for the idea of progression direct to worldwide integration stems from the widespread diffusion of a potential *world culture,* of which the primary elements are Western technology and Western norms toward the use of material objects. Western technology has penetrated virtually everywhere, with some of the culturally most revolutionary instruments being modern means of communication and transportation. Nearly every country of Asia and Latin America, plus many in Africa, now has one or more television stations. Sets still are owned by only a minority, sometimes a tiny one, of the population, but in many areas receivers have been put in public places where a whole village can have access. To a very great degree these media have become carriers of Western mass culture, perhaps with local subtitles. The impending impact of communications satellites in spreading this mass culture is certain to be enormous. Among the elites, intercontinental jet transport has also had enormous influence, which may be even greater when the era of supersonic transports arrives. Largely as a result of these developments certain very basic cultural norms are widely accepted in areas where they are quite novel. The ideals of equality, national independence, and economic development are at least

---

[3] This would correspond rather closely to what Southall (1953, pp. 229-63) has described as "the segmentary state," composed of highly autonomous sub-systems within a larger system, with only weak central authority.

given lip service by the leaders of almost every country.[4] Everywhere men are coming more and more to accept the idea, previously quite specific to modern Europe, that their destinies are to a large degree controllable and can be improved by their own efforts.

In recent years, at least, the earth has become somewhat more tightly bound by *economic transactions*. Obviously the total value and volume of world commerce has expanded over the past two decades, but again we must have some benchmark against which to measure that growth. In chapter eight we have used as a measure of interdependence the ratio of trade to total product. For the entire world this relationship has changed moderately since the end of World War II. The most reliable long-term world production indices are for manufacturing production. From 1948 to 1965 world commerce grew an estimated 306 per cent, as compared with an increase of manufacturing production of 259 per cent. The relative growth of the former has been quite steady over the whole span. To some degree this may be attributed to recovery from the war, which disrupted trade even more than it did production. But since foreign trade continued slowly to outpace manufacturing even into the 1960's, something more permanent is probably at work.[5] The flow of investment capital abroad has grown much faster even than trade. Benoit (1966, p. 13) estimates that the sale of goods and services produced by American-controlled companies abroad has gone up twice as fast as American exports, and now has a value about three times as great as all United States exports.

Other bits of evidence, however, are less compelling. Changes in the *relative incomes* of rich and poor nations present a very complicated pattern, but certainly not one that leads to any conclusion of a still-narrowing gap. The great difference first appeared during the Nineteenth and early Twentieth Centuries, when the West industrialized rapidly while productivity in Asia and Africa changed hardly at all. World War II did little to change the difference between the extremes (the United States and Afro-Asia), but wartime damage in the European countries temporarily reduced the distance between them and the bottom of the scale. By the late 1950's Europe recovered from the war, and along with Japan and the communist

[4] Cf. the essay by Talcott Parsons (1962).

[5] Data for recent trends in world trade and production are from United Nations (1966c, pp. vii—ix), and for previous years from Deutsch and Eckstein (1961, p. 290). Manufacturing production probably in fact *understates* the trend, because it has grown much faster since World War II than have either mining or agriculture. These more recent data modify the conclusions of Deutsch and Eckstein, whose analysis stopped in 1959. They emphasized the low trade/production ratio of postwar years compared with that of the 1920's and even earlier, and appear not to have anticipated the continued recovery of world trade in the 1960's. At the same time, their basic conclusion is unharmed, since even the 1964 trade production ratio was well below that of the interwar years.

nations of Eastern Europe showed a very rapid rate of growth in per capita income, averaging twice the rate manifested in North America. The result was a substantial reduction in income differentials among industrialized nations. Communist China also recovered and grew rapidly during this period (though not later, after the great leap forward had tripped), at a rate roughly approximating the states of Eastern Europe, so this was another instance, and one involving a quarter of the world's population, where the income gap was being narrowed. Yet China was almost the only major underdeveloped country to make such notable progress, and the other large poor states (e.g., India, Indonesia, Pakistan) began to industrialize but fell behind Europe's rate of advance, though in some cases they did keep up the pace of the United States. Measured by any of the common overall summary statistics for the entire distribution from rich to poor the degree of inequality on the globe was indeed, by the 1960's, slightly diminished. But if one looks only at the non-communist states, and in addition excludes North America, the picture is different—of a growing gulf between Europe and the non-communist third world.[6]

The number of *international organizations* in the analyses of chapters six and seven grew, over the decade, by 52 per cent (from 107 to 163). This suggests a strengthening of the institutional bonds joining the nations of the world, as new structures, to serve a variety of functions, arise to link one with another. Certainly some nations, especially those of Western Europe, were indeed enmeshed in more organizational strands than ever before. But actually the increase in the number of organizations closely paralleled the emergence of new nations, and the number of countries included in the two analyses grew at almost the same pace—48 per cent (from 77 to 114).

Whatever the suggestions of a very modest growth in some of the conditions for world political integration, these same data, when examined for the growth of regional integration, give a more clearly positive answer *for certain areas.* On the side of impressions about *cultural homogeneity,* one can make a rather powerful case for an increasing similarity at least in Western Europe and in Eastern Europe. Whatever trends toward convergence may also exist, the major social and cultural fact of recent years may well be the success of the two chief centers in homogenizing their periphery. In addition, a major struggle over one other peripheral area is now underway in Southeast Asia, and the result will almost certainly be the homogenization of the area with the system of the winner.

If world trade has grown a little faster than production, intra-regional

---

[6] This picture can be pieced together from a variety of sources, including Kuznets (1958), Andic and Peacock (1961), Zimmerman (1965, p. 39), and Russett (1965, ch. 7). Andic and Peacock also support the earlier assertion that inequalities *between* countries are much greater than those *within* nations.

trade has not consistently developed more rapidly than has commerce between regions. The only spectacular regional increase has been in Western Europe, where from 1953 to 1964 trade within the area grew almost 40 per cent faster than did that region's trade with the entire world. Eastern Europe shows a minor (about two per cent) relative gain in intra-regional trade. Other major areas of the globe, however, exhibit a contrary trend. Slightly in Latin America, and much more in Asia, Africa, and the Middle East, world-wide trade grew faster than commerce within each of the areas—more than twice as fast in the case of Africa (United Nations, 1966a, pp. 398–405).

Among *international organizations,* by far the fastest growth has occurred in the number of regional institutions. Of the 107 intergovernmental organizations analyzed for 1951, a total of 45 could be called "regional." (They either had the name of a region in their titles, or in fact were limited in membership to a clearly identifiable and virtually contiguous geographic region.) By 1962 the figures were 163 organizations in all, of which 93 met these same regional criteria: an increment of 107 per cent in the latter, but of only 13 per cent in the non-regional category. As shown in chapter 12 this applies to each of the major regions. Similarly, Robert Angell (1965), in his study which included the more than 1000 non-governmental (private) international organizations, reported a growth of 167 per cent in regional organizations over his six-year period, and an increase of only 32 per cent in all other types. In both of these studies the most striking was in the EEC area (600 per cent for inter-governmental organizations, 167 per cent for non-governmental organizations), but even excluding the EEC institutions the rates for other countries are also high (98 per cent and 77 per cent, respectively).

Of the major institutional attempts at economic regionalism over the past decade, without doubt the most successful has been the European Common Market. This coincides with the area's outstanding performance on the above criteria. Some distance behind it in impact has been the more modest, but in its way successful, Central American Common Market. COMECON too can claim limited gains in Eastern Europe. And well behind them come the European Free Trade Area (EFTA) of the peripheral seven, and the Latin American Free Trade Area (LAFTA).

The strongest argument against the conclusion that the conditions for regional integration are on the increase at the expense of worldwide integration concerns the overall correlations between studies that we examined in the last chapter. The average correlation among all studies during the 1950's was 0.81; for the 1960's it dropped down to 0.77, a fall of four points. This is not an enormous difference—it is far less, for instance, than the average difference in correlations *within* each time period—but it still is not in the hypothesized direction. For this purpose, however, the figures in Table 13.1

are deceptive, because in the 1950's many African and some Asian states were not members of the United Nations, were not independent and therefore could not be included in the international organization analysis, and in some cases did not even report their trade figures. As a result, most of the early 1950's comparisons are based primarily on countries in Europe, the Western Hemisphere, and the older Asian countries, and especially for the first two categories, this is where integration was highest anyway. But in the 1960's analysis the overall level of congruence is brought down by the addition of many new states, where the level of international integration is comparatively low. If the 1960's comparisons are recalculated to include only the same countries as were matched in the earlier years, the average correlation becomes 0.79, not enough drop from the 1950's to have much significance. Thus while in some sense the "worldwide average" potential for regional integration has declined, there has been no notable fall for those areas on which we have comparable data over the decade.[7]

Yet this is not the same as finding that capabilities for integration in those areas have increased. For that, the best we can do is return to the evidence cited above, which is after all a more direct test than the simple presence or absence of high congruence between studies. (The latter bears more on the question of boundaries and the creation of subsystems.) Wars have become rare in several regions. We found modest growth in capabilities in both Eastern and Western Europe, though greater in the latter. If there was some increase in ties between the two halves of Europe it was so small and started from such a low baseline as not to show up in the analyses. In the rest of the world the trends showed no clear slope either way; *possibly* there was a growth in the Arab world and in Central America, but not much in other parts of Afro-Asian or Latin America. As we have already established, the process of building regional integration is a slow one, and if we were not yet convinced the ambiguous evidence we have about just what *did* happen from the 1950's to the early 1960's should clinch the argument.

The major prediction of this section is thus for some further integration in certain regions, but not for any very great change in the number or composition of the principal coalitions operating at present in world politics. To forecast some *integration* is not to expect *unification* of the areas in question. The changes of the last five or six years, with the splits in the Atlantic Alliance and among the communist states, are probably as great as or greater than any subsequent political changes that will be witnessed during the next 15 years or so. Assuming of course that nuclear war is avoided, we probably have already passed through the most notable realignments of the postwar period, as the early bipolarity has loosened moderately but without creating a clearly multipolar or "balance of power" system.

[7] This is reinforced by examination of the graphs for specific regions in chapter 11.

REGIONAL INTEGRATION vs. WORLDWIDE INTEGRATION

Imagine a debate between a World Federalist and an advocate of Atlantic Union. The Federalist emphasizes the need for over-arching worldwide institutions. He knows that the world is a diverse and variegated place, but insists that only a global organization can prevent war and promote cooperative effort for the good of all mankind. The advocate of Atlantic Union may accept much of this argument as the statement of a long-term goal, but for now he dwells on the divisions and heterogeneity so manifest among nations. For the present, he says, we must take whatever islands of relative similarity we find, and integrate them as units which can solve their own internal problems and contribute to the stability of the larger international system without transforming it drastically. In the long run a world community may well be built by aggregating these units at a yet higher level of organization, in which they, not the existing nation-states, might be the basic building blocks in a global federal hierarchy.

Political events are not *determined* by the operation of background influences and aggregate events of the sort we have examined in this book. But such events do set the conditions within which statesmen must act; they close off some options and make others more feasible. An individual leader can sometimes halt or even reverse a trend which he opposes, but it is harder for him to create conditions that may be required for the achievement of his desires. President De Gaulle may be able to throw some sand in the gears of political union on the continent, but President Nasser cannot, by an act of will, produce an Arab union.[8]

If we consider the observed developments to be material for acts of creative statesmanship, some of the bases for further regional integration undoubtedly exist. Bonds linking the countries of Western Europe, Eastern Europe, and Latin America are clearly discernible, and others exist elsewhere. So far the regional subsystems of the world are far less well delineated than are the boundaries of national systems. For a nation the level of transactions, the institutional arrangements, and frequently the culture all change sharply at the political border. Neither the regional limits as defined operationally by any one criterion, nor the congruence of several different definitions, are as sharp or uniform for groups of countries. But if the path of regional integration is followed either as an intended step toward a world state or a substitute for it, the boundaries of those groups will become clearer. Their transactions with other countries within the region will grow faster

---

[8] See the useful distinction by Sprout and Sprout (1965, p. 199) between the prediction of specific events and "negative prediction," or narrowing the range of possible outcomes by eliminating the most unlikely.

than transactions with states outside the group, institutions within the group will grow even stronger and more numerous than institutions linking countries in different groups, and homogeneity within the region will increase at the cost of heterogeneity at the boundaries.

Many of the elements of such a trend are already present, but the developments of the past decade or so have been very moderate, mixed, and could be slowed or reversed. Politics is seldom so simple as the mere extrapolation of past rates and patterns of development. (Persistence forecasting is easy, but hardly the way to identify *change*!) A combination of autonomous forces and political will must be behind any continuation or quickening of the pace. Whether it can be made to move rapidly enough to solve pressing political problems in the world is a very open question.

A more serious question is whether regional integration would in fact ease or exacerbate the most dangerous political threats in world politics. Would the regional fractionation of the world improve or damage global abilities for the promotion of peaceful change? For some, the attraction of regional institution-building lies in its implication of the regional settlement of disputes, that a strengthened Organization of American States, for instance, would deal with Western Hemisphere problems without external interference. Too often in the past this scheme has been primarily a cover for great powers' spheres of influence, such as under the Monroe Doctrine or Japan's former predominance in East Asia. Those days are past and will not return. Most regional integration in the Western Hemisphere will only marginally include the United States, especially any movement that involves creating coercive institutions.

Other proponents of regional union without global integration above it seem to expect the emergence of several subsystems or superpowers in something like a balance of power system.[9] Advocacy of a "balance of power" opens up myriad questions, for it is a highly ambiguous concept that seems to mean all things to all men.[10] For many of its enthusiasts it becomes largely a nostalgic longing for a distant past that the advocates themselves could never have known first hand.

Regional integration would have the undoubted advantage of greatly reducing the risks of war within large areas of the world. From that point of view we could not but welcome it. Yet regional integration *alone* would introduce other potential threats to a stable and peaceful globe. At present the bonds among various groups of countries are too weak to permit the

[9] A notable bit of enthusiasm for this point of view is written by Masters (1966) with a more systematic theoretical statement in his earlier (1961) paper. See also the report of the Commission to Study the Organization of Peace (1953).

[10] Of many critiques of the concept, the most penetrating probably remain those of Haas (1953) and Claude (1962, ch. 2).

groupings to act in a highly unified way on very many regional or global issues. But the political integration of several large "regions," with a sharpening of the boundaries between groupings, implies a weakening of the worldwide cement that joins nations *across* regions. This would almost surely produce rigidities and heightened conflicts between groupings. The vision of a "Europe from the Atlantic to the Urals" is a distant one indeed. Regional integration along the presently-indicated lines would do nothing to bridge the gaps either of the Cold War or between rich and poor. Much of the opposition to Atlantic Union in American intellectual circles stems from precisely this fear.[11]

If not accompanied also by stronger global ties, regional integration in itself is a choice against the cross-pressures or cross-cutting solidarities that bind, however weakly, the diverse nations from all parts of the world. The role of cross-pressures in preventing rigidity in political alignments has long been recognized as crucial. Originally the concept was applied to *sociological* cross-pressures, primarily differences in demographic attributes like the religion, occupation, or ethnic background of individuals. If groups of people as identified by one attribute, like occupation, were found to be heterogeneous by another which was also salient for them, such as religion, it was suggested that the likelihood of polarized, severe conflict between groups, such as two occupational groupings, was lower than if each group was homogeneous. Workers in one trade would be unable to present a unified front against another trade because of ties of sentiment and common interest which would make some of their number unwilling to oppose their counterparts in the other group too vigorously. Empirical studies in the United States have shown that individuals who are cross-pressured are likely to postpone making up their minds on a decision, to shift allegiance, and often to avoid taking a clear-cut position at all. It is not unreasonable to think that much the same kind of mechanisms would apply to the men in official positions in cross-pressured governments. A sharpening of regional boundaries in the world, making ties of similarity, interdependence, and institution coincide, would involve a reduction in the number of cross-pressures that currently exist in the world, and thus reduce the effectiveness of a major influence for controlling conflict between groups.

Even when considering only the groupings of a single criterion, the cross-pressure idea is still relevant. A nation with ties to two organizationally-

[11] The concept of cross-pressures first gained currency in studies of voting in the United States, primarily that of Lazarsfeld, Berelson, and Gaudet (1944), and has also been given great theoretical attention by Parsons (1959, 1961a). I have applied it to international politics elsewhere (Alker and Russett, 1965, ch. 12). For a perceptive discussion of regional integration as threatening to widen inter-regional gaps see Yalem (1965), ch. 6, passim.

defined groupings, for instance (e.g., the United States, which belongs to many institutions in common with the Western Europeans as well as with the Latin Americans) also can serve as a useful bridge and help prevent the emergence of sharp conflicts between the two. To the extent that cleaner lines of demarcation between groups develop, these ties are lost.

To some degree the absence of sociological cross-pressures might be compensated by *attitude* cross-pressures, or shifting alignments of the major groupings on different issues.[12] Western Europe would have some political interests in common with Latin America, and others with Eastern Europe. But the crucial question is how long such a multi-bloc system would remain fluid and flexible. The mere existence of several actors of more or less equal power guarantees nothing about the ease with which coalitions would be made or broken. Building blocs might well create several units closer to an equality of economic and military power than now exist, but the coalescence of these units does imply a reduction in the number of political actors in the system, and in that sense a loss of maneuverability. The price of greater equality is the sacrifice of former opportunities for alliance formation among small powers. And one of the primary virtues of having a large number of small uncommitted states arises when that group is sufficiently incohesive that they may be split off, some aligning with one side and some with another, in patterns that change over time. But historical experience with "balance of power" systems of just four to eight roughly equal states is not altogether reassuring. If the international system becomes highly polarized between two grand coalitions as in 1914, any risk of defection by or damage to a major actor can be extremely threatening to the entire system's stability. Should a system with only a few major actors become highly polarized in the next decade or two, World War I might look like a skeet-shoot.

One wonders if the more recent counter example, the bipolar world with two great super-powers, each flanked by a retinue of much smaller states with few in between, is necessarily such an undesirable situation. It may be worse than a truly flexible and shifting multi-polar system, and it certainly seemed bad in the 1950's, primarily because the risk of nuclear war appeared so great. But was the nuclear threat present because the world was bipolar, or merely because of technological developments, especially those that created deterrents which seemed for a time to be so vulnerable to surprise attack? The best-known builder of models of world politics (Kaplan, 1957, ch. 2) seems to say that the bipolar system is *inherently* unstable and tension-producing, but the evidence is not all that clear. One of his chief critics (Waltz, 1964) argues forcefully (in what he admits is perhaps a bit of nostalgia on his own part) that the bipolar system of ten years ago was

[12] Cf. Campbell et al. (1960), pp. 80-88.

really neither so unstable nor dangerous as it may have looked to those who lived in it, as compared with what may arise in a multi-bloc world.[13]

The shift toward a modification of the bipolar conflict of the 1950's, bringing greater independence for China and for Europe, has without doubt permitted a reduction in United States-Soviet tensions. Many of the hostilities that the peoples and governments of the two great powers used to direct toward each other, however, have instead of vanishing merely been redirected toward China. For the most part this has been a consequence of China's growth in power and bellicosity, but the shift seems also to have been aided by deliberate governmental action (with some second thoughts evident in parts of the United States government as I wrote this in the late spring of 1966). Communist China is for the moment an almost ideal scapegoat. It is just big and powerful enough almost to be a credible threat to America or the Soviet Union, and visions of a billion Chinese and the "yellow horde" can be invoked. But even though the Peking regime could cause great trouble to small states around its perimeter, and a long-run world danger from China is surely no chimera, Chinese current military and economic strength is not now sufficiently great to threaten the basic sources of Russian or American power. But conscious diversion of popular hostility toward China, if indeed it is a deliberate policy of the government of either major power, carries more risks than may immediately appear from an inventory of current Chinese military hardware or a count of Chinese nuclear weapons. It is quite conceivable that the Chinese could respond to this hostility—for which, in all fairness, they can to a very large degree blame only themselves—by building the equivalent of a Doomsday machine. Such a feat is within the foreseeable capabilities of communist China, even though a sophisticated second-strike deterrent force may not be.

These comments about the dangers that remain and perhaps even are magnified as we move from a bipolar world to one with some significant second-rank powers are meant simply to emphasize the intellectual difficulties in talking too abstractly about the virtues of having more big blocs in the system. A number of other structural aspects of the system must be taken into account, and we may pertinently ask just *which* blocs are being advocated. Of the candidates for regional integration discussed in chapter eleven,

---

[13] A "balance of power system" with a small number (but at least three) of major powers is different from the system with many independent states looked upon with favor by Deutsch and Singer (1964). It is not necessarily correct to imply, however, as Deutsch and Singer seem to do, that such a balance of power system is somewhere in between the bipolar and many-power systems in stability. For an interesting attempt to analyze these models, resulting in advocacy of a system (with the ungainly label of bi-multipolarity) containing two great powers but with the flexibility provided by a number of significant states not attached to either pole, see Rosecrance (1966).

the best possibility seemed to lie in Western Europe. While such a vision may not please the ex-colonial nations, and the potential of a free-floating Europe that could make some tactical arrangements with the Soviet Union ought to give Americans some pause, it is certainly the grouping that would pose the fewest threats either to American foreign policy or to the peace of the world. And from both considerations we may regret the lack of a regional unit capable of off-setting the Chinese threat. A movement toward the integration of Southeast Asia or of India and Japan would have its distinct uses, but unfortunately we found no signs pointing toward its fulfillment. With this exception, however, it is not amiss to inquire whether we would want to see the emergence of another have-not power—which like China might combine frustration with some new power, to produce dangerous aggression. Would many people, even in the underdeveloped areas, really welcome the achievement of Arab unity? It could only mean either the erasure of Israel in war, or irresistable pressures for Israeli acquisition of nuclear weapons.

Pragmatically, both the theorist and the policy-maker may favor the promotion of regional integration in some areas but not in others. Integration may in some circumstances further the solution of local conflicts, such as border disputes; in others it may relieve the threat of great power intervention or other dangers to broader peace. Many areas of Africa may well fit these descriptions. To express reservations about the wisdom of generally and indiscriminately promoting regional integration, and especially about the effort to build up aggregates that can become near-great powers, is not to be in favor of the worst aspects of Balkanization. Nor of course can we expect the political leaders of these areas always to share our doubts—their perspectives are neither those of an American State Department hand nor of a political theorist.

Nevertheless, we should retain our own perspectives and not go around the world actively fostering regional unity everywhere, but must additionally concentrate on the integration of the international system as a whole. Regional integration without concurrent pressures, and probably deliberate effort, toward integrating the entire international system would be at best a short-term and at worst a highly volatile "solution." If we take the Atlantic Unionist seriously, we must also take the World Federalist seriously. If creative statesmen choose to go down the path of regional integration they had better look far enough down that road to see the fork that will not be far ahead. The choice about what to do for *global* unity will determine whether the regional blocs will build a stable political edifice for man, or merely a shaky temple he can pull down upon his head.

These are not yet mutually exclusive roads. We must not allow the World Federalist and the Regional Unionist to polarize the debate and force us to take one of the options they offer. The world is not now ready for amalgamation in the style of the Federalist; the basic ecological underpinnings just do not exist. Maybe we will want to work in that direction in the long run. At this stage, however, a central choice of strategy is not forced upon us. The early steps toward world political unification based on amalgamating what are more or less the existing units are not so very different from the actions that should be taken for building world-wide mutual responsiveness within a pluralistic framework. We can lay a multi-purpose foundation without now choosing the eventual form of the structure to be built, leaving room for the ingenuity and learning of later architects to devise a stronger habitation than we now know how to construct.

REFERENCES

1. Ackerman, Edward A. "Regional Research—Emerging Concepts and Techniques in the Field of Geography." *Economic Geography,* 29 (1953), pp. 188–97.

2. Adelman, Irma, and Cynthia Taft Morris. "Factor Analysis of the Interrelationship Between Social and Political Variables and Per Capita Gross National Product." *Quarterly Journal of Economics,* 79, 4 (1965), pp. 555–78.

3. ———. "A Quantitative Study of Social and Political Determinants of Fertility." *Economic Development and Cultural Change,* 14, 2 (1966), pp. 129–57.

4. Ahmavaara, Yrjo. *Transformation Analysis of Factorial Data.* Helsinki: Suomalaisen Kirjallisuuden Seuran Kirjapainon Oy, 1954.

5. ———. *On the Unified Theory of the Mind.* Helsinki: Suomalaisen Kirjallisuuden Kirjapainon Oy, 1957.

6. ———, and Touko Markkanen, *The Unified Factor Model.* Helsinki: Uudenmaan Kirjapainon Oy, 1958.

7. Alexander, Christopher. *HIDECS 3: Four Computer Programs for the Hierarchical Decomposition of a Set Which Has an Associated Linear Graph.* Cambridge, Mass.: Civil Engineering Systems Laboratory, M.I.T., 1963.

8. ———. *Notes on the Synthesis of Form.* Cambridge, Mass.: Harvard University Press, 1964.

9. ———, and Marvin L. Manheim. *HIDECS 2: A Computer Program for the Hierarchical Decomposition of a Set Which Has an Associated Linear Graph.* Cambridge, Mass.: Civil Engineering Systems Laboratory, M.I.T., 1963.

10. Alger, Chadwick F. "Non-Resolution Consequences of the United Nations and Their Effect on International Conflict." *Journal of Conflict Resolution,* 5 (1961), pp. 128–45.

11. ———. "Personal Contact in Intergovernmental Organizations," in Herbert C. Kelman, ed., *International Behavior: A Social-Psychological Analysis,* New York: Holt, Rinehart and Winston, 1965.

12. Alker, Hayward R., Jr. "An IBM Program for the Gross Analysis of Transaction Flows." *Behavioral Science,* 7 (1962), pp. 498–99.

13. ———. "Dimensions of Conflict in the General Assembly," *American Political Science Review,* LVIII, 3 (1964).

14. ———, and Bruce M. Russett. *World Politics in the General Assembly.* New Haven, Conn.: Yale University Press, 1965.

15. Almond, Gabriel, and Sidney Verba. *The Civic Culture.* Princeton, N.J.: Princeton University Press, 1963.

16. Anderson, Lee, Meredith Watts, and Allen Wilcox. *Legislative Roll-Call Analysis.* Evanston, Ill.: Northwestern University Press, 1966.

17. Andic, Suphan, and Alan Peacock. "The International Distribution of Income, 1949 and 1957." *Journal of the Royal Statistical Society,* Series A (General), 124, 2 (1961), pp. 206–18.

18. Angell, Robert C. "Analysis of Trends in International Organizations." *Peace Research Society, Papers,* 3 (1965), pp. 85–96.

19. Aron, Raymond, and Daniel Lerner, eds. *France Defeats EDC.* New York: Praeger, 1957.

20. Balassa, Bela. *The Theory of Economic Integration.* Homewood, Ill.: Richard D. Irwin, 1961.

21. Ball, Geoffrey H. *Data Analysis in the Social Sciences: What About the Details?* Menlo Park, Calif.: Stanford Research Institute, Mimeo., 1965.

22. Bank for International Settlements. *28th Annual Report.* Basel: Bank for International Settlements, 1958.

23. Banks, Arthur S., and Robert Textor. *A Cross-Polity Survey.* Cambridge, Mass.: M.I.T. Press, 1963.

24. ———, and Phillip M. Gregg. "Grouping Political Systems: Q-Factor Analysis of 'A Cross-Polity Survey.' " *American Behavioral Scientist,* 9, 3 (1965), pp. 3–5.

25. Bauer, Raymond A., Ithiel De Sola Pool, and Lewis Anthony Dexter. *American Business and Public Policy.* New York: Atherton Press, 1964.

26. Benoit, Emile. "Interdependence on a Small Planet." *Columbia Journal of Business,* 1, 2 (1966), pp. 9–18.

27. Berelson, Bernard, and Gary A. Steiner. *Human Behavior: An Inventory of Scientific Findings.* New York: Harcourt, Brace, and World, 1964.

28. Berrien, F. K. "Homeostasis in Groups." *General Systems: Yearbook of the Society for General Systems Research,* 9 (1964), pp. 205–18.

29. Berry, Brian J. L. "An Inductive Approach to the Regionalization of Economic Development," in Norton Ginsburg (ed.). *Essays on Geography and Economic Development.* Chicago: University of Chicago Press, 1960.

30. ———. "Basic Patterns of Economic Development," in Norton Ginsburg (ed.). *Atlas of Economic Development.* Chicago: University of Chicago Press, 1961a.

31. ———. "A Method for Deriving Multi-factor Uniform Regions." *Polish Geographer,* 33, 2 (1961b), 263–79.

32. ———. *Identification of Declining Regions: An Empirical Study of the Dimensions of Rural Poverty.* Kingston, Ontario: Queen's University, Conference on Areas of Economic Stress, 1966.

33. ———. *Proceedings of the Brno Conference on Economic Regionalization.* Brno: Czech Academy of Sciences, 1966.

34. ———. "A Synthesis of Formal and Functional Regions Using a General Field Theory of Spacial Behavior" in Brian J. L. Berry and Duane F. Marble (eds.) *Spacial Analysis.* Englewood Cliffs, N. J.: Prentice-Hall, 1967.

35. ———, and Thomas D. Hankins. *A Bibliographic Guide to the Economic Regions of the United States.* Chicago: University of Chicago, Department of Geography, 1963.

36. Bhoutros-Ghali, Bhoutros. *Contribution á L'Etude des Ententes Regionales.* Paris: A. Pédone, 1949.

37. Binder, Leonard. "The Middle East as a Subordinate International System." *World Politics,* 10, 3 (1958), pp. 408–29.

38. Blalock, H. M. "Four-Variable Causal Models and Partial Correlations." *American Journal of Sociology,* 58, 2 (1962), pp. 182–94.

39. ———. *Causal Inference in Non-Experimental Research.* Chapel Hill: University of North Carolina Press, 1964.

40. Bloomfield, Lincoln P. "The United States, the United Nations, and the Creation of Community." *International Organization,* 14, 4 (1960), pp. 503–13.

41. ———. "The New Diplomacy in the United Nations," in Francis O. Wilcox and H. Field Haviland (eds.) *The United States and the United Nations,* Baltimore: Johns Hopkins Press, 1961.

42. Bogue, Donald J. "The Need for an International System of Regions and Subregions." *Proceedings and Papers, Regional Science Association,* I (1955), pp. 1–11.

43. Bonner, R. E. "On Some Clustering Techniques." *IBM Journal of Research and Development,* 8, 1 (1964), pp. 22–32.

44. Boulding, Kenneth E. *Conflict and Defense: A Theoretical Statement.* New York: Harper & Row, 1962.

45. Brams, Steven J. "A Generalized Program for the Analysis of Transaction Flows." *Behavioral Science,* 10 (1965a), pp. 487–88.

46. ———. *Flow and Form in the International System.* Evanston, Ill.: Northwestern University, Ph.D. Dissertation, 1965b.

47. Brecher, Michael. "International Relations and Asian Studies: The Subordinate State System of Southern Asia." *World Politics* 15, 2 (1963), pp. 212–35.

48. Brehm, Jack W., and Arthur C. Cohen. *Explorations in Cognitive Dissonance.* New York: Wiley, 1962.

49. Brzezinski, Zbigniew, and Samuel Huntington. *Political Power: U.S.A./ U.S.S.R.* New York: Viking, 1964.

50. Bull, Hedley. "What is the Commonwealth?" *World Politics,* 11, 4 (1959), pp. 577–87.

51. Bunge, William. *Theoretical Geography.* Lund, Sweden: G.W.K. Gleeruys, 1962.

52. Campbell, Angus, Philip Converse, Warren Miller, and Donald Stokes. *The American Voter.* New York: Wiley, 1960.

53. Cantril, Hadley. *The Pattern of Human Concerns.* Brunswick, New Jersey: Rutgers University Press, 1966.

54. Carr, E. H. *Nationalism and After.* London: Macmillan, 1945.

55. Casetti, Emilio. *Multiple Discriminant Functions,* Technical Report # 11 of ONR Task No. 389–135. Evanston, Ill.: Office of Naval Research, Geography Branch, Northwestern University, 1964.

56. Cattell, Raymond B. "The Dimensions of Culture Patterns of Factorization of National Characters." *Journal of Abnormal and Social Psychology,* XLIV, 4 (1949), pp. 443–469.

57. ———. "The Principal Culture Patterns Discoverable in the Syntal Dimensions of Existing Nations." *Journal of Social Psychology,* 32, 2 (1950), 215–53.

58. ———, H. Breul, and H. P. Hartman. "An Attempt at More Refined Definition of the Cultural Dimensions of Syntality in Modern Nations." *American Sociological Review,* 17, 4 (1951), pp. 408–21.

59. ———, and Richard Gorsuch. "The Definition and Measurement of National Morale and Morality." *Journal of Social Psychology,* 67, 1 (1965), pp. 77–96.

60. Chamberlin, Edward. *The Theory of Monopolistic Competition.* Cambridge, Mass.: Harvard University Press, 1933.

61. Claude, Inis L. *Swords Into Plowshares.* New York: Random House, 1959.

62. ———. *Power and International Relations.* New York: Random House, 1962.

63. Cohen, Saul Bernard. *Geography and Politics in a World Divided.* New York: Random House, 1963.

64. Cole, J. P. *Geography and World Affairs.* London: Penguin, 3rd ed., 1964.

65. Commission to Study the Organization of Peace. *Regional Arrangements for Security and the United Nations.* New York: Commission to Study the Organization of Peace, 1953.

66. Coombs, Clyde. *A Theory of Data.* New York: Wiley, 1964.

67. Coser, Lewis. *The Functions of Social Conflict.* Glencoe, Ill.: Free Press, 1956.

68. Davison, Roderic. "Where is the Middle East?" in Richard Nolte (ed.). *The Modern Middle East.* New York: Atherton Press, 1964.

69. De Rusett, Alan. *Strengthening the Framework of Peace.* London: Royal Institute of International Affairs, 1950.

70. Denton, Frank H. *A Handbook of Factor Analysis for International Relations.* Los Angeles: University of Southern California, School of International Relations, mimeo, 1965.

71. Deutsch, Karl W. et al. *Political Community and the North Atlantic Area,* Princeton, New Jersey: Princeton University Press, 1957.

72. ———, and Alexander Eckstein. "National Industrialization and the Declining Share of the International Economic Sector." *World Politics,* 8, 2 (1961), pp. 267–99.

73. ———, and J. David Singer. "Multipolar Power Systems and International Stability." *World Politics,* 16, 3 (1964), pp. 390–406.

74. Duncan, Otis Dudley, Ray P. Cuzzort, and Beverly Duncan. *Statistical Geography: Problems in Analyzing Areal Data.* Glencoe, Ill.: Free Press, 1961.

75. Etzioni, Amitai. "The Dialectics of Supranational Unification." *American Political Science Review,* 56, 4 (1962), pp. 927–36.

76. ———. "The Epigenesis of Political Communities at the International Level." *American Journal of Sociology* 28, 3 (1963), pp. 407–21.

77. ———. "Atlantic Union, the Southern Continents, and the United Nations," in Roger Fisher (ed.). *International Conflict and Behavioral Science.* New York: Basic Books, 1964.

78. ———. *Political Unification.* New York: Holt, Rinehart & Winston 1965.

79. Festinger, Leon. *A Theory of Cognitive Dissonance.* Evanston, Ill.: Row, Peterson, 1957.

80. Finch, V. C. "Geographical Science and Social Philosophy." *Annals of the Association of American Geographers,* 29, 1 (1939).

81. Fitzgibbon, Russell, and Kenneth Johnson. "The Measurement of Latin American Political Change." *American Political Science Review,* 55, 3 (1961), 515–26.

82. Foltz, William. *From French West Africa to the Mali Federation.* New Haven, Conn.: Yale University Press, 1965.

83. Free, Lloyd A. *Six Allies and a Neutral.* Glencoe, Ill.: Free Press, 1959.

84. Gladwyn Lord. "World Order and the Nation-State—A Regional Approach." *Daedalus*, 95, 2 (1966), pp. 694–703.

85. Goodman, Leo. "Statistical Methods for the Preliminary Analysis of Transaction Flows." *Econometrica*, 31 (1963), pp. 197–208.

86. ———. "A Short Computer Program for the Analysis of Transaction Flows." *Behavioral Science* (1964), pp. 176–86.

87. Gregg, Phillip M., and Arthur S. Banks. "Dimensions of Political Systems: Factor Analysis of 'A Cross-Polity Survey.'" *American Political Science Review*, 3 (1965), pp. 602–14.

88. Grumm, John. "A Factor Analysis of Legislative Behavior." *Midwest Journal of Political Science*, 7, 4 (1963), pp. 336–56.

89. Haas, Ernst B. "The Balance of Power: Prescription, Concept, or Propaganda?" *World Politics*, 5, 4 (1953), pp. 442–77.

90. ———. *The Uniting of Europe*. Stanford Calif.: Stanford University Press, 1957.

91. ———. "The Challenge of Regionalism." *International Organization*, 12, 3 (1958), pp. 440–48.

92. ———. "International Integration: The European and the Universal Process." *International Organization*, 15 (1961), pp. 366–92.

93. ———. "Dynamic Environment and Static System: Revolutionary Regimes in the United Nations," in Morton A. Kaplan (ed.). *The Revolution in World Politics*, New York: Wiley, 1962.

94. ———. *Beyond the Nation-State: Functionalism and International Organization*. Stanford: Stanford University Press, 1964.

95. ———, and Philippe Schmitter. "Economics and Differential Patterns of Political Integration: Projections About Unity in Latin America." *International Organization*, 18, 4 (1964), pp. 705–37.

96. Haggett, Peter. *Locational Analysis in Human Geography*. New York: St. Martin's Press, 1966.

97. Hagood, Margaret, "Statistical Methods for Delineation of Regions Applied to Data on Agriculture and Population." *Social Forces*, 21, 3 (1943), pp. 287–97.

98. ———, Nadia Danilevsky, and Corlin O. Beum. "An Examination of the Use of Factor Analysis in the Problem of Sub-regional Delineation." *Rural Sociology*, 6, 3 (1941), pp. 216–34.

99. Hamblin, Robert. "Group Integration During a Crisis." *Human Relations*, 9, 1 (1958), pp. 67–76.

100. Harman, Harry H. *Modern Factor Analysis*. Chicago, Ill.: University of Chicago Press, 1960.

101. Hawley, Amos H. *Human Ecology: A Theory of Community Structure*. New York: Ronald Press, 1950.

102. Hodgkin, Thomas. "The New West African State System." *University of Toronto Quarterly*, 31 (1961) pp. 74–82.

103. Hoffmann, Stanley. "Discord in Community: The North Atlantic Area as a Partial International System." *International Organization*, 17, 3 (1963), pp. 521–49.

104. Homans, George C. *The Human Group*. New York: Harcourt, Brace, 1950.

105. Horst, Paul. *Factor Analysis of Data Matrices*. New York: Holt, Rinehart, and Winston, 1965.

106. Hovet, Thomas, Jr. *Bloc Voting in the United Nations.* Cambridge: Harvard University Press, 1961.
107. *International Conciliation,* 544 (1963).
108. *International Organization,* 18, 2 (1964) pp. 313–467.
109. Isard, Walter. "Regional Science, the Concept of Region, and Regional Structure." *Papers and Proceedings of the Regional Science Association.* Cambridge, Mass.: Regional Science Association, 1956.
110. Jackson, Elmore. "The Future Development of the United Nations: Some Suggestions for Future Research." *Journal of Conflict Resolution,* 5, (1961), pp. 119–28.
111. Jacob, Philip E. et al. *Report of the First International Roundtable.* Philadelphia: University of Pennsylvania, International Studies of Values in Politics, mimeo, 1965.
112. ———, and Alexine Atherton. *The Dynamics of International Organization,* Homewood, Ill.: Dorsey Press, 1965.
113. ———, and Henry Teune. "The Integrative Process: Guidelines for the Analysis of the Bases of Political Community," in Philip Jacob and James Toscano (eds.). *The Integration of Political Communities.* Philadelphia: Lippincott, 1964.
114. Kaiser, H. F. *Relating Factors Between Studies Based Upon Different Individuals,* mimeo, 1960.
115. Kaplan, Abraham. *The Conduct of Inquiry.* San Francisco: Chandler, 1964.
116. Kaplan, Morton A. *System and Process in International Politics.* New York: Wiley, 1957.
117. Kendall, Maurice G. "The Geographical Distribution of Crop Productivity in England." *Journal of the Royal Statistical Society,* Series A., 102 (1939), pp. 21–62.
118. Keohane, Robert. *Political Practice in the United Nations General Assembly.* Cambridge, Mass.: Harvard University, Ph.D. Dissertation, 1965.
119. Klingberg, Frank. "Studies in Measurement of the Relations Among Sovereign States." *Psychometrika,* 6, 4 (1941), pp. 335–52.
120. Kruskal, J. B. "Multidimensional Scaling by Optimizing Goodness of Fit to a Nonmetric Hypothesis." *Psychometrika,* 29 (1964a), pp. 1–27.
121. ———. "Nonmetric Multidimensional Scaling: A Numerical Method," *Psychometrika,* 29 (1964b), pp. 28–42.
122. Kuznets, Simon. "Regional Economic Trends and Levels of Living," in Philip Hauser (ed.). *Population and World Politics,* Glencoe, Ill.: Free Press, 1958.
123. Lakdawala, D. T. "Trends in Regional Cooperation in Asia," in Margaret Grant (ed.). *National Development and the World Community.* New York: Dodd, Mead, 1964.
124. Lawson, Ruth D. *International Regional Organizations: Constitutional Foundations.* New York: Praeger, 1962.
125. Lazarsfeld, Paul, Bernard Berelson, and Hazel Gaudet. *The People's Choice.* New York: Duell, Sloan and Pierce, 1944.
126. Leech, Margaret. *In the Days of McKinley.* New York: Harper, 1959.
127. Lerner Daniel. "French Business Leaders Look at EDC." *Public Opinion Quarterly,* 20, 1 (1956), pp. 212–21.
128. Lewin, Kurt. *Field Theory in Social Science.* New York: Harper, 1951.

129. Lijphart, Arend. "The Analysis of Bloc Voting in the General Assembly." *American Political Science Review,* 57, 4 (1963), pp. 902–17.

130. Lindberg, Leon. *The Political Dynamics of European Economic Integration.* Stanford: Stanford University Press, 1963.

131. Lingoes, James C. *Multivariate Analysis of Contingencies: An IBM 7090 Program for Analyzing Metric/Nonmetric or Linear/Nonlinear Data.* Computation Report, #2. Ann Arbor, Michigan: University of Michigan Computing Center, 1963.

132. ———. *New Computer Developments in Pattern Analysis and Nonmetric Techniques.* Blaricum, Netherlands: IBM Symposium, Computers in Psychological Research, 1964.

133. ———. "An IBM Program for Guttman-Lingoes Smallest Space Analysis." *Behavioral Science,* 10, 2 (1965a), pp. 183–84.

134. ———. "An IBM-7090 Program for Guttman-Lingoes Smallest Space Analysis—II." *Behavioral Science,* 10, 4 (1965b), p. 487.

135. Liska, George. *Nations in Alliance.* Baltimore: Johns Hopkins University Press, 1962.

136. Lundberg, George. "Regionalism, Science, and the Peace Settlement." *Social Forces.* 21, 2 (1942) pp. 131–37.

137. McClelland, David. *The Achieving Society.* Princeton, New Jersey: Van Nostrand, 1961.

138. MacKinder, Halford J. *Democratic Ideals and Reality.* New York: Henry Holt, 1919.

139. McQuitty, L. L. "Capabilities and Improvements of Linkage Analysis as a Clustering Method." *Educational and Psychological Measurement,* 24, 3 (1964), pp. 441–56.

140. ———. "Single and Multiple Hierarchical Classification by Reciprocal Pairs and Rank Order Types." *Educational and Psychological Measurement,* 26, 2 (1966), pp. 253–65.

141. MacRae, Duncan, Jr. "Direct Factor Analysis of Sociometric Data." *Sociometry,* 23, 4 (1960), pp. 360–71.

142. ———, and James A. Meldrum. "Critical Elections in Illinois: 1888–1958." *American Political Science Review,* 54, 3 (1960), pp. 669–83.

143. ———. "Cluster Analysis of Congressional Votes with the BC TRY System." *Western Political Quarterly,* 19, 4 (1966), pp. 631–38.

144. March, James G., and Herbert Simon. *Organizations.* New York: Wiley, 1958.

145. Masters, Roger D. "A Multi-Bloc Model of the International System." *American Political Science Review,* 55, 4 (1961), pp. 780–98.

146. ———. "Goals for American Power." *Yale Review,* 55, 3 (1966), pp. 365–88.

147. Megee, Mary. "Problems in Regionalizing and Measurement." *Peace Research Society Papers,* 4 (1966), pp. 7–35.

148. Meier, Richard L. "Information, Resources, and Economic Growth," in J. J. Spengler (ed.). *National Resources and Economic Growth,* Washington, D.C.: Resources for the Future, Inc., 1961.

149. Merritt, Richard. *The Growth of American Community.* New Haven Conn.: Yale University Press, 1966.

150. Merton, Robert. *Social Theory and Social Structure.* Glencoe, Ill.: Free Press, 1957.

151. Miller, James G. "Living Systems: Cross-Level Hypotheses." *Behavioral Science,* 10, 4 (1965), pp. 380–411.

152. Mishler, Anita L. "Personal Contact in International Exchanges," in Herbert C. Kelman (ed.). *International Behavior: A Social-Psychological Analysis.* New York: Holt, Rinehart, and Winston, 1965.

153. Mitrany, David. *A Working Peace System.* New York and London: Royal Institute of International Affairs, 1946.

154. Modelski, George. "International Relations and Area Studies: The Case of South-East Asia." *International Relations,* 2 (1961a), pp. 143–55.

155. ———. *The Communist International System,* Research Monograph No. 9. Princeton, N.J.: Center of International Studies, Princeton University, 1961b.

156. Mood, Fulmer. "The Origin, Evolution, and Application of the Sectional Concept," in Merrill Jensen (ed.). *Regionalism in America.* Madison, Wisconsin: University of Wisconsin Press, 1951.

157. Mortara, Georgio. "Indices of the Intensity of International Trade." *PROD Translations,* 3, 6 (1960), pp. 14–20.

158. Moser, C. A., and Wolf Scott. *British Towns.* Edinburgh and London: Oliver and Boyd, 1961.

159. Myrdal, Gunnar. *An International Economy.* London: Routledge and Kegan Paul, 1956.

160. Namenwirth, J. Zvi, and Thomas L. Brewer. "Elite Editorial Comment on the European and Atlantic Communities in Four Countries," in Philip J. Stone; Dexter Dunphy; and Daniel Ogilvie (eds.). *The General Inquirer: Computer Methods for Content Analysis in the Behavioral Sciences.* Cambridge, Mass.: M.I.T. Press, 1966.

161. National Resources Committee. *Regional Factors in National Planning and Development.* Washington, D.C.: Government Printing Office, 1935.

162. Neubauer, Deane. *On the Theory of Polyarchy: An Empirical Study of Democracy in Ten Countries.* New Haven, Conn.: Yale University Press, 1967.

163. North, Robert C., H. E. Koch, and Dina Zinnes. "The Integrative Functions of Conflict." *Journal of Conflict Resolution,* 4 (1960), pp. 355–74.

164. Nosanchuk, Terance A. "A Comparison of Several Sociometric Partitioning Techniques." *Sociometry,* 26, 1 (1963), pp. 112–24.

165. Nye, J. S. "Patterns and Catalysts in Regional Integration," *International Organization,* 19, 4 (1965a), p. 878.

166. ———. *Pan-Africanism and East African Integration.* Cambridge: Harvard University Press, 1965b.

167. Odum, Howard W. *Southern Regions of the United States.* Chapel Hill, N.C.: University of North Carolina Press, 1936.

168. ———, and Harry Estill Moore. *American Regionalism: A Cultural-Historical Approach to National Integration.* New York: Henry Holt, 1938.

169. Okita, Saburo. "Japan and the Developing Nations." *Contemporary Japan,* 28, 2 (1965), pp. 1–14.

170. Olsen, Bernard M., and Gerald Garb. "An Application of Factor Analysis to Regional Economic Growth." *Journal of Regional Science* 6, 1 (1965), pp. 51–56.

171. Osgood, Charles, and Percy Tannanbaum. "The Principle of Congruity and the Prediction of Attitude Change." *Psychological Review,* 62, 1 (1955), pp. 42–55.

172. ———, George Suci, and Percy Tannenbaum. *The Measurement of Meaning.* Urbana, Illinois: University of Illinois Press, 1957.

173. Padelford, Norman J. "A Selected Bibliography on Regionalism and Regional Arrangements." *International Organization,* 10, 3 (1956), pp. 575–603.

174. Parsons, Talcott. "Voting and the Equilibrium of the American Political System," in Eugene Burdick and Arthur J. Brodbeck (eds.). *American Voting Behavior,* Glencoe, Ill.: Free Press, 1959.

175. ———. "Order and Continuity in the International Social System," in James N. Rosenau (ed.). *International Politics and Foreign Policy,* New York: Free Press, 1961a.

176. ———. "The Point of View of the Author," in Max Black (ed.). *The Social Theories of Talcott Parsons.* Englewood Cliffs, N.J.: Prentice-Hall, 1961b.

177. ———. "Polarization and the Problem of International Order," in Quincy Wright, William Evan, and Morton Deutsch (eds.). *Preventing World War III,* New York: Simon and Schuster, 1962.

178. Pool, Ithiel de Sola. "Effects of Cross-National Contact on National and International Images," in Herbert C. Kelman (ed.). *International Behavior: A Social-Psychological Analysis,* New York: Holt, Rinehart and Winston, 1965.

179. Puchala, Donald J. *European Political Integration: Progress and Prospects.* New Haven, Conn.: Yale University, Political Science Research Library, 1966.

180. Regnier, S. *Sur Quelques Aspects Mathematiques des Problems de Classification Automatique.* Paris: Maison des Sciences de l'Homme, Centre de Calcul, 1964.

181. Resources for the Future. *Design for a Worldwide Study of Regional Development.* Baltimore: Johns Hopkins Press, 1966.

182. Richardson, Lewis Frye. *Statistics of Deadly Quarrels.* Pittsburgh and Chicago: ·Boxwood and Quadrangle, 1960.

183. Riemer, Svend. "Theoretical Aspects of Regionalism." *Social Forces,* 21, 3 (1943).

184. Robinson, Joan. *The Economics of Imperfect Competition.* London, Macmillan, 1933.

185. Robinson, John. *Multidimensional Analysis as a Comparative Framework for Political Systems.* Ann Arbor, Mich.: University of Michigan, seminar paper, 1965.

186. Rock, Vincent P. *A Strategy of Interdependence: A Program for the Control of Conflict Between the United States and the Soviet Union.* New York: Scribner, 1964.

187. Rosecrance, Richard N. "Bipolarity, Multipolarity, and the Future." *Journal of Conflict Resolution,* 10, 3 (1966), pp. 314–27.

188. Rosenau, James N. "Pre-Theories and Theories of Foreign Policy," in R. Barry Farrell (ed.). *Approaches to International and Comparative Politics.* Evanston, Ill.: Northwestern University Press, 1966.

189. Ross, John, and Norman Cliff. "A Generalization of the Interpoint Distance Model." *Psychometrika,* 29, 2 (1964), pp. 167–76.

190. Rummel, R. J. "Dimensions of Conflict Behavior Within and Between Nations," in A. Rapoport and L. von Bertalanffy (eds.). *General Systems: Yearbook of the Society for General Systems Research,* 8. Ann Arbor, Mich.: Mental Health Research Institute, 1963.

191. ———. "Testing Some Possible Predictors of Conflict Behavior Within and Between Nations." *Peace Research Society, Papers,* 1 (1964), pp. 79–112.

192. ———. "Domestic Attributes and Foreign Conflict," in J. David Singer (ed.). *Quantitative International Politics: Insights and Evidence: International Yearbook of Political Behavior Research,* 6, New York: Free Press, 1967a.

193. ———. *Applied Factor Analysis.* Evanston, Ill.: Northwestern University Press, 1967b.

194. ———, Jack Sawyer, Harold Guetzkow, and Raymond Tanter. *Dimensions of Nations.* Evanston, Ill.: Northwestern University Press, 1967, forthcoming.

195. Russett, Bruce M. "Cause, Surprise and No Escape." *Journal of Politics,* 24, 1 (1962) pp. 3–22.

196. ———. *Community and Contention: Britain and America in the Twentieth Century.* Cambridge, Mass.: M.I.T. Press, 1963.

197. ———. *Trends in World Politics.* New York: Macmillan, 1965.

198. ———. "Discovering Voting Groups in the United Nations." *American Political Science Review,* 2 (1966), pp. 327–39.

199. ———. "Delineating International Regions," in J. David Singer (ed.). *Quantitative International Politics: Insights and Evidence: International Yearbook of Political Behavior Research,* New York: Free Press, 1967.

200. ———; and Hayward R. Alker, Karl W. Deutsch, Harold D. Lasswell. *World Handbook of Political and Social Indicators.* New Haven, Conn.: Yale University Press, 1964.

201. Salvadori, Massimo. *NATO: A Twentieth-Century Community of Nations.* Princeton, N.J.: Van Nostrand, 1957.

202. Savage, I. Richard, and K. W. Deutsch. "A Statistical Model of the Gross Analysis of Transactions Flows." *Econometrica,* 28, 3 (1960), pp. 551–72.

203. Sawrey, W., L. Keller, and J. Conger. "An Objective Method of Grouping Profiles by Distance Functions and Its Relation to Factor Analysis." *Educational and Psychological Measurement,* 20 (1960), pp. 651–73.

204. Sawyer, Jack, and Terrance Nosanchuk. "Analysis of Sociometric Structure: A Method of Successive Grouping." *Proceedings of the Social Statistics Section, American Statistical Association,* 1960, pp. 206–11.

205. Sewell, James P. *Functionalism and World Politics.* Princeton: Princeton University Press, 1965.

206. Shepard, Roger. "The Analysis of Proximities: Multidimensional Scaling with an Unknown Distance Function. I." *Psychometrika,* 27, 2 (1962a), pp. 125–40.

207. ———. "The Analysis of Proximities: Multidimensional Scaling with an Unknown Distance Function. II." *Psychometrika,* 27, 3 (1962b), pp. 219–46.

208. Sherif, Muzafer, *et al. Intergroup Conflict and Cooperation: The Robber's Cave Experiment.* Norman, Okla.: University of Oklahoma, Institute of Group Relations, 1961.

209. Silvert, K. H. (ed.). *Expectant Peoples.* New York: Random House, 1963.

210. Simmel, George. *Conflict and the Web of Group Affiliation.* Translated by K. H. Wolff and Reinhard Bendix. Glencoe, Ill.: Free Press, 1955.

211. Simon, Herbert A. *Models of Man.* New York: Wiley, 1957.

212. ———. "The Architecture of Complexity." *Proceedings of the American Philosophical Society,* 106, 6 (December 1962), pp. 467–82.

213. Singer, J. David. "The Level of Analysis Problem in International Relations." *World Politics,* 14 (1961), pp. 77–92.

214. ———. "The Global System and Its Subsystems: A Developmental View." Paper presented to the Annual Meeting of the American Political Science Association, New York, September 1966.

215. Sokal, Robert R., and Peter H. A. Sneath. *Principles of Numerical Taxonomy.* San Francisco: W. H. Freeman and Co., 1963.

216. Southall, Aidan. *Alur Society,* Cambridge: W. Heffer & Sons, 1953.

217. Sprout, Harold, and Margaret Sprout. *The Ecological Perspective on Human Affairs.* Princeton, N.J.: Princeton University Press, 1965.

218. Sypkman, Nicholas. *America's Strategy in World Politics.* New York: Harcourt, Brace, 1942.

219. Stein, Eric. "Assimilation of National Laws as a Function of European Integration." *American Journal of International Law,* 58, 1 (January 1964), pp. 1–40.

220. Stigler, George. *A Theory of Price.* New York: Macmillan, 1952.

221. Stone, Richard. "A Comparison of the Economic Structure of Regions Based on Concept of Distance." *Journal of Regional Science,* 2, 2 (1960), pp. 3–20.

222. Szalai, Alexander, et al. "Multinational Comparative Research." *American Behavioral Scientist,* 10, 4 (1966), pp. 1–30.

223. Tanter, Raymond. "Dimensions of Conflict Behavior Within and Between Nations, 1958–60." *Journal of Conflict Resolution,* 10, 1 (1966), pp. 41–64.

224. Thompson, John, S. Sufrin, P. Gould, and M. Buck. "Toward a Geography of Economic Health: The Case of New York State," in John Friedmann and William Alonso (eds.). *Regional Development and Planning: A Reader.* Cambridge, Mass.: M.I.T. Press 1964, pp. 187–206.

225. Torgerson, Warren S. *Theory and Methods of Scaling.* New York: Wiley, 1958.

226. ———. "Multidimensional Scaling of Similarity." *Psychometrika* 30, 4 (1965), pp. 379–94.

227. Truman, David B. *The Congressional Party.* New York: John Wiley & Sons, 1959.

228. Tryon, Robert C., and Daniel Bailey. *The BC TRY Computer System of Cluster and Factor Analysis. Multivariate Behavioral Research,* 1, 1 (1966), pp. 95–111.

229. Turner, Frederick Jackson. *The Significance of Sections in United States History.* New York: Henry Holt, 1932.

230. Union of International Associations. *Yearbook of International Organizations,* 1951–52. Brussels: Union of International Associations, 1952.

231. ———. *Yearbook of International Organizations,* 1962–63. Brussels: Union of International Associations, 1963.

232. United Nations. Statistical Papers, series T., Vol. 8, No. 7. *Direction of International Trade,* New York: United Nations 1957.

233. ———. *Yearbook of National Accounts Statistics, 1963.* New York: United Nations, 1964.

234. ———. *Statistical Yearbook, 1965.* New York: United Nations, 1966a.

235. ———. *Yearbook of National Accounts Statistics, 1965.* New York: United Nations, 1966b.

236. ———. *Monthly Bulletin of Statistics,* 20, 7 (July 1966)c.

237. United Nations Conference on International Organization. *Documents of the United Nations Conference on International Organization, San Francisco, 1945, 12.* London and New York: UN Information Organization, 1945.

238. U.S. Congress, Joint Economic Committee. *Annual Economic Indicators for the U.S.S.R., February, 1964.* Washington, D.C.: U.S. Government Printing Office, 1964.

239. Vance, Rupert B. "The Regional Concept as a Tool for Social Research," in Merrill Jensen (ed.). *Regionalism in America.* Madison, Wis.: University of Wisconsin Press, 1951.

240. Waltz, Kenneth N. "The Stability of a Bipolar World." *Daedalus,* 93, 3 (1964), pp. 881–909.

241. Ward, Joe H., and Marion Hook. "Application of an Hierarchical Grouping Procedure to a Problem of Grouping Profiles." *Educational and Psychological Measurement,* 23 (1963), pp. 69–81.

242. Wigmore, John Henry. *A Panorama of the World's Legal Systems.* St. Paul: West Publishing Co., vol. 3, 1928.

243. Wilcox, Francis O. "International Confederation—The United Nations and State Sovereignty" in Elmer Plischke (ed.). *Systems of Integrating the International Community.* Princeton, N.J.: Van Nostrand, 1964.

244. Wirth, Louis. "Limitations of Regionalism" in Merrill Jensen (ed.). *Regionalism in America.* Madison, Wis.: University of Wisconsin Press, 1951.

245. Wooley, Herbert B. *Measuring Transactions Between World Areas.* New York: Columbia University Press, 1966.

246. Wright, B., and M. Evitts. "Direct Factor Analysis in Sociometry." *Sociometry,* 24, 1 (1961), pp. 82–98.

247. Wright, Quincy. *A Study of War.* Chicago: The University of Chicago Press, 2 vols., 1942.

248. ———. *The Study of International Relations.* New York: Appleton-Century-Crofts, 1955.

249. Yalem, Ronald D. *Regionalism and World Order.* Washington, D.C.: Public Affairs Press, 1965.

250. Young, O. R. "The Impact of General Systems Theory on Political Science," *General Systems: Yearbook of the Society for General Systems Research,* 9 (1964), pp. 239–54.

251. Zimmerman, L. J. *Poor Lands, Rich Lands.* New York: Random House, 1965.

INDEX